The America's Cup

Also by Bob Bavier

SAILING TO WIN
THE NEW YACHT RACING RULES
FASTER SAILING
A VIEW FROM THE COCKPIT
KEYS TO RACING SUCCESS

The America's Cup

AN INSIDER'S VIEW—1930 TO THE PRESENT
A Revision of *America's Cup Fever*

by Bob Bavier

 A TRITON BOOK

Dodd, Mead & Company   New York

All photographs are by Stanley Rosenfeld, copyright © Stanley Rosenfeld, with the following exceptions: p. 109, copyright Wide World Photos; p. 115, courtesy *Yachting* magazine; p. 178, copyright © Robert P. Foley; pp. 54, 186, 189, 193, 202, 231, 236, Guy Gurney; pp. 197, 198, 199, 204, 230 Bob Bavier.

Library of Congress Cataloging-in-Publication Data

Bavier, Robert Newton, 1918–
  The America's Cup.

  1. America's Cup races—History.   2. Yacht racing—
History.   I. Title.
GV829.B378   1986   797.1′4   86-13511
ISBN 0-396-08679-9

Contents

Foreword

Because my own involvement with America's Cup competition happens to coincide precisely with the period on which this account is focused, and because during that period I was fortunate to become acquainted with many of the leading characters of that period, I can say with conviction that the author is "spot on" throughout the text.

In addition, circumstances placed me very close, both physically and mentally, during the key part of an unforgettable campaign—*Constellation* 1964. I have some insight into how Bob Bavier, the sailor and the author, is so highly successful.

I also had the good fortune of knowing Bob's parents—during what would be called a formative period—and both Olin and I had respect and admiration for them and learned many important basics of sailing from Bob, Sr., who clearly earned the name some of us had for him—The Brain.

One particular detail was Bob, Sr.'s clear explanation of the relative merits of yawl versus ketch, which has helped keep me on course in an area where there is more than a little misunderstanding. Neither Bob, Sr., nor his son has ever forgotten the importance of sailing efficiently and, still more important, enjoying it.

During my involvement with *Constellation* in '64, I continued to learn from the author. It has been my good fortune to sail with many wonderful helmsmen, but none who could get a boat from one tack to the other with less loss of speed or with an easier job for the crew.

The way Bob could delegate responsibility reminded me of Tom Watson, whose success with I.B.M. has certainly been helped by the most successful application of this skill. Bob never second guesses his tactical advisors, nor his navigator, and the way he would walk up the dock for dinner in the evening with his family, even when there were relatively intricate mechanical details to sort out before an early harbor start the next morning, emphasizes this ability. This practice has astonishingly beneficial results.

First and foremost, Bob always arrived on board for the next race with the benefit of having had an enjoyable and relaxed evening, plus a good night's sleep, so that *Constellation* always had the benefit of his best potential.

Meanwhile, the nut and bolt boys realized that the ball was in their court, so they gave it all they had and again and again, jobs were done better and quicker than would have been possible if the "old man" was asking questions and complicating the situation with various alternative possibilities.

This delegation of responsibility did much to build mutual trust and confidence among the various components that very rapidly became an efficient crew. The relation between skipper, navigator, tactician, midship crew and those on the foredeck was never strained and this did much to provide a successful end result.

With such appropriate basic credentials, Bob has been able to clearly explain so much relating to the key personalities, including enlightening information on designers and also helmsmen, and wonderfully clear explanations of key races and tactics involved.

When I read Bob's comments on the "black box," it seemed almost like E.S.P.—almost as though I should have credit for writing from that particular viewpoint; likewise "Why Twelve Meters?"

Bob's great understanding of right-of-way rules permits him to provide vividly clear explanations of pivotal protests—particularly the '34 and '70 matches, and the latter are documented by an excellent sequential series of pictures.

I would like to add small personal comments on four of the designers Bob has chronicled so appropriately.

I was introduced to Capt. Nat Herreshoff by Mike Vanderbilt in the middle of the 1937 campaign. My job was to show and explain some movies of *Ranger* and some of her competitors in Capt. Nat's home, where he was bedridden at the time. However, Capt. Nat proved to be one person who had such complete basic knowledge that he clearly saw more in the pictures than either Mike Vanderbilt or I had seen, and after I had made a few introductory explanations, both Mike Vanderbilt and I were able to sit back and listen to the myriad of details that that wonderful man spotted with such immediate precision and clarity. At that occasion, I realized that one could not possibly exaggerate his capabilities and his contributions to all types of nautical development, all of which was well corroborated by contacts with his son, Sydney, and later with his grandson, Halsey.

Mike Vanderbilt was also responsible for my contact with Starling Burgess during the design, construction and sailing of *Ranger*. There was no possible doubting of Starling Burgess's credentials, but what really impressed me was his willingness to share his great knowledge with his co-designer, my brother Olin. The alacrity with which Mr. Burgess could reach the bottom line was clearly demonstrated when he solved a complex raking problem aloft on *Enterprise,* when she was in danger of losing her mast, by quickly clipping port and starboard spinnaker halyards over both middle and top shrouds to effectively tie these together and control the lower spreaders, which were overswinging by failure of the gear that secured them.

Olin has been given deserved credit for his amply demonstrated skill in the field of yacht design and I would like to add that while I have been lucky enough to sail with many of the very best, there is no better shipmate, whether it's around the buoys or a hard offshore sail, nor is there a better tactician, nor one more knowledgeable in sail analysis, weather judgment, navigation, as well as being a fine helmsman. Although *Mustang* was my own boat, she always did her best when Olin was aboard and at those times that he was skipper, and I moved down to mate—an arrangement which provided the best possible results.

Finally, while David Boyd did not achieve the desired results with *Sceptre* and *Sovereign*, we must not forget the great Six Meter *Circe*, which he designed. She was the only Six to defeat *Goose* in the 1938 season. By coincidence, this match, which was for the Seawanhaka Cup, was the only 1938 series that Bob was unable to race aboard *Goose*.

Bob Bavier has given us a wonderfully perceptive, personal look at America's Cup competition. I hope others enjoy it as much as I have.

ROD STEPHENS

Preface

Much has been written about the America's Cup, some of it fascinating reading, some factual, some phony. Its history is so well chronicled that a rehash would be pointless. This book will focus instead on what I like to think of as the inside story of the last fifty-seven years.

The America's Cup is a revision of a book entitled *America's Cup Fever,* but is sufficiently different to warrant a new title. In the preparation of this edition, I wish to acknowledge above all the help of Guy Gurney, not only for his excellent photos but also for his thoughts on the strengths of the various contenders for the 1987 match.

To present an inside story one has to have *been* inside, and in this respect I consider myself fortunate. My association with the America's Cup started in 1930 when my father was a member of the afterguard of the J-boat *Weetamoe,* one of the four candidates for defense. At the age of twelve I was aboard *Weetamoe* in an actual race, the youngest (to my knowledge) ever to race on a Cup boat. Throughout the J-boat era in the 1930s, I was a close spectator and got to meet and even know the participants. Since the renewal in 1958 of America's Cup racing in Twelve Meters, I have known the men who sailed in every successive match up to the present day. I know what it means both to win and lose, having been helmsman and "quarterback" of the defender *Constellation* in 1964 and skipper of the winning *Courageous* in 1974 up to the final race of the final trials, when I was bounced in favor of Ted Hood. And to round off the picture, I was on the Selection Committee to pick the American defender in 1977, and again in 1980 and 1983. Even when not directly involved I was on the scene, knew the players, saw and felt firsthand both the exhilaration of victory and the anguish of defeat in this grueling contest.

I will not go into the years prior to 1930 in any depth because to do so would depend on the written word or secondhand information, hardly the inside story I would like to tell. But for those readers who may be unfamiliar with the America's Cup races a capsule account of its history and significance might be of interest.

It all began in 1851 when the schooner yacht *America* sailed abroad to race against the best British yachts. It was like the Super Bowl game between the New York Jets and the Baltimore Colts in 1969 when Namath and Company were given no chance but still won.

The United States was making seagoing history with its clipper ships in the mid-nineteenth century, but in yachting we were still a fledgling nation, while Britannia was conceived as ruling the waves. At that time we had but one yacht club, the New York Yacht Club, founded in 1844. We had no tradition and precious little experience in yacht racing, but John Stevens, commodore of the New York Yacht Club, was far from daunted. Yachts of that era were designed along the cod's head and mackerel tail configuration, with full bows and long fine runs. *America,* on the other hand, was designed by George Steers more along clipper ship lines with a fine entrance and powerful quarters. She was a refinement of the New York pilot boats which had to be both fast and seaworthy if they were to be the first to get a pilot aboard a ship entering New York harbor.

After a fast transatlantic passage, *America* put in at Le Havre, France, to be put into racing trim. When sailing from France to Cowes, England, she met one of England's fastest yachts and in an informal brush tipped her hand by sailing away from the British boat. This made it difficult for her to arrange matches, which in those days were for substantial cash prizes or wagers. Finally she was allowed to enter a race around the Isle of Wight for what was then known as the 100 Guinea Cup. Arrayed against her was the cream of the English yachting fleet, yet *America* trounced them so thoroughly that Queen Victoria, when asking who was second, was told, "Alas, Your Majesty, there is no second."

Not only was *America*'s hull form revolutionary, but so also were her sails—far flatter and better able to hold their shape than the baggy sails carried by the British yachts. In all respects she was a breakthrough, and the magnitude of her triumph was such as to shatter the myth of England's yachting supremacy.

In 1857 the owners of *America* deeded their trophy, known ever since as the America's Cup, to the New York Yacht Club as an international challenge trophy. The first challenge came in 1870 when the schooner *Cambria* sailed to America in hopes of regaining the trophy. Like *America* she was forced to sail against a fleet of defenders, but unlike her she didn't come close to winning. She finished in the middle of the fleet, beaten even by the nineteen-year-old *America*. The winner was *Magic*.

The next year the schooner *Livonia* challenged, and in the interest of fairness she was compelled to sail against but one defender at a time. But the Americans didn't go overboard in being fair! Whereas *Livonia* now had to race only one boat at a time, two defenders *(Columbia* and *Sappho)* were selected, one to race if light air was expected, the other in a breeze. Again the Americans were easy winners, but rather than discouraging challenges, the beginning of a winning tradition was making the prize even more coveted.

Commencing with the 1876 match and forever after, the races have been a true match race affair, with but one defender to meet the challenger.

The first three matches were between large schooners, but since 1881 only sloops and cutters have competed, the largest and still fastest on a reach being the 143-foot sloop *Reliance*. *Reliance* carried a huge sail plan of 15,000 square feet, double that of a J-boat and more than seven times the area carried by a Twelve Meter. It took a crew of forty-three to handle her. While a J-boat would have beaten her around the course because of its greater efficiency upwind, *Reliance* had the highest maximum speed of any Cup boat. Her sail plan is shown on page 93.

While some matches were close, and while we even lost an occasional race in the competition, which evolved into a best two out of three, then three out of five and finally a four out of seven series, until 1983 the American boat was always the eventual winner.

In the 117 years since the first match and the 136 years since *America* sailed to glory, challenges have come from England, Canada, Scotland, Australia, France, Sweden, and Italy. There were no fewer than six different challengers for the twenty-fifth match in 1983. The longer the Americans continue to win, the greater incentive to be the first to beat us. I well remember watching the 1970 match between *Gretel II* and *Intrepid* with Tony Boyden, who had backed *Sovereign*'s 1964 challenge against *Constellation*. I was a bit surprised to find him rooting for *Intrepid*. "But of course," said Tony, "I want to be the first to beat you bloody Americans."

Now that the string has been broken with the stirring victory of *Australia II* over *Liberty,* there seems to be no slackening of interest. There are more American syndicates than ever vying for the honor of becoming the challenger and getting the cup back "where it belongs." Nor is there any less interest from other nations. Italy, New Zealand, France, Canada, and Britain have joined the chase. Germany and Sweden issued challenges, but have since backed off due to difficulty in raising enough money to mount a meaningful effort.

Once bitten by America's Cup fever, it is almost impossible to recover.

The most persistent challenger was Sir Thomas Lipton, whose *Shamrock* challenged in 1899 and whose *Shamrock V* challenged in 1930, with three other *Shamrocks* making futile efforts in 1901, 1903, and 1920. Baron Bich of France first got bitten in 1970, and 1980 marked his fourth effort to win the cup. The fact that until 1980 his yachts did not win a single race in America's Cup trials only made him redouble his efforts and spend even more millions of dollars in the quest of yachting's Holy Grail. In 1980, his *France III* did much better, finishing second to *Australia* among the four challengers. Despite this improvement the Baron did not challenge in 1983. He left the scene as one of the most beloved challengers.

If you think of Twelve Meters as large and glamorous boats, the drawing on page 93 puts them in proper perspective and reveals how gargantuan some of the earlier boats were.

Twelve Meters are large by today's standards, and they are also highly refined racing machines. The fact that they are impractical for anything but closed course racing and that each one costs at least one-and-a-half million dollars to design, build, and race for a single summer may be considered negatives by some. But these very impracticalities, combined with the fact that they are such superb performers, especially upwind, heightens the romance of the event. It is the one sailing contest that captures the imagination and the attention of the nonyachting public, the one event that any keen sailor would like to race in and win more than any other.

The America's Cup—a symbol of excellence, of man's striving to improve himself and his boat, and a goal so unattainable as to kindle fierce desires, sacrifices, and effort in hopes of achieving it. People don't laugh when it is called the greatest sporting event in the world.

It's worth looking into, so with no further ado, let's get started.

The America's Cup

Chapter I
A 1930 Race on Weetamoe

It was a beautiful day in the early summer of 1930 as I steamed down Long Island Sound on a Fall River liner bound for Buzzards Bay. But I wasn't very happy. The year before, when I was eleven, my dad had bought me a Bullseye Class sloop, otherwise known as a Herreshoff 12½ (for her waterline length). I had great fun racing her and even took a few overnight cruises with a friend my own age. It had been the best summer of my life. I thought I was a pretty hot sailor and was looking forward to more of the same.

It came as a shock to me, therefore, when I was told in the spring of 1930 that I was going to camp on Buzzards Bay. The fact that Camp Mashnee was supposed to have a good sailing program (I later found out it didn't—the boats, like those at all camps of my acquaintance, were pretty poor and no match for my Bullseye) didn't sell me. But my parents told me it was an opportunity most boys would leap at, I would have lots of fun, meet new friends, and, besides, it would be good for me to have a summer away from home.

When none of these arguments came close to convincing me, I was finally told the real reason. My dad had been asked to be part of the afterguard on the J-boat *Weetamoe,* one of four American boats vying for the right to defend the America's Cup, and would be away all summer. I couldn't tag along without being in the way and couldn't stay home alone.

Being brought up in a family where sailing monopolized most of our thoughts and conversation, even at age twelve I knew something about the importance of the America's Cup. I was excited about Dad being part of it, but at that age my own boat seemed more important. That's why I felt a bit put upon and more than a little homesick as we steamed east.

Camp Mashnee turned out fine, and, despite its typical camp fleet of boats, I had fun not only sailing but in all other camp activities. Even so, the weekly highlight was a letter from Dad.

He was never a prolific letter writer, but that summer I received a brief note from him at least once a week telling me about the races between *Weetamoe* and the other three contenders: *Enterprise, Yankee,* and *Whirlwind.* The news was usually good since *Weetamoe* had the best record in the early races. I remember Dad cautioning me not to be too optimistic— saying that the final races in the latter part of August were all that really counted and that by then the others, especially *Enterprise,* might find themselves. I dismissed this as just so much adult conservatism and found it hard to conceive any boat my dad had a key role in failing at the end after such a strong start. I felt pretty good about the whole thing except that I would have liked to see them race.

A Race on Weetamoe

At the beginning of August a letter arrived with the exciting news that the J-boats would be sailing on the New York Yacht Club cruise and on 5 August would be racing on Buzzards Bay off Mattapoisett, just a few miles from my camp. I thought the next lines would read that I could get a chance to watch them race. Instead Dad wrote that he had squared it with both *Weetamoe*'s skipper George Nichols and with the director of the camp for me actually to race on board *Weetamoe*. I let out a clarion yell which might still be reverberating on the eastern reaches of Buzzards Bay.

The morning of the race was sparkling with a light-to-moderate NNW wind ruffling the waters of Buzzards Bay. I felt like a big shot as *Weetamoe*'s tender with my dad standing in the bow eased alongside our dock at camp to take me on board. But as we neared *Weetamoe* I began to feel even smaller than my four feet four and seventy-three pounds. Her freeboard was five and a half feet and I had to climb rather than step aboard. Dad introduced me first to George Nichols and the rest of the afterguard, all resplendent in white flannels, white shoes, and yachting jackets. "Mr. Nichols, as I thought of him then (and ever after, even when I was to crew with him eight years later on the Six Meter *Goose* to win the Scandinavian Gold Cup), couldn't have been nicer. He shook my hand, smiled with all his face and eyes, and told me how glad he was that I had come for the race and that if I was anything like my dad I would bring them luck. Though awed, I liked him immediately, and in subsequent years learned that my instinctive reaction was justified. There were better sailors than George Nichols but no better or kinder men.

Dad introduced me to many of the crew, all decked out in spotless white sailor suits. I remember most the calluses on their hands as I shook them—hard as concrete and equally rough. They were polite in a hearty way but, I sensed, a bit surprised that such a young squirt would be allowed aboard for a real race. The part of their "uniform" that most intrigued me was a hank of cotton string looped through a leather thong at their waists and then braided. Dad told me that these were for stopping the light sails.

Dad told me about one particular brute of a man I had just met. He had been swept overboard the day before on the hard reach from Newport to Mattapoisett. *Weetamoe* was battling for the lead at the time, and as the crewman came to the surface, he hollered—"Keep going, I can swim to shore"; this despite the fact that the nearest shore was three miles away and no boats were near. No one doubted his sincerity, but of course they went back for him and had him back aboard within minutes, none the

3

worse for wear. When he complained, it was explained to him that a boat was disqualified if it finished without its full crew, which made him feel even worse for costing *Weetamoe* a possible victory. This man, whose name I unfortunately can't remember, epitomized the spirit of the entire crew—a tough, hearty group with as fierce a will to win as any crew I've ever seen. Perhaps they were influenced by the fact that every member of the professional crew received a cash bonus for each victory, and while I'm sure that motivated them, I felt then and still feel that pride was the main stimulant.

Perhaps Dad told me this story to warn me against the danger (and disgrace) of falling overboard but he gave me the dignity of not saying "Be careful." He showed me a place slightly behind the helmsman and the rest of the afterguard, as the amateur yachtsmen were called, which was to be my station for the race. I appreciated the fact that he didn't tell me to keep quiet, to ask no questions, and to be sure to keep out of the way once the race started. I knew enough about racing so that he didn't have to, but it made me feel more grown-up not to be so warned by him, "Mr." Nichols, or the others.

Dad also showed me below deck. I remember it as a cross between a machine shop and a storage warehouse, with huge cranks to activate the winches on deck, drums for lines, bins for an endless variety of enormous sails. More than anything else it seemed huge, extending seemingly forever and with headroom above a man's reach.

Weetamoe's larger tender came alongside soon after we were back on deck with the light weather main the afterguard had decided to use that day. It was flaked like a long sausage and more than twenty crew carried it aboard over their shoulders. I later learned it weighed over a ton. It took twenty minutes to bend on the main while we towed slowly out to the starting line. Several more minutes were required to hoist it, and I almost got dizzy craning my neck aloft as it went to the masthead more than 152 feet above deck.

Weetamoe making knots in 1930. That's my dad standing by the main sheet. The crew member sitting farthest off is in the spot I occupied in the race off Mattapoisett.

We cast off and reached about under main alone, taking a compass bearing of the line and checking course signals. I could hear the navigator reporting that there was to be a 21-mile triangular course, a 10-mile beam reach to FL White Bell "5" abeam of Robinsons Hole in the middle of Buzzards Bay, a slightly broader reach to a buoy near Falmouth, northeast of Woods Hole, and then a beat to the finish.

The leeward end of the line was favored, and I could hear the afterguard discussing which end to cross at. I remember to this day my dad recommending the leeward end and others suggesting the weather end on the assumption that *Weetamoe* was fast on a light reach and that all she needed was clear air. Dad countered by saying he expected the morning breeze to slacken before it freshened late in the day and that if the wind did die it would be important to be to leeward and thus able to increase speed by heading higher late in the leg. Mr. Nichols listened to all hands, looked at the wind on the water, and then announced they would start at the windward end. My dad made no remonstrance, but I could swear he looked my way and gave me an imperceptible shrug and a wry grin. I, of course, said nothing but thought plenty, especially since Dad had castigated me on several occasions the previous summer for getting too high on a reach in light air and dying when I tried to get down to the mark.

Shortly after the warning gun we broke out our genoa and started reaching away from the line. At first *Weetamoe* seemed sluggish, but speed increased steadily, first five, then six, seven, eight, and then nearly nine knots despite a wind which couldn't have been over seven or eight. With five minutes to go we jibed back for the line on a tight reach. It looked like we might be okay, except that *Yankee* was just ahead of us and blanketing our wind. At the gun *Yankee* had a fine start at the weather end with *Weetamoe* a length behind. At the leeward end were *Whirlwind* and *Enterprise* in that order.

I remember our being luffed as we tried to pass *Yankee* to windward and the afterguard advising not to try again because we were getting too high. Down to leeward *Whirlwind* held her lead and rounded the first mark twelve seconds ahead of *Enterprise* with *Yankee* third one minute forty seconds later and *Weetamoe* ten seconds farther back.

On the next reach *Whirlwind* set a ballooner with a small balloon staysail set inside it and had her finest leg of the entire summer. She drew away from *Enterprise* in startling fashion, until the latter set a staysail inside her genoa and thereafter did better. Unfortunately the wind up ahead was stronger and while we did pass *Yankee* after changing jobs (a long protracted operation), *Whirlwind*'s lead at the second mark was two minutes over *Enterprise*, nine over *Weetamoe,* and nine and a half over *Yankee.*

Whirlwind was sailing into a dying northerly with *Enterprise* gaining rapidly and *Weetamoe* and *Yankee* closing on both of them. Halfway up we had cut the deficit in half when I heard my dad, without pointing but looking toward the west, saying, "There it is." No one else could see it but he had detected the first ruffling of a westerly. We tacked at once to starboard and as we did I too could see the new breeze.

We sailed for several lengths before the boats ahead tacked to cover but with *Yankee* close aboard. We switched to working sails just before the new breeze hit, tacked to port in the header, and started boiling for the line four miles away. Down to leeward I could see *Whirlwind* virtually flat and *Enterprise* little better off. *Weetamoe* heeled till her rail was just above the water. I had never seen water move past so fast, but what I remember most is the sound. There was a steady hiss as we sped along. *Weetamoe* seemed to be on a railroad track and a smooth one at that, with no pitching whatsoever.

When our speed through the still smooth water had reached nearly eleven knots an oceangoing tug crossed our bow close aboard at full speed, creating a huge quarter wave. As we approached the wave I looked for something to hang on to. I needn't have bothered. *Weetamoe*'s 143 tons sliced into the wave as though it wasn't there. There was no lurching, no loss in speed, just the barest nod of a lift to her long, lean bow as we smashed through the sea, throwing spray thirty feet to leeward. By the time the spray had settled we had left the wave astern. The feeling of power and of irresistible force is one I've never before or since even remotely experienced on any boat.

The excitement I felt by the speed of the graceful brute I was riding was heightened by the thrill of what had developed into a real race. *Yankee* was boiling along close astern but not really gaining. Down to leeward *Whirlwind* was still flat, now barely ahead of us and already behind *Enterprise*. For a while it appeared that we might sweep past *Enterprise* before she got into our breeze. We could see the wind approaching her but if it delayed just a few minutes more we might just sail around her. Then I saw her sails harden, saw her heel even before the wind on the water reached her, and knew we were too late. Sherman Hoyt, the wily member of Mike Vanderbilt's afterguard, was too smart to get too far out on a limb. While concentrating on passing *Whirlwind,* he had focused also on the boats behind and any new wind they might bring. As a result he had suggested to Mike that *Enterprise* match our tack even though it meant leaving *Whirlwind,* thus escaping the hole she sank into.

At the finish *Enterprise* beat us by more than two minutes. *Yankee* was eighteen seconds behind us and poor *Whirlwind* more than two and a half minutes farther back.

I was too excited at sailing on such a magnificent machine and about our good last leg to feel any disappointment about not winning. Despite the long periods of light air we had averaged 8.57 knots for the course, which not only was the fastest I had traveled around a closed course but also ever since that momentous day fifty-seven years ago.

After the finish the jib was dropped and George Nichols asked if I would like to steer for a moment. It must have been an incongruous sight to see me hanging onto that huge wheel and peering *between,* not over, the spokes. It was so finely geared, however, that I could turn it without too much effort, and when I turned, *Weetamoe*'s huge bulk responded. It would be thirty-four years before I would again touch the helm of a Cup contender in quite a different role.

Chapter II
America's Cup Skippers

One begins to appreciate the special significance of the America's Cup by scrutinizing the men who have raced for it. Not just by getting to know them but by exploring what it meant to them, the sacrifices they made, and the energies they squandered in the great pursuit. By probing the exhilaration they felt in victory and the depth of their despair in failure, we might begin to understand what makes the America's Cup so very special.

Many people feel it is easier to win the America's Cup than, say, a Star or Soling Class World Championship or an Olympic gold medal. There is some truth to this *once the competition begins,* simply because in a world championship or the Olympics there are scores of boats to beat, whereas in the America's Cup there are fewer contenders in the trials and only one opponent in the match itself. Hence through pure weight of numbers, there is a strong case for the claim that an Olympic medal is harder to win. Despite this the America's Cup remains the least attainable prize and the hardest to win for two reasons. First, you cannot win it (or lose it)

Rod Stephens is never happier than when something needs fixing aloft.

until or unless you are selected to be skipper or crew. And with almost every top sailor willing to give his eye teeth for the chance, the competition is fierce. Second, once selected, you are up against top sailors who got there because they were superbly qualified and had demonstrated their excellence in other major yachting events.

It is discouraging in a way but also stimulating and challenging to compete for the America's Cup and to know that the skippers and crews against you are going to sail superlatively well. One of the most fruitful ways to win in big fleets is to avoid mistakes, while waiting for your opponents to make errors in tactics, in helmsmanship, or in sail selection. Unless you have a much faster boat, that is a discouraging way to attempt to win in America's Cup competition. The other skippers and crew make so few mistakes and the ones they do make are so minor that you have got to be aggressive to win.

There have been a few examples in the past when men of wealth who were good but not brilliant sailors raced for the America's Cup because they were major contributors and to a certain degree bought themselves in. Not so anymore. Only top sailors compete and very few top sailors who are asked decline the honor. One such was Buddy Melges, without question one of the world's finest sailors. For many years, he felt he could not take time away from business for the months on end required to become a defender. But he finally succumbed and will skipper the Chicago challenger in 1987.

Others who have been asked either beat their bosses over the head until they give in, take a leave of absence without pay, or, in more than a few instances, quit their jobs in order to participate. While the syndicate takes care of your living expenses during the summer, everyone who competes incurs a financial sacrifice. Still, no one who competes seems to mind.

Harold S. Vanderbilt—Skipper of Enterprise *1930,* Rainbow *1934 and* Ranger *1937*

In reviewing the America's Cup skippers I have known over fifty-seven years, I have to start with Harold S. Vanderbilt, known to his intimates as

Mike. He is the only three-time winner of the Cup, as skipper of *Enterprise* in 1930, *Rainbow* in 1934, and *Ranger* in 1937. It was not too easy to become intimate with Mike. He had a brilliant mind, as proven by his prowess in bridge and his business acumen. He was socially prominent and supremely confident to the point of being overbearing. When I first knew him as a teenager I thought of him with a mixture of awe and fear. When we served together on the Appeals Committee and Racing Rules Committee of the North American Yacht Racing Union in later years, the fear vanished but the awe remained. His mind was razor sharp and the power of his conviction so strong that, even if you thought he was wrong, you sure as hell thought twice before disagreeing. And even on the rare occasions when he was wrong, it was tough to convince him.

As an America's Cup skipper, however, he was not hard to sail with. He ran his yachts like a business. Everyone knew who was boss but he delegated authority and seldom countermanded a decision of his afterguard. Mike was not a good small boat sailor, but J-boats were anything but small. He showed great judgment in the early decisions so necessary to make such a complicated venture gel and come together at the time of the final trials. He was a great student of the weather and seldom had the wrong sail up and seldom was caught on the wrong side of a wind shift. He was also a psychologist, as witness the fact that he always removed the mainsail from the boom each evening even though he was going to race the next day and the main already bent was probably the right one for the next day's weather. J-boat mains weighed over a ton, and it was a backbreaking and time-consuming job to unbend one and bend another, but Mike was smart enough to realize that if a main was already in place in the morning there was the danger, human nature being what it is, to conclude that maybe it would be okay for the expected weather. All mains therefore were put ashore each night so that his judgment of which would be right for the next day would not be colored by which was easier to get at.

He was an innovator, too, being the first to develop the timed start, known forevermore as the Vanderbilt start. To illustrate: Knowing it took

Mike Vanderbilt at Ranger's *wheel, surrounded by his afterguard Rod Stephens, Olin Stephens, Zene Bliss, Mike's wife Gertie, and Artie Knapp.*

forty seconds to jibe a J-boat and reverse course 180°, and assuming you were on the line and reaching away from it with five minutes to go, when should you jibe to head back? In this instance, the formula would read $\frac{5^1 + 40^{11}}{2} = 2'30'' + 20''$ or 2 minutes 50 seconds being the amount of time *remaining* at which you should commence your jibe to return to the line. For years keen skippers had been doing something similar, but Mike was the first to reduce it to a mathematical formula, which is one reason why his starts were superb. He was smart enough to realize that the formula had to be modified in the event of current, or if he was blanketed or expected to be blanketed either leaving or returning to the line, but having the formula to rely on gave great confidence when returning to the line at eleven knots. In the absence of variables, if the formula said you were not going to be early, you were not early, and this made for gutsy starts with full headway.

Mike was a superb helmsman of J-boats in a strong breeze. He could sense when she was in the groove, not by looking at the sails, but by a combination of feel and by looking at the leeward rail to ensure heel angle was not excessive. Conversely he had a poor feel sailing to windward in light air, tending to drive too much, thus building too much speed but not getting to the windward mark as fast as if he had pointed higher at reduced speed. But he was smart enough to recognize this weakness and that is why others, Sherman Hoyt in 1930 on *Enterprise* and in 1934 on *Rainbow* and Olin Stephens in 1937 on *Ranger,* were the windward helmsmen in light air.

Mike's other great attribute was a mastery of the racing rules and a ruthlessness in using them. This led to some unpleasantness (see Chapter VIII on famous protests) but it helped him win races.

Two of the three times Mike Vanderbilt defended the Cup, it might well have gone overseas if he had not been in the picture. In 1930 he won in *Enterprise* but it is likely that any of the four American boats of that year could have beaten *Shamrock V.* In 1934, however, *Endeavour* was certainly a faster boat than *Rainbow* and without Mike's key decisions I feel *Endeavour* would have won (see Chapter X). In 1937 *Ranger* was a super boat and clearly superior to *Endeavour II.* But had it not been for Mike recognizing that unless a new defender was built we would lose the Cup, lose it we surely would have. Remember, those were recession years and the syndicate Mike tried to organize to pay for a new defender never got off the ground. Mike was, of course, a wealthy man but when other wealthy men were keeping their hands in their pockets, he financed *Ranger* virtually singlehandedly. He did so in realization that our existing J-boats were not up to the job of beating *Endeavour II* and for anyone bitten with America's Cup fever no sacrifice was too much to ensure that the Cup stayed here.

*Charles Francis Adams, the first amateur skipper to defend the Cup (*Resolute, *1920), came within one foot of defending in* Yankee *when she lost the final trial race to* Rainbow. *Charlie was a spry 68 at the time and would have been the oldest skipper to defend.*

Charles Francis Adams—Skipper of Resolute *1920 and* Yankee *1934*

Many of the skippers Mike raced against in the J-boat were better all-around sailors and would have beaten him in smaller boats where it is more of a one-man show, with organization assuming less importance.

One such was Charles Francis Adams. Charlie Adams came from the illustrious Adams family. Two of his direct forebears were presidents of the United States and Charlie himself was a Secretary of the Navy. He could sail anything well and was the first amateur skipper to win the Cup as skipper of *Resolute* in 1920 against *Shamrock IV.* In 1934 in his sixty-eighth year he beat Mike Vanderbilt's *Rainbow* in their first ten head-to-head races. *Rainbow* did win the last two races prior to the final selection trials, but as Mike Vanderbilt wrote in *On the Wind's Highway:* "We were in desperate straits when the trial races began."

When *Yankee* won the first race against *Rainbow* in the final trials by over six minutes, the straits looked even more desperate.

Chapter IV, entitled "Why the Early Leader Often Loses," describes how *Rainbow* won the next four races to gain selection. She won the final race by a split second—so close that no one on either boat knew who had won. When Charlie Adams, that strong, silent and apparently imperturbable man, learned that *Yankee* had lost and that *Rainbow* was to be the defender he broke down and cried—not the only time this has happened to losers of close matches. America's Cup fever will bring men back to try again, will leave winners with a high they have never felt before, but can leave losers with long-lasting scars. I saw tears running down the cheeks of more than one member of *Intrepid*'s crew in 1974 when, after being tied entering the last race against *Courageous*, they lost in weather they had expected to win in. Others like Bill Cox in *American Eagle,* 1964, and Artie Knapp in *Weatherly* in 1958, while outwardly calm after being eliminated, went through a long period of being withdrawn and lacking their usual bounce. The competition extends over so many months that when you get the axe, especially after you smelled victory, it takes a long time to recover your equilibrium. I know of no one who has ever suffered a nervous breakdown after a Cup campaign, but there have been some near misses. It is not a game for the faint of heart.

George Nichols—Skipper of Weetamoe *1930*

With rare exceptions I will portray only the skippers who actually raced for the Cup in the match itself, not those many fine sailors who failed to survive the trials. One such exception who nearly went all the way was George Nichols, skipper of *Weetamoe* in 1930. You have already met him through a boy's eyes in Chapter I, but allow me to expand a bit. George was a gentleman in the finest sense as well as the narrow sense of being in

George Nichols, skipper of Weetamoe in 1930. Better sailors have raced for the Cup, but no finer or kinder men.

the social register. He epitomized the term yachtsman, looking and dressing the part. His paid crew of Scandinavians revered him. His afterguard considered him a great person and gave him high marks for organizing a campaign. Their only complaint was the fact that he did not always delegate responsibility or rely on their advice. But the real rub was that he simply was not a very good helmsman. He knew the game from A to Z but was not adept at keeping *Weetamoe* in the groove.

I saw this weakness firsthand when I crewed for George Nichols in the Six Meter *Goose* when we won the Scandinavian Gold Cup in three straight races. Counting the selection trials, I raced on *Goose* in thirty races that summer of 1938 and with George Nichols as skipper we won every race. It would seem, therefore, that he was pretty hot stuff in a boat. Of course he was good, but far from great. We were usually behind at the start, and all too frequently *Goose* was either being driven too hard or pinched. We won because we had a super boat, far faster than her competitors, and when George had her in the groove we walked away from the competition.

After losing the trials to *Enterprise,* George Nichols told her designer, Clinton Crane: "Clinton, it is all my fault. The boat was better, but I let you down." I believe he was right. But this remark at the moment of defeat also is a measure of the man. Better sailors than George Nichols have raced for the America's Cup but no better men.

In the modern era a syndicate would probably have switched skippers when *Weetamoe* began to lose. That simply was not done in those days. Had it been, my dad would have been the logical choice. Yes, I am prejudiced, but I also know he was a superb helmsman and an instinctively great sailor. I am confident that in his hands *Weetamoe* would have won.

In respect to my dad's memory, let me emphasize that he *never* told me this, and it never crossed his mind that he would be given *Weetamoe*'s wheel. He never complained about George, but in describing to me how certain races were lost, I knew he was hurting inside. One race was lost by overstanding the mark, and it happened in an odd way. Dad had the finest eyesight of any sailor I know and could see a buoy or a wind shift sooner than anyone. On the day in question, he spotted the tug marking the weather mark and told both the navigator and the skipper that they could tack and fetch it. Unfortunately, there was another vessel which looked like a tug closer than the one standing by the mark. Dad assumed that everyone could see the real mark, but none of them could and they assumed he was referring to the other vessel which indeed they could not fetch. Hence, they overruled him despite his insistence that they could fetch. By the time he realized they saw only the nearer boat and pointed out that he sure as hell did see the mark farther upwind, *Weetamoe* was already well past the lay line. Dad blamed himself, not the others, for this breakdown in communication, but if he had been skipper they would have tacked in time and would have retained the lead they had at the time. Instead, it developed into a damaging loss to *Enterprise*.

Ernest Heard—Skipper of Shamrock V 1930

Ernest Heard was the last of a breed—the professional skipper. Until Charles Francis Adams sailed *Resolute* to victory in 1920, the skipper of defenders and challengers alike were professionals. For many years there had been many good amateur skippers but none of them sailed the really big boats. Perhaps it took so much time to campaign a big boat and to train her crew (which in those days were professional too) that the amateurs couldn't get off from work long enough to do the job. Perhaps the big boats cost so much even in those days that only a few men of

Ernest Heard, the last of a now extinct breed—the professional racing skipper. He sailed Shamrock V *against* Enterprise *in 1930.*

enormous wealth could afford them. Being wealthy or a smart businessman doesn't guarantee that you're also a hot sailor. It could be that the owners, knowing they were not up to the job, preferred a professional skipper rather than having to admit that some other amateur was better than they, but then it may have just been bowing to the custom of the days.

I never knew Ernest Heard, though I do remember seeing him—a rugged no-nonsense sort of man, yet with a pleasant demeanor. In the 1930 match he sailed *Shamrock V* competently but was done in by two things. He was up against that master strategist and fine big boat sailor, Mike Vanderbilt. He was also in the hopeless position of sailing a slower boat—a faster boat makes anyone look smart and a slower one makes the best of us look dumb. Heard might have been more aggressive, but even if he had, it wouldn't have done him any good. As it was, I hope he got satisfaction from sailing for the Cup even though his cause was hopeless.

Tom Sopwith—Skipper of the British Challengers Endeavour *1934 and* Endeavour II *1937*

I met Tom Sopwith but I never did know him. I will here break my rule about reporting only on people I really knew for two reasons. First, he came closer in *Endeavour* to lifting the Cup in 1934 than anyone ever had before, and second, I have talked to people who knew him well, as recently as 1978. He is obviously a brilliant man, not only as proven by his great success in the aircraft business but in the way he organized *Endeavour*. He also sailed her with a fine touch and with faultless tactics until his colossal error in the third race when an unnecessary tack cost *Endeavour* her third straight win and instead made the score 2–1.

That's one way *Endeavour* lost. She also lost the America's Cup through Sopwith's determination to stand on principle and not bow to pressure he considered unwarranted. Shortly before *Endeavour* left England for America her professional crew struck for higher wages. They probably assumed that they had Sopwith where they wanted him since without

Tom Sopwith at Endeavour's *wheel in 1934 came the closest of any challenger to winning the Cup, taking the first two races from* Rainbow. *He sailed even better three years later but* Endeavour II *was no match for* Ranger.

them the whole challenge would have to be aborted. But Sopwith felt the wages were eminently fair, considered the demands blackmail, and refused to give in. Instead, he fired them all and recruited a crew of amateur sailors. The amateurs were excellent but not only did they have insufficient time to train and become a well-oiled machine, but there was not time to develop the calluses required to cope with handling the lines efficiently. *Endeavour's* crew quite literally had bleeding hands before the series was over, and this might have been a real factor in some of their slow sail handling.

In 1937, with a well-trained crew, Sopwith sailed *Endeavour II* superbly, but her cause was hopeless against *Ranger,* the super boat of all America's

Cup matches. Had *Endeavour* been as well sailed in 1934 as *Endeavour II* was in 1937, the Cup would surely have gone overseas.

A friend of mine talked to Tom Sopwith in 1978, found him in fine spirits and remembering his two unsuccessful challenges as one of the great experiences of his life—remarkable for one who came so close yet lost and who was involved in bitter protests which were decided against him (see Chapter VIII).

Briggs Cunningham—Skipper of Columbia *1958*

Since the rebirth of America's Cup racing in Twelve Meters, the successful skippers have all had brillant records in small boats and have made their marks not only in open classes but also in one-design competition. Briggs Cunningham is a quiet man, an unassuming man, but a fierce competitor. He raced sports cars on the European circuit and competed at Le Mans not with a Ferrari, a Porsche, or a Maserati, but with a Cunningham! She was a great car but not quite up to the European cars which had been engineered for road racing for generations. But this effort epitomizes Briggs's delight in a stern challenge.

In sailing he had great success in the 1930s in a series of Six Meters, and in 1947 I had the pleasure of crewing for him in *Goose* when we once again won the Scandinavian Gold Cup. By that time *Goose* was no longer the super boat she was in 1938. In fact, some of the newer designs were faster. But Briggs got good starts, sailed an error-free series, and got the most out of the old girl.

His was always the boat to beat in the Atlantic class, winning several national championships in an era when Atlantics were a highly competitive class.

Briggs is not a flamboyant sailor or a brilliant one. He can best be characterized as a solid sailor and a very good one who waits for other, flashier sailors to make mistakes. His boats are always in superb working order and a breakdown is almost unheard of. He keeps a notebook of things to be done to sails or gear, and this preventive maintenance pays off not only in avoiding breakdowns but in building boat speed.

Briggs Cunningham, the likable, modest skipper of Columbia *in 1958. Great attention to detail develops the full potential from the boats he sails.*

Briggs is also modest. When *Vim* was beating *Columbia* in a number of trial races it was Briggs's idea to let the famed sailor Corny Shields take a crack at her helm. But Corny, good as he is, got no more out of *Columbia* and when Briggs resumed the role of skipper he brought her home. When one realizes that he was up against the brilliant Bus Mosbacher in *Vim* and that great sailor Artie Knapp sailing *Weatherly,* Briggs's solid performance is even more noteworthy. *Columbia* competed in three more campaigns under other skippers but never again won, while *Weatherly* became the successful defender in 1962. Briggs may not rank with the best Cup skippers but he is very little behind them and, in my view, underrated except by those who have sailed with or against him.

Bus Mosbacher is no one to fool with on the race course.

Bus Mosbacher—Skipper of Vim *1958,* Weatherly *1962,* Intrepid *1967*

Bus Mosbacher gets my vote as the best America's Cup skipper. He learned the game in Atlantics in the 1930s and in the International One-Design class immediately after World War II when it was in its heyday and populated by such sailing greats as Corny Shields, Bill Cox, Artie Knapp, George Hinman, and others. Bus didn't win each year, but he did emerge as the cream of a tough crop. He sailed dinghies well when at Dartmouth, he won the Mallory Cup and before entering Twelve Meter competition in 1958 had established himself as one of the country's top-ranking small boat sailors.

When he signed aboard the twenty-year-old *Vim* for the 1958 campaign, it was not clear whether or not he was skipper. It did not take long for Bus's brilliance to be recognized, however, and he soon had the wheel. *Vim* was still a good Twelve but in anyone else's hands would not have been a contender against the newer boats. Bus kept her in there right through to the very end of the final trials simply by more aggressive, sharper sailing. He was especially good at starts and devised what were then new tactics of blocking his opponent from getting back to the line on time. His helmsmanship was superb and *Vim* was always in the groove.

Coupled with an instinctive feel and innovative and sound tactics, Bus had the same organizational ability as Mike Vanderbilt. Things seldom went awry on any of his Twelves. You had to beat them and not count on either breakdowns or mistakes to let you through. One rare exception was the second Cup race in 1962 against *Gretel* when *Weatherly* broke her spinnaker pole when the guy was not snagged up soon enough and *Gretel* went on to win. You can bet *Weatherly*'s crew heard about it that night. Bus was tough. He drilled his crew harder than anyone and there was never any doubt as to who was boss. One night a key crew member went out on the town and missed curfew. Despite the fact that *Weatherly* was in the midst of a key set of trial races, the recalcitrant was beached for the next two races. Neither he nor any others were late thereafter.

While Bus was tough he was also fair, and I doubt if any skipper had a more loyal crew.

I found out firsthand how adept he was at starts. After we had been selected to defend the Cup in *Constellation* in 1964 and prior to the match, I invited Bus to come to Newport and practice starts against us. Bus had not raced Twelves for a couple of years, but he brought some of his old crew with him, hopped into our trial horse and proceeded to beat me at the start more often than not. His sense of timing was impeccable, as was his proclivity for handling Twelves like a dinghy, maneuvering within a few feet of us with a daring based on keen judgment of both distance and how fast he could maneuver to clear our stern, jibe inside us, or otherwise give us grief. Yes, we won some starts, something I have always felt I was good at, but Bus won more.

His keen sailing was instrumental in winning the right to defend in *Weatherly* in 1962 as well as in retaining the Cup against *Gretel*. *Weatherly* was improved with hull and rig modifications after her unsuccessful bid in 1958. Still she was no super boat and *Nefertiti,* our only new boat that year, was good only in a breeze. We were vulnerable against *Gretel,* a boat most observers felt was a faster Twelve. *Weatherly* lost one race, another was a real squeaker, but superior handling and tactics brought *Weatherly* home.

In 1967, sailing *Intrepid* against *Dame Pattie,* Bus had it easy. *Intrepid* lost only one trial race all summer, caused by a navigational error in a preliminary race in June—a loss which still rankles Bus. In the match it was no contest. *Dame Pattie* was not the dog many people thought. It was just that *Intrepid* was a super boat, just as *Ranger* had been thirty years before, and in the hands of Bus and his crew she was virtually unbeatable.

Graham Mann—Skipper of the British Challenger Sceptre *1958*

I have little to say about Graham, partly because although I met him in 1958 I never got to know him well. But the pervading reason is the fact that *Sceptre* was so badly outclassed by *Columbia* that it was impossible to get much of a reading on him. Graham did get adequate starts, was tactically sound, and appeared to have *Sceptre* on the wind and in as good a groove as was capable. After losing in light air, the British kept saying "Just wait for a breeze." When the breeze did come, *Columbia* annihilated her. No one could have won in *Sceptre,* not only because her hull was slow, particularly in a seaway, but also because her sails appeared inferior. They also insisted on using huge spinnakers, despite the lesson which could have been learned from our trials to the effect that small chutes were faster, especially in light air. The British were stubborn (stupid might have been a better word) and kept using huge spinnakers; the lighter the air, the larger the chute. Although it sounds like that would work, the big chutes collapsed more, lifted less, and were invariably slower. *Sceptre*'s campaign seemed to lack intensity; they seemed more

Graham Mann, shown at Sceptre's *wheel in 1958—one of a long line of genial Englishmen who had "a go" at the Cup in outclassed boats.*

intent in proving the British adage: "It matters not whether you win or lose—it's how you play the game." Mann lost big but he was a fine gent, much liked by all, especially *Columbia*'s crew which felt winning was pretty darned important. I'm being too hard on Mann, except for his stubbornness in not using smaller spinnakers. His cause was hopeless no matter what he did. He gets full marks for the seamanlike way his crew jury-repaired a broken main boom in the last race and carried on to the finish, losing little in the process. They were gracious losers.

Jock Sturrock (left) won one race in Gretel *against Bus Mosbacher (right), who sailed* Weatherly. *Bus on* Vim *(1958),* Weatherly *(1962), and* Intrepid *(1967) impressed me as the best of all the fine skippers who defended the Cup. Jock had the misfortune of meeting him twice, the second time in 1967 sailing an outclassed* Dame Pattie *against* Intrepid. *Bus's genial shoreside manner could readily change into that of a bucko skipper.*

Jock Sturrock—Skipper of the Australian Challengers Gretel *1962 and* Dame Pattie *1967*

One of the best liked skippers ever to challenge for the Cup was Jock Sturrock. He is a straightforward, hard-working man with a fine sense of humor and the belief that yacht racing, even when, or perhaps especially when, racing for the America's Cup should be fun. He and his crew captivated Newport with their good humor, their proclivity for drinking beer after and between races accompanied by much loud (and surprisingly good) singing of *Waltzing Matilda* and other more earthy songs. They discovered a little waterfront restaurant called The Black Pearl and made it their evening headquarters and in the process put it on the map as the "in" place to be. The Black Pearl has since been enlarged, but ever since the Aussies put it on the map it is perpetually jammed. And Jock and his crew knew how to sail. Even though pitted against Bus Mosbacher, in each challenge he got good starts. Their sail handling and general crew work was good, and in the case of *Gretel* in 1962 they came very close to lifting the Cup. Their syndicate head Frank Packer didn't help the cause by switching the navigator on the eve of the first race, nor did he help by keeping Jock up in the air as to whether he would remain as skipper. A navigational lapse may have cost *Gretel* the first race. She won the second, and in another race lost by a scant twenty-six seconds. *Gretel* was surely faster then *Weatherly* in a breeze and was helped by having the first cross-connected coffee grinders, allowing four men to grind the genoa home instead of two for the Americans, a great help in heavy weather tacking duels. Had it been a windy series we would almost certainly have lost in the 1962 match, but it blew hard on only one day.

In light air *Gretel* and *Weatherly* seemed evenly matched. The difference was slightly better sail selection and an absence of tactical errors by Bus and his *Weatherly* crew. Still, Jock sailed well and hard. He was there to win and came closer than the 4–1 score would indicate.

In 1967, sailing *Dame Pattie* against *Intrepid,* it was no contest but only because *Intrepid* was so outstanding. *Dame Pattie* was a pretty good Twelve, especially in light air. After their first challenge the Aussies apparently decided that designing a light air Twelve was the way to win and got crossed up when it blew stronger than in 1962. But even in light going *Intrepid* was faster and in a breeze it was no contest. As is often the case with an outclassed boat, Jock didn't seem to sail with the same fire as he had five years earlier. He suspected before the series and had it confirmed in the first race that *Dame Pattie* was the slower boat. It was surprising, therefore, that Jock didn't try aggressive starts. Sure, it might not have worked, but his only hope of beating *Intrepid* was to smother her at the start; yet he seemed content with getting clear air starts, a hopeless tactic against *Intrepid*. Other than that he sailed well in a hopeless cause.

Eric Ridder organized Constellation*'s 1964 campaign but didn't quite have the touch at the wheel to bring her home.*

Eric Ridder—Skipper of Constellation *1964*

Most books and articles on the America's Cup record that I was skipper of *Constellation* in 1964. Not so. Eric Ridder was. It's true that in the final trials and in the match itself I not only was helmsman but also called the shots, with Eric deferring to me should we be in disagreement. Still, Eric retained the title of skipper. After all, he was a major contributor to the syndicate and had worked for many months getting *Constellation* and her crew organized. When the syndicate managers decided to let me sail the boat, they asked if Eric could remain as skipper although I was to have full authority, especially from the sounding of the ten minute gun until the finish. I demurred at first because I felt it might be difficult to assume the role of skipper without being acknowledged as same. But once assured by Eric that I was to have a free hand, I agreed. Here I am talking about myself when we are really talking about Eric, but we became so intertwined that it's impossible not to.

Eric is a good sailor, with an Olympic gold medal to his credit in the Six Meter class. He also has had a fine record in ocean racing. His other great attribute was a flair for organizing the boat and ensuring all was in readiness. He was calm and bore up well under the pressures of a Cup campaign. Moreover, he is a perfect gentleman and a real fine guy. What's more, on the race course he has a complete grasp of match race tactics.

He had several shortcomings, however, which proved to be fatal. First, he didn't have the sense of timing or of distance to get good starts. Second, he had great trouble keeping *Constellation* in the groove and going her best when on the wind. Often we were either pinching or driving too much and very seldom just right. In these regards he reminds me of George Nichols. Eric also was stubborn in sticking to systems he believed in, even when all the evidence indicated they were wanting. For example, he had developed an intricate jibing method with lines leading into the end of the pole to cam cleats. The cams often slipped and we kept botching our jibes; we even lost a couple of early races because of the system before a near mutiny on the foredeck persuaded Eric to switch to the tried and proven *Vim* jibing method.

Eric sailed *Constellation* in the June and July trials and amassed a record of seven wins and eight losses, including five losses against *American Eagle*, which had a record of fourteen wins and no losses for the same period.

It is a matter of record (and I hope not to be construed as boasting on my part) that once Eric turned *Constellation* over to me her record for the rest of the summer was thirteen wins and three losses, with ten of the wins coming against *American Eagle*.

Eric demonstrated the fact that even in a fast boat it's not enough to be just a good sailor to win in America's Cup competition. You've got to be better than good. But he remained a great guy to the very end, never showing any sour grapes or envy when I managed to turn *Constellation* into a winner. When we approached the finish line of the final America's Cup race, I asked Eric to take the wheel. He refused and refused even to share the wheel with me as we crossed the line. That's the kind of guy he is.

Bob Bavier—Helmsman of Constellation *1964, Skipper of Courageous 1974*

This is a tough one. How do you analyze yourself without sounding like a pompous ass or a shrinking violet? But since I was involved in two successful Cup campaigns an attempt must be made. In his foreword to my book *A View from the Cockpit,* Peter Scott describes me as a modest man. I'll try to not prove him wrong and at the same time present an objective appraisal.

I've raced small boats ever since I was eleven years old, with good success in keen classes. I've also done a great deal of ocean racing. Probably my strongest attribute is the ability to steer a boat fast on all points of sailing, coupled with a good sense of the special tactics of downwind sailing. In his foreword to *A View from the Cockpit,* Peter wrote: "The point should not be missed that *Constellation* was sailed with superlative skill by a great natural Twelve Meter helmsman—probably the best in the world."

That bit of hyperbole should be taken in context as coming from someone I had beaten decisively and hence perhaps not completely objective or accurate. But Peter is right on the natural part. I'm not a particularly scientific sailor but do have a good touch and an instinctive feel when a boat is going her best and the ability to keep her there, as well as a good knowledge of tactics.

In 1964 I was loose. When I took over, *Constellation* had never beaten our main adversary, *American Eagle.* Hence I had nothing to lose and could be relaxed. I also had the benefit of feeling that *Constellation* was a shade faster than *American Eagle* and a lot faster than the other contenders, knowledge which allowed me to sail *Constellation* conservatively, concentrating on getting the maximum speed out of her with the assurance that if I didn't hack it this would be enough to see us through. It worked, as witness our thirteen win, three loss record thereafter, one loss occurring when we were dismasted. Since we had never beaten *Eagle* before, it is evident that *Constellation*'s slightly better boat speed wasn't the full answer, but it sure helped. As for the match itself against *Sovereign,* we

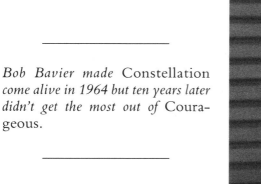

Bob Bavier made Constellation *come alive in 1964 but ten years later didn't get the most out of* Courageous.

won by the greatest margins in America's Cup history but I take little pride in that. A trained monkey could have sailed *Constellation* to victory over the hopelessly outclassed *Sovereign.*

Ten years later, in *Courageous,* it was quite a different story. Here we were the preseason favorite and this made for a less relaxed atmosphere. Early races against *Mariner* and *Valiant* to whom we never lost all summer reaffirmed our favorite's role. But when we hooked up against *Intrepid* in the preliminary trials at Newport it was quite a different story. Upwind we were definitely slower than *Intrepid,* primarily because our experimental Kevlar main was a dog. Downwind we had a decided edge, however, partly because of better spinnakers, partly, I feel, because we sailed better. We had an even record against *Intrepid* in June but each win was such a struggle that this accomplishment didn't build my confidence.

In all honesty I think I sailed *Courageous* very well in June. We shared starting honors against *Intrepid,* we won the tacking duels and we were superior on the downwind legs. Inferior boat speed did us in to windward.

The syndicate, however, was not pleased and between the June and July trials insisted we spend hours sailing upwind checking against our computer to determine whether I was getting the most out of her. We also practiced tacking, with the computer being used as a gauge to determine the most efficient tacking speed. In retrospect I should have insisted on spending more time perfecting our sails. In July we started losing the tacking duels. Our windward speed had improved a trifle but was still inferior to *Intrepid.* Downwind they had closed the gap to where there was little to choose. Worst of all, I started losing the majority of the starts against *Intrepid.* Strangely, I won most of the starts against Ted Turner in *Mariner.* Ted in turn edged Gerry Driscoll who was sailing *Intrepid,* yet I was losing the starts to Gerry. Obviously I was getting tight and not sailing as well as I should against our main rival.

In between the July trials and the selection trials of August we got new sails. The only rub was that we didn't have enough time to determine which sails were best in the various wind ranges. When the final trials began, it was apparent at once that *Courageous* was much improved and for the first time a shade faster upwind. Not so her skipper. I had been fed so much advice that I was no longer sailing instinctively but rather trying to follow the advice, some of which I didn't believe in. Result—I was sailing pretty poorly. I kept beating Turner at the starts, while losing most of the starts to Driscoll. The syndicate quite wisely directed me to let Ted Hood sail upwind after the start, with me sailing downwind. Then, after *Mariner* and *Valiant* had been eliminated, Dennis Conner came aboard as starting helmsman, Ted sailed upwind, and I sailed downwind. It could have been a good combination, but by this time I had lost so much confidence that I wasn't making sound decisions or very forceful ones. You have to have one overall boss on a boat and in effect we had three, with me being the titular boss but not acting as such. Hence we delayed in our decisions, each deferring to the other. Still, with this combination we managed a 4–4 record against *Intrepid.* Everyone knew that the next boat to win a race would be selected, and the syndicate felt that they had to make a decisive move to improve our chances. They voted to kick me off, promote Ted Hood to skipper, and retain Dennis as starting helmsman and tactician.

I have no quarrel with the decision. I wasn't sailing well, I was not sufficiently forceful and Ted was better than I. Under Ted's leadership *Courageous* did win the next race and that gave her the selection. Maybe I could have won it, maybe not, but the decision was a sound one. I quarrel only with the way I got the word, being notified as I was walking down the dock to step aboard as skipper for the climactic race and being told that I was no longer wanted. Had we discussed the situation the evening before (as the public was led to believe), I am sure I would have agreed and then it would have been a joint decision by me and the syndicate to make what was a logical move. But it was not discussed! I was simply told I was beached, which was a tough way to end three months of racing, with but one race to go.

My biggest mistake, I feel, was in not insisting on doing things my own instinctive way and also in not insisting that we get new sails before the July trials. I requested them, but when told I should wait till August, I backed down and went along.

So how do you rate Bob Bavier as an America's Cup skipper? Probably pretty high marks for 1964, pretty low ones for 1974. I still feel that doing things my own way I could have pulled it off in 1974, but I allowed myself to be coerced into doing it other people's way instead, with disastrous results. I made one other mistake. When things were so tight in the final trials, I should have taken myself off the boat instead of having to be kicked off. What is that saying about aging prize fighters being the last to recognize or to admit that they are over the hill and not the hot stuff they still consider themselves to be?

Peter Scott—Skipper of the British Challenger *Sovereign* 1964

Peter Scott, now Sir Peter Scott, is as close to being a renaissance man as anyone I know. He excels at anything he does. His father, Robert Falcon

One of Sir Peter Scott's few failures was his lost cause with Sovereign *in 1964. He has hardly sailed since.*

Scott, was the noted explorer who reached the South Pole in 1912, only to die from hunger and cold on the return to his headquarters on Ross Island. Peter inherited his father's adventuresome spirit and love of a stern challenge as well as a fierce determination to excel.

And excel he does. He took up airplane soaring in middle age and within a few years was European champion. He became a television commentator and soon had one of Britain's leading programs. He is a superlative painter, specializing in depicting waterfowl (Canada geese are his favorite subject) in their natural habitat but also was a good enough portrait painter to be commissioned to do a portrait of the Queen. He is one of the world's leading ornithologists and now head of the Wildfowl Trust at Slimbridge, England. In recent years he has gotten interested in scuba diving and snorkeling and travels worldwide on underwater expeditions recording what he has seen through magnificent photos. He is a polished and successful author.

He was for a number of years president of the International Yacht Racing Union and responsible for making it international in fact as well as in name. The skill with which he conducts a stormy meeting, keeps it on course, and gains decisions from widely diverse factions has to be seen to be believed.

And in yacht racing like anything else he was a past master, winning an Olympic Medal in his youth and the famed Prince of Wales Cup for the International 14 class when it was in its heyday.

The quest for the America's Cup is the very sort of challenge Peter would revel in. And it turned out to be one of the few challenges that he failed to win. In his foreword to *A View from the Cockpit* he writes: "To me the words 'America's Cup' mean the most publicized and spectacular failure of my life." He was right but the failure was due to the boat and the sails, not the way he sailed her. Peter did almost all anyone could hope to, given the tools he had to work with. First of all, his sails were no match for ours. Second, her hull shape was such as to slow her and induce hobbyhorsing in a seaway. I sailed *Sovereign* in one race against *Constellation* two years later (1966) in Marseilles and won with her. But, and it's an enormous but, *Sovereign* was then equipped with new Hood sails and the water was smooth. When seas built up, *Constellation* gained like crazy. And at Newport in 1964 there was always a sea caused both by the wash from the spectator craft and the wind.

Peter seemed not too tough to beat at the start in the two races we were trying to win the start. In the other two we went just for clear air since we knew we had such an edge in speed we could lose only through a foul or perhaps a severe deficit at the start. Peter should have been more aggressive at starts, and he and his crew were stubborn in flying too large a spinnaker for the bumpy conditions. But in other respects he sailed as well as could be expected. In a match race it is very difficult to look smart and sharp with a vastly slower boat.

Peter was his charming, witty self at the press conferences after each race. He is not typically British in that he came to win, not just to play the game, but he knew how to lose with dignity.

He had the following to say about losing in his foreword to my book:

So we were beaten—badly beaten—a combination which failed miserably to compete with a superior combination, but after all we had done our best. The series had been conducted without a single unhappy incident or protest. Much had been learned about Twelve Meters, their design, their sails, their handling. New friendships had been made and old ones confirmed. Even as we sailed back into Newport Harbor after the last race of the Cup series I knew that for me the effort had been worthwhile. Tony Boyden, *Sovereign*'s owner, has told me that he felt the same, even on that last bitter evening.

To my knowledge, Peter Scott has never raced a boat since, but only because he has sought other worlds to conquer and also because he is too smart to race for the Cup again with inferior tools. But sixteen years later Tony Boyden backed a new British challenge with *Lionheart,* a much better boat.

Bill Ficker—Skipper of Intrepid 1970

Bill Ficker looks like Mr. Clean but sails a lot smarter. An architect by profession, he brought a scientific analytical mind to Cup sailing, and pitted against *Gretel II* it is lucky he did. Bill is an ex-Star Class world champion, proof positive of his small boat prowess. But he's particularly adept at organizing a larger boat like a Twelve. Bill worked efficiently in training his crew and perfecting the boat and sails and in the actual races delegated much authority to his tactician Steve Van Dyke and his navigator Peter Wilson. The tactics were left largely in their hands, with Bill reserving a veto power which he seldom exercised. This allowed him to concentrate on steering—a good thing because *Intrepid* was not an easy boat to sail, especially in light air. She had been modified by Britton Chance after her triumph in 1967, and most knowledgeable yachtsmen feel she was slowed in the process. Her keel was shortened and her displacement increased. In a breeze she was probably faster than before

Bill Ficker looks like Mr. Clean but sails a whole lot better. Only masterful sailing of Intrepid *in 1970 staved off* Gretel II.

but in light air was sluggish, accelerating slowly after tacks and making excessive leeway until she regained headway.

The other new American boats *Valiant* and *Heritage* had similar weaknesses. All three were excessively heavy. The history of boats built to the International Rule had been that the larger and heavier the boat the better the performance. This time all three American designers (Chance on *Intrepid*, Sparkman and Stephens on *Valiant* and Charles Morgan on *Heritage*) had gone too far. They hoped to remain competitive in light air by reducing wetted surface but all three boats came to have too great a resemblance to a dinosaur. The handwriting was on the wall when the venerable and over the hill *Weatherly* gave them fits during the trials in light air. The Cup was up for the grabbing and only a superlative job by Ficker and his afterguard kept *Gretel II* from taking it to Australia.

We will get back to Ficker and how he won the 1970 match in Chapter X where we discuss the times the Cup was nearly lost and in Chapter VIII which covers famous protests. Let it be recorded here, however, that he did one whale of a job.

Jim Hardy—Skipper of the Australian Challengers Gretel II *1970,* Southern Cross *1974 and* Australia *1980*

He became known as Gentleman Jim Hardy, and with good reason. No more likable skipper ever challenged for the Cup. He was polite, affable, diplomatic in his statements and fun to be with. Underneath this smooth veneer was a fierce will to win. While he was charming Newport ashore he was out to get us afloat, and he came so very close! Helping him was the fact that he was a fine sailor, with a good touch at the wheel. Had he realized soon enough that in *Gretel II* he had the fastest Twelve of that year in light and moderate air, and had he governed his tactics accordingly, I believe he would have won. He could well have won also if he had known racing rule 42.3 which restricts the rights of a leeward yacht at the starting line after the starting signal. *Gretel II* did win one race and would have won another if Hardy had known this rule, but instead he was disqualified.

We will revisit Hardy and learn how he lost in Chapters VIII, X and XIII. Suffice it to say now that in 1970 he had the tools to win the Cup, and in 1980 he had an outside chance, but despite sailing well he let the greatest prize of all escape his grasp.

In 1974, sailing *Southern Cross* against *Courageous* he was outgunned. Again he sailed well, though not brilliantly. Although no match against Dennis Conner at the starts, in the first two races he was in the fight. He had the lead on the first leg of one of them and could have won if he had not overstood the mark. In the other he had a chance to round the first mark first, and since *Southern Cross* was a fast reaching boat would be expected to hold her lead thereafter. Still *Courageous* was enough faster upwind to make the Australian's cause extremely difficult. In the second race, however, *Cross* lost by little over a minute, though trailing all the

If "Gentleman Jim" Hardy had known Rule 42 he might well have lifted the America's Cup with Gretel II *in 1970. He also came close in 1980.*

way, proof that she was no dog and in fact capable of winning if she outsailed *Courageous.*

After the first two races, Hardy in a desperation move switched sails. The replacement sails were inferior, however, and *Courageous* won big. Again I feel he did not recognize how competitive his boat was. In *Gretel II* against *Intrepid* he had the slightly faster boat. In *Southern Cross* he was very slightly slower than *Courageous* until the sail switching. It would have been far better, I feel, for him to have stuck with the sails which a summer of experience indicated were his best rather than indulging in wishful thinking by trying different ones and thus putting himself completely out of it.

In 1980, he was also close. He did win one race and with better starts could have won the first three races. This match is described in Chapter

XIII, but let it be recorded here that with the exception of Tom Sopwith, Jim Hardy has come the closest to lifting the Cup. He has won two races outright and a third on the race course, which was later taken away from him through a protest. That is more than any other challenging skipper had accomplished until John Bertrand won in *Australia II* in 1983.

Ted Hood—Skipper of Courageous 1974

I have sailed more against and with Ted Hood than any of the other America's Cup skippers, and often I still do not know what he is thinking. He is an extremely quiet and shy man. I have raced with him as navigator on two Newport-Bermuda races, one of which he won. I have raced with him in the SORC. I raced against him in the America's Cup trials in 1964 when he was skipper of *Nefertiti,* and finally we spent the summer together on *Courageous* when he was my number two before I got bounced. We are good friends but still I do not feel I know him all that well, for he is a very private man.

He lets his sailing and his sailmaking speak for him. He delegates authority almost to an extreme, picking good people to sail with him and then counting on them to do their job. For example, when I was navigating for him in the Bermuda Race, the second day out there was a decision to be made as to whether we should tack. I thought we should, but it was an iffy thing and I really wanted to discuss the options with Ted. I planned to show him on the chart exactly where we were and explain the pros and cons of tacking as I saw it. But I prefaced my remarks by saying I thought we should tack, and Ted never let me explain my reasoning. True, I had raced to Bermuda many times and this was Ted's first, but still I wanted to share the burden of the tack with Ted. He wouldn't sit still for any reasoning and instead hollered to the helmsman: "The navigator says we should tack, so let's go." Thank God, it turned out to be a wise tack; we hit the Gulf Stream at the point of the most favorable current and went on to win. What I am pointing out is that Ted not only trusts you to do a good job, he expects it. When you don't, you

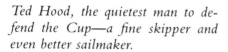
Ted Hood, the quietest man to defend the Cup—a fine skipper and even better sailmaker.

don't get chewed out, but later on the error of omission or commission is discussed quietly but forthrightly.

A passenger sailing for the first time and viewing him operating with a good crew might come to the erroneous conclusion that Ted lacks leadership. Not so. He never says anything unnecessary but when leadership is required he is there to give it. He has an uncanny feel for when a boat is not going her best. On that first Bermuda Race Ted was apparently dozing in his bunk below but popped his head up the companionway and without even looking around asked: "What are you guys doing? Cruising? Get the number one jib on." We had been debating whether we should replace the number two but were not sure. Ted in his bunk *was* sure and as usual he was right.

I do not feel that Ted is a top organizer except for surrounding himself with able people, but he can sure sail a boat. He steers well and has a superb knowledge of tactics. He is only a fair match race starter but not averse to letting someone else start for him (providing that someone is named Dennis Conner or someone else of similar competence). Still, in the climactic race against *Intrepid* in the final trials of 1974 Ted started himself. It was blowing so hard that Ted probably didn't want Dennis trying any fancy stuff and risking a breakdown. Instead Ted got a conservative start, slightly behind *Intrepid* but on the side of her he wanted to be and with clear air. It was a good start for the conditions and it did the job. I am also sure that Ted felt *Courageous* would be faster in that going and hence a safe clear air start was all that was needed. In that he was right.

While Ted was serving as my tactician on *Courageous,* his reticence in speaking out was a detriment. There were times I would have welcomed far more input. Ted is, I feel, a better skipper than he is a crew or an advisor.

There is another side of Ted's character which needs airing. As everyone knows, he is a superb sailmaker and in the 1964 trials was building sails for all the contenders. He was racing *Nefertiti* against us, but I could swear he spent even more time on our sails, and as recut by him they became even better than the ones he had on his own boat. Ted would come aboard, look at our sails, and even when we thought they were perfect, he would ask for them to go ashore for a bit of recutting. I never questioned Ted on this and seldom even asked what he intended to do with them. They would come back a day later better than ever. Ted is a man you can trust.

In the match against *Southern Cross* he sailed an error-free series, and with his slightly faster boat that was the ball game.

Ted Turner—Skipper of Mariner *1974 and* Courageous *1977 and 1980*

What do you say about Ted Turner, "the mouth of the South," that has not been chronicled many times over? Roger Vaughan has written two

Ted Turner is never at a loss for words, a fact that tends to obscure the fact that he is a fine sailor. He works hard at it and has fun doing it.

books about him. He has been interviewed by *Playboy* and been featured in *People* magazine as well as all the boating magazines. The press loves him because he is such good copy, quick with one-liners, and never dull. As the flamboyant owner of the Atlanta Braves baseball team and the basketball Atlanta Hawks, he has become known to the general public, not just to yachtsmen. In the long history of the America's Cup no skipper has done more to draw attention to the contest. Now, not only yachtsmen but cab drivers, ball players, rural housewives and, in fact, people of all ages and all walks of life know about the races. They may call it the "American Cup" races, "that sailboat race at Newport," or some outlandish name, but they know about it as never before. And they care! Many misguided yachtsmen wanted the challenger to win, but the great American public wanted Ted Turner to beat the Australians. He was the people's choice.

Ted reveled in the publicity. He genuinely loves being in the limelight and gets such a charge out of it that it becomes infectious and no one really minds that he is a ham. The fact that his talk is well-laced with humor keeps people from taking offense at most of his outlandish remarks. I remember when we were having a drink together after the first Admiral's Cup Race several years ago at Cowes, England. The German team had won the first race and sailors from many nations were gathered around the bar. Ted announced in a loud voice: "Don't worry about those Germans—they're always fast starters. Remember what happened to them after 1914 and 1939?" Even the Germans laughed (but in this instance, they had the last laugh by holding on to win the Admiral's Cup).

Vain, cocky, brash, loud, proud—all these adjectives fit Ted Turner. Less flattering words like crude and rowdy apply occasionally, but even more accurate are such terms as straight, honest, loyal. There is nothing phony about Ted Turner, and, strange as it may seem, he does not have an exalted view of himself. He knows he is a good sailor and will freely admit it, but he also knows and acknowledges when he goofs or when someone else has done a better job, either in sailing or in business. When he wins he is apt to come ashore and announce: "We annihilated them. It was just like Sherman marching through Georgia." When he loses he is apt to say: "I sailed a lousy race." And speaking of business, in his twenties he inherited a family business that was on the verge of bankruptcy and developed it so well that he is now a self-made multimillionaire.

If you are not sure whether Ted Turner likes you, do not ask. If he thinks you are a jerk, he will tell you so. But if he likes you do not expect flattery. He shouts at his crew, often in uncomplimentary fashion, but I know this is just to keep them on their toes. Still, he is not one to sail with if you have got a thin skin. In 1978 I was crewing for Ted on *Tenacious* at Newport week. Handling the main sheet was Wally Stenhouse, a strong, well-conditioned man in his fifties. Wally is a great sailor, having preceded Ted as World Ocean Racing Champion, and was doing a good job trimming the main during prestart maneuvering. But not fast enough to suit Ted who hollered to his crew: "Get that geriatric case off the main and find someone who can trim it." Wally did not bat an eye and he still sails with Ted. All of us who have sailed with Ted receive abuse in the heat of battle, but we all realize that it is Ted's way of letting off steam and keeping everyone sharp and that no offense is intended. It is significant that every single crew member who sailed with him on the 1977 defense of the Cup was with him in 1980.

How good a sailor is Ted Turner? If you had asked me that in 1974, I would have said: "Good, but far from great." Sure, he had a slow boat then and slow boats tend to make anyone look bad. Still, he was not too tough to beat at the start and some of his tactics seemed questionable. But three years later sailing *Courageous* he was outstanding. He clearly out-sailed Lowell North and Ted Hood, and that is no small achievement. Not only was he sharp personally but he trained his crew so well that *Courageous* was the best handled of the lot. Ted was quieter in 1977, relying more on his crew rather than trying to direct everything himself, a prior weakness. Gary Jobson on tactics and Robbie Doyle on sail trim were given quite a free hand, thus letting Ted concentrate on steering fast. He almost always had *Courageous* going her best.

In 1980, Ted and his crew once again sailed *Courageous* well but with a bit less fire than in 1977. While getting good starts he lost more than he won, especially to Dennis Conner. Ted's business activities prevented all-out preparation and might well have also distracted his concentration on the racing. He was done in more by the fact that both *Freedom* and *Clipper* were probably faster hulls and particularly in comparison to *Freedom*'s, the sails on *Courageous* were inferior. It was the old story of looking bad in a match race because your boat and sails were a shade slower, com-pounded by the fact that Dennis Conner and his crew were a bit sharper.

Ted Turner is a self-made sailor rather than one born with unusual natural skills. He sailed Lightnings for a number of years before even winning his home club's championship. But hard work and a great deal of sailing in boats of all sizes and types have made him a truly fine sailor. Let there be no mistake—Ted Turner loves sailing, loves the competition, and does more of it than anyone I know. Once he got on top there was no slackening. He kept putting it on the line, kept racing in top competition even though he had no new worlds to conquer. I feel he did it more

47

because he loves racing than he did to keep in the limelight. Having won in *Courageous* as an underdog in 1977 one could expect that he would rest on his laurels. But that is not Turner.

In the 1977 match *Courageous* was up against a tough challenger. If *Australia* had as good jibs, if she had gotten as good starts, and if her tactics had been as sharp, she could have beaten *Courageous*. The apparently easy victory scored by *Courageous* was not due to far better boat speed but instead to the fact that Turner and Company did a better job. They were usually ahead at the start and invariably went the right way thereafter. They often made a loose cover after *Australia*'s initial clearing tack, and each time made a big gain by letting their opponent go the wrong way. Having built a commanding lead, they then sailed conservatively with the margin between the two boats remaining virtually constant. Yes, *Courageous* was a shade faster but just a shade.

I rate Ted Turner as a fine America's Cup skipper, based on his performance on the race course in 1977. His contribution to Cup awareness, however, has to be rated at the very top. No one else has gotten the public so involved, no one else was such a sentimental favorite. True, he was drunk at the final press conference after *Courageous* won in 1977, but how many baseball players are sober three hours after winning the World Series? When Ted Turner and *Courageous* were the first to be eliminated in the 1980 defender trials, all of Newport was in virtual mourning. The people's choice was gone, never to return. Ted says, quite rightly, that three times is enough. But he will be missed, because in his inimitable way he has made more people be aware and care about what happens in races for the America's Cup than anyone else in the event's long history.

Noel Robins—Skipper of the Australian Challenger Australia *1977*

While Noel Robins is a very pleasant chap and a sound sailor, there seemed little to distinguish him. Maybe it was all bottled up within, but

Noel Robins is a thoroughly pleasant chap, perhaps too pleasant to get the aggressive starts Australia *needed to have a chance against* Courageous *in 1977.*

he seemed to lack any fierce will to win and, in fact, appeared to expect *Courageous* to win and to accept it. He got decent starts but not the aggressive ones to be expected from a challenger who expects his boat to be slower. He lost a great chance to win the third race. Turner got too far away from the line with several minutes to go. When he started back, Robins, who was nearer the line, instead of tacking on *Courageous*'s wind fell in on her weather beam. *Courageous* from that time on went full out for the line but was still twenty-two seconds late, and with a safe leeward on *Australia*. Had Robins tacked on her wind he could have slowed *Courageous* down enough to win the start by thirty seconds. Had he covered well thereafter he should have been able to stay on top because *Australia* was going well in that race, and after getting behind early lost only two seconds on the last five legs of the course. It was a golden opportunity to capitalize on the one big error made by Turner in the entire series.

Most observers thought the match was a rout. I will admit the outcome seemed inevitable after the first leg of the first race, but I feel that if the crews had switched boats and jibs the Americans still would have won. Match racing can seem far more one-sided than it is if a slightly faster boat is also the better sailed boat. The Aussies should be disappointed with their performance but not discouraged. They came closer to being really in it than most people realize.

Dennis Conner—Skipper of Freedom 1980 and Liberty 1983

In 1980, Dennis Conner finally got his chance to skipper a Cup defender and he made the most of it. He had replaced Ted Turner as skipper of the ill-fated *Mariner* late in the 1974 campaign. After *Mariner* was eliminated Dennis came aboard *Courageous* as starting helmsman. He did such a good job that I am sure he expected to be invited to skipper a contender in 1977. When no invitation was forthcoming Dennis sailed both small boats and ocean racers with such distinction that he was an obvious choice for the 1980 campaign. He has world championships in the Star class to his credit and was an Olympic medalist in the Tempest class in the 1976 Games. In big boats he has won the SORC and has excelled in Admiral's Cup competition. His match-racing prowess was proved by winning the Congressional Cup with a perfect 9–0 record.

Few Cup skippers can boast such a dazzling record and he most obviously is a fine sailor. But his greatest forte was awareness of the importance of preparation, coupled with determination to work harder than anyone else. In previous campaigns, less than a year was devoted to getting ready, but Dennis and his crew sailed *Freedom* for close to 300 days over a two-year period—days that started early and often ended after dark. Scores of sails were tested and catalogued so meticulously that *Freedom* almost always had the right one flying for the wind at hand.

Knowing that his equipment and crew were honed to perfection en-

Dennis Conner, the confident, competent skipper of Freedom *in the 1980 match, and of* Liberty *in 1983, where he was much less confident. No one ever prepared for the event so exhaustively. His easy smile is seldom seen on the race course and belies his fierce will to win.*

abled Dennis to be confident, and when he is confident he is very tough to beat, getting good starts, steering fast, and sailing tactically sound races.

All of this paid off in the 1980 match, where Conner sailed brilliantly and established himself as an outstanding Cup skipper. There was little to choose between *Freedom* and *Australia* and without superior sailing by Dennis and his crew the Cup could easily have been lost. Americans were so used to winning that *Freedom*'s victory was almost taken for granted, but it shouldn't have been.

Those who know Dennis Conner only off the race course will find him most ingratiating. He says all the right things, is pleasant and (unless you ask him who is the best sailor in the world) makes a big front of appearing modest. On the race course he becomes Mr. Hyde of the Jekyll and Hyde syndrome, particularly in match racing. Match racing is a dog-eat-dog affair and Dennis sees nothing wrong in being the meanest dog. He will shout at his opponent at the start and whenever close on the race course, often citing possible rule infractions. This is designed to ruffle the opponent and often it works. Dennis is overly quick to fly a protest flag. In the second race of the 1980 America's Cup match he protested *Australia* for failure to carry running lights after sundown. *Australia* was in direct violation of the conditions of the match in not carrying them but even so most everyone thought this was a Mickey Mouse-type of protest. Dennis did too after he had a night of sleep on it (and after the syndicate and some of his key crew members advised him that this was a low-blow way to win a race he had lost fairly and squarely). The next morning he withdrew the protest, much to everyone's relief.

Based on his 1980 performance, Dennis has to be rated among the all-time great Cup skippers. Some people felt he gained even greater stature in defeat in 1983. I don't agree. He brought to the 1983 campaign the same long period of preparation, the same hard work. But, some of the confidence was lacking by the time the match for the Cup started. First, he had a harder than anticipated time gaining selection. But more damaging was the great record *Australia II* had amassed in the challenger trials. Dennis and his crew were obsessed by the boat with the strange new keel and, in fact, were running scared. The Aussies had done a great job in extolling *Australia II* as a superior boat, where in reality she was just another good Twelve quite comparable in speed to *Challenge 12.* But Dennis and his crew feared that *Liberty* was much slower than *Australia II,* and hence entered the match in almost a defeatist mood. Dennis Conner sailing without confidence is simply not going to sail effectively. John Bertrand, in his book *Born To Win,* revealed that he was glad he was going to race against Conner as opposed to John Kolius because he felt Kolius did not have as many hang-ups as Dennis. Bertrand stated that Kolius's attitude would be, "I don't give a damn about that goddamn keel. Let's just get out there and race boats."

Conner did a good job in the first four races to make the record three to one in his favor. He was helped, of course, by breakdowns on *Australia II* in two of the races he won, but a lesser skipper might well have lost in four straight races. Still, Dennis lacked confidence and if he hadn't, in my opinion, he could have won any of the last three races. Instead Bertrand had him so psyched out that Conner made atypical errors. True, *Australia II* was a great Twelve, in most conditions better than *Liberty,* but she was not unbeatable.

Final judgment on Conner's ranking as an America's Cup skipper will have to wait until we see how he fares in the campaign for the 1987 match. Based on his 1980 performance he has to rank right near the all-time top, but this image became slightly tarnished in 1983, despite a good effort. He has proved already to be the most persistent, most hard-working of all Cup skippers. No matter what the future brings he will also be remembered as one of the best.

John Bertrand—Skipper of Australia II, *1983*

Just as Hilary and Tenzing will always be remembered as the first to scale Mt. Everest, and just as Roger Banister's place in history is secure as the first to break the four-minute barrier in the mile run, so, too, will John Bertrand be forever remembered by sailors as the first challenger to win the America's Cup. It was he who brought the longest winning streak in sports (132 years) to an end, and that in itself is enough to gain sports immortality. John avows he will never again race for the America's Cup and I believe him. He has already done it four times—three as crew and once as skipper—and is therefore well aware of the sacrifice a Cup campaign entails on self and family. Having a good sense of priorities, he says this was his last fling.

Many people credit the boat more than the skipper for *Australia II's* great victory. I don't. *Australia II* was a fine Twelve, perhaps the finest ever designed up to that time, but she was far from unbeatable, far from a super boat. It was John Bertrand first, and *Australia II* second, who won the America's Cup.

When I won the Cup in 1964 in *Constellation,* our boat was so superior to *Sovereign* that any good club racing skipper could have won. I take

pride in the fact that we won by the greatest margin in America's Cup history but I deplore the fact that we had insufficient competition to determine whether or not the skipper (me) was as hot stuff as he thought he was. John Bertrand has a similar problem. Almost everyone feels he won simply because *Australia II* was a super boat, whereas I feel he won primarily because for the first time a challenger was not intimidated and sailed at least as well as the defender.

Bertrand himself was a major contributing factor to this image of *Australia II*. He and Alan Bond realized early in the summer that the Americans (especially Conner) were worried sick about *Australia*'s new keel design. They both figured that this worry would destroy their usual confidence and make them sail erratically. Therefore, whenever *Australia II* won a trial race, Bertrand gave all the credit to his boat. Whenever they lost, he blamed only himself. The truth of the matter was that *Australia II* was little, if any, faster than *Challenge 12,* and nearly on a par with *Victory 83* and *Azzura.* But Bertrand is a great believer in the power of positive thinking, or perhaps more accurately in the harm of negativism in relation to sports. That's why he insisted on having a combat psychologist, Laurie Hayden, as a member of *Australia II's* team. And that's why he felt that if the Americans, especially Conner (who as Bertrand himself put it "likes to have the dice loaded in his favor"), believed *Australia II* was a super boat they would not sail as well. I believe he was right and believe this above everything else enabled him to win the last three races.

But it is far more than the right psychology that made Bertrand a winner. He came from a sailing family that lived close to the ocean and claims he cannot remember life without boats and sailing. At school, when he was supposed to be doing his homework, he did almost nothing but draw boats.

He owned his first boat at age seven. At age thirteen he was the State of Victoria junior champion. In his first Junior National Championship (1962) he won every race by a huge margin and sailed right into the middle of the senior fleet that had started ten minutes earlier. By age twenty-two he had won three Junior National Championships, one senior, two runners-up and one third. He raced in two Olympics (fourth in 1972 and third in 1976, both times in Finns). The first time he skippered a Soling, in 1976, he won the Australian championships with six straight firsts. Like his father, he is an engineer, which may account for his orderly mind. His mother was a champion swimmer, which may have contributed to his drive. He practiced sailing incessantly, explaining, "because we loved it. The pursuit of excellence has always driven me. We did not do it for acclamation but to achieve sailing perfection. In this way we were ahead of our time."

With all this top-level experience and achievement behind him, Bertrand at age thirty-six was well equipped to win the America's Cup in 1983. And unlike any previous challenger I know of, he was convinced in his own mind that he *would* win. What's more, he was able to convince at least half of his crew that they would win, and at the same time at least half of *Liberty's* crew that they would lose.

One might think Bertrand is cocky. I didn't find him so. Yes, he has an ego, but confident is a better adjective than cocky. Above all he seems unflappable. We invited him and his charming wife Rasa for dinner on board the America's Cup committee yacht, along with Alan Bond and a few other principals. It was right in the middle of the final trial races when the Americans were declaring *Australia II*'s keel illegal. There seemed at that time a real chance that *Australia II* would not be allowed to race, and there is some reason to believe Bertrand hated all our guts.

If so, he didn't show it. We spent a delightful evening talking about boats in general (not keels) and through it all Bertrand seemed loose as the proverbial goose. I remember thinking at the time that here was a supremely confident, likable young man who would have to be beaten if we were to retain the Cup. He surely wasn't going to beat himself through self-doubt. And since at that time I, too, was caught up in the super-boat mystique, I remember feeling that the Cup was very shaky on its pedestal, where it had rested for so many years.

How to rate John Bertrand as an America's Cup skipper? Surely the best challenger, and in the same league as many top Americans.

Let's Hear It for the Crews

It is axiomatic in yacht racing and certainly true of the America's Cup that the skipper gets the lion's share of the credit for victory and most of the blame for losing. It is not fair either way but that is how the ball bounces. Actually, the skipper is like the quarterback of a football team, certainly a key man but needing a good line (winch grinders), good ends (foredeck), good backs (the afterguard). Twelve Meters sail with a crew of eleven. J-boats sailed with approximately thirty and the huge sloops like *Reliance,* at the turn of the century, had forty-three on board.

Without a good crew and especially without a good tactician and crew boss or sail trimmer, no skipper has a chance in America's Cup competition.

Most skippers who have sailed for the America's Cup feel they had the best crew ever to sail in the epic event, which is not surprising since they have never had as good a crew before nor ever will again. America's Cup racing has such allure that the finest sailors try out for it, and only the finest of the fine are finally chosen and go all the way to the match itself.

I will let you in on a secret which other Cup skippers will deny but which is true nonetheless—the finest America's Cup crew of all time was the one which sailed *Constellation* to victory in 1964. They were the best not because of being better sailors than many other Cup crews but because of their character. Most crews would have wilted and become discouraged when we went all through the June and July trials, never once beating our main rival *American Eagle*. Not so *Constellation*'s crew. They just worked harder, kept their cool, and sailed better than even they thought they could. And they kept having fun. Their names in alphabetical order: Bob Bavier, Buddy Bombard, Put Brown, Bob Connell, Dick Enersen, Dun Gifford, Dick Goennel, John Handel, Fenny Johnson, Fred Kulicke, Eric Ridder, Larry Scheu, Rod Stephens, Steve Van Dyke. You will note that I have mentioned fourteen names. This includes three alternates, who made a tremendous contribution to our success.

It is too bad that space does not permit describing these sailors and the other great men who have defended and challenged for the America's Cup. Let's talk about just one to represent the hundreds who have sailed so brilliantly. I refer to Rod Stephens, who has crewed on three Cup defenders over a period of twenty-seven years: *Ranger* 1937, *Columbia* 1958, and *Constellation* 1964. On *Ranger* his assigned job was rover in charge of the crew and rig. He was tougher and more agile than any of *Ranger*'s professional crew and delighted in some snafu aloft which would allow him to climb the rigging hand over hand to fix it before a bosun's chair could be rigged.

On *Constellation* he came aboard late, primarily at my suggestion, when I became helmsman. I wanted someone I could rely on to be a second pair of eyes and as tactician. I also wanted someone who could get that little extra out of the crew, not in effort, because they were all putting out to their utmost, but in welding them into a more efficient team. Having crewed with Rod, I knew he was just what we needed. His title was navigator but in actuality he was also my number two, the crew

Rod Stephens kept things working and was an outstanding crew on three defenders—
Ranger *(1938),* Columbia *(1958), and* Constellation *(1964). He never crewed on a losing Cup boat.*

boss, rover, and general expert. His contribution was enormous and a big factor in our turnaround.

Actually, I did not want him as navigator because we had a superb one in Dun Gifford who, with his ability and affability, was, I felt, important to our success. There was no one I *wanted* to get rid of to make room for Rod because all were good. But I did want to keep Dun almost above all others and recommended beaching someone else to make way. This was the only matter the syndicate overruled me on, but let it be recorded here and now that the best sailor ever to be replaced on a Cup defender was

Dun Gifford. I did, however, get him back on board for the third race against *Sovereign*.

Though Rod's contribution was far more than that as navigator, his innate sense of navigation iced one win against *American Eagle*. We had a narrow lead over *Eagle* a few minutes after the start when we sailed into a pronounced header. As we did Rod scrambled below, made a quick plot on the chart and emerged seconds later with the remark, "You can tack and fetch." "Are you sure?" I asked. When Rod said "yes" that was good enough for me. We tacked away from *Eagle* while on her weather beam. It had never occurred to them that we were at the lay line. It was amusing to see the consternation in their cockpit and to see their navigator rush below. It was a full minute before they matched our tack, a minute thrown away when we fetched ("of course," Rod would say) with fifty yards to spare after sailing on that tack for three and a half miles.

One other thing about Rod which bears telling is the way he feels about boats. A good one is to him not just a conglomeration of wood, steel, aluminum, and dacron but instead something which almost lives and breathes. After a good performance he will pat the boat's topsides and will talk to her like a rider patting a horse after a successful steeplechase. Rod is so caught up in everything that makes a boat go fast, everything that makes her hold together that the boat becomes a part of him and of his thinking. Hence she almost becomes alive. He is not a timid sailor but is a conservative one, knowing how hard a boat should be driven, but stopping just short of driving beyond the brink and perhaps injuring her (or the crew). On ocean racers he is apt to shorten down sooner than others and usually just before the other boats go into a wild broaching act. Rod Stephens is a superlative seaman as well as a superlative sailor. A good man to have on your team! He epitomizes the sort you sail with when racing for the America's Cup.

Chapter III
Match Race Tactics

While it is unlikely that many readers of this book will ever compete in match racing and fewer still in the premier match race of all, an understanding of match racing is essential to a full appreciation of the America's Cup. It's a dog-eat-dog affair where the emphasis must focus on how you can hinder the other boat. Second is a pretty good finish in most races. In a match race second is last and hence both in philosophy and in tactics one's approach must differ from fleet racing.

The start is always important in a yacht race. In match racing it assumes even greater importance. This is particularly true if the two boats are even in speed or if you feel your boat is slower. In a slower boat, getting on top at the start is just about the only realistic way you could hope to win. That's why it is surprising to see slower challengers not sailing aggressively at the start. They have so little to lose by trying. If

Constellation *is squeezing up under* Sovereign *into a safe leeward position. Note how much flatter* Constellation*'s sails are.*

their aggressive approach backfires and they get clobbered at the start, it means only that they lose by a greater margin than they would have. If the tactics work it gives them a shot at victory.

With two even boats the start is also vital since the early leader has a tremendous edge. Only if you know your boat is faster should you be conservative at the start. Then you should go for a clear air start and not a dramatic one. This is easy to achieve and makes it almost impossible for the slower boat to stay ahead for long. In the first Cup race in 1964 we on *Constellation* were aggressive at the start because we were not sure we were faster. It was fun to win that start. The first race showed us that we were so much faster than *Sovereign* that the only way we could lose was by being beaten badly at the start. Hence we let *Sovereign* have her own way, let her edge us at the start in the next two races, *but in the process* we ensured that we were close behind and had clear air—all we needed to assume the lead within a mile of the start. I got angry, however, when the daily press, in reporting on those races, indicated that "Bavier sure couldn't start as well as Scott, but his boat bailed him out." Hence in the fourth race, much against our advisors' wills, we went after *Sovereign* hard at the ten minute gun and got her into such a position that in trying to beat us across the line they were early. It was, I suppose, a childish reaction on my part, since we knew by then that all we needed was clear air in order to win. But just winning isn't everything. You've got to be proud about how you won, how you sailed, and I knew for an absolute certainty that even if I blew the start completely, was over ahead of the gun or a half dozen lengths dead to leeward of *Sovereign* and dead in the water at the start, we could still catch her. Hence in this instance a conservative start wasn't necessary.

But in watching future America's Cup matches, if in the first race one boat proves faster, don't castigate her skipper if he is edged in all subsequent starts. That great starter Bus Mosbacher had indifferent starts in *Intrepid*'s 1967 match against *Dame Pattie*. He was absolutely right in so

Prestart circling wasn't invented by the Twelve Meter skippers. Here the J-boats Rainbow *and* Endeavour *go at it in 1934.*

doing because everyone knew *Intrepid* was a super boat. The blame should rest on Sturrock's shoulders, not Bus's, for accepting even starts in a slower boat. The fact that he suspected Bus would outmaneuver him if he tried to mix it up is no excuse. *He had to try.*

OK, we've established the importance of starts in a match race. How do you go about winning the start? There is no single simple answer, but the goal is to maneuver so as to be able to control the other boat's action to your benefit. The circling maneuvers are done in an attempt to get on the other boat's tail and so close that she is unable to tack or jibe without fouling. The trailing boat can thus control the actions of the boat ahead and hopefully keep her from returning to the line on time. When time has run out you can then go for the line and the other boat has no recourse but to follow. Remember, in a match race it matters not at all how late you are at the start provided you are ahead of your adversary.

This tactic will work only if you can block the other boat while maneuvering outside the extremities of the starting line. If within the extremities and to leeward of the line and able to fetch one or both ends, the leading boat, even if blocked from tacking or jibing, can stall and wait until time has nearly run out and then go for it. The trailer still has a slight advantage since he can keep forcing the action, continually trying to prod the leader closer to the line. If he times his start well, he can accelerate sooner, break through, and if all is timed to perfection, can probably either get a safe leeward or choose which end of the line to cross at, with the boat he had been tailing often forced to go for the unfavored end to avoid being blanketed. In short, the tailing position is a good one if you can pull it off—dramatically good if you have lured your adversary beyond the extremities and helpful even if you haven't.

How best to get on the tail? If possible, when you first hook up it is desirable to be on port tack, reaching with full speed and attempt to pass close to leeward of the other boat which is reaching on starboard tack. If he is smart he will try to get to leeward of you, but attempt to forestall this by bearing off yourself. Above all, allow enough time to build maximum boat speed before you meet, even if this means sharpening up on a reach and passing to windward of your adversary, who would now be broad off to get to leeward of you and hence going slow. With your extra speed you might be able to jibe or tack (depending on where he goes) and get on his tail before he can regain speed.

Let's assume, however, that everything has gone well and you do approach on port tack and are reaching to leeward of your opponent on starboard tack. A favorite and excellent maneuver is to head up just as you pass, as if to tack with the assumption that he will jibe in hopes of getting on your tail. After you fake a tack, then bear off and jibe. If he continues to bear off and jibe, when you jibe you are on starboard tack and he on port. Even if no foul ensues he has to think then of avoiding a foul, and has to maneuver so that he can't think of getting on your tail. If he jibes back you will be on his tail. If he attempts to tack clear, it will have to be such a sudden tack that he will lose way and you might again be able to get on his tail.

The first time you get together presents the most propitious opportunity for tailing. That's why it is preferable to approach on port, so your first tack or jibe will put you on starboard with right of way.

If you want to be aggressive, it's preferable to circle in a clockwise direction. You will then be jibing onto starboard tack and less speed is lost in a jibe, if well executed, than a tack, and better speed coupled with the starboard tack advantage is helpful to achieve tailing.

More often than not, since both skippers are pretty savvy in an America's Cup match, a tailing position is seldom achieved with the first tack or jibe. To gain it eventually, it is essential to achieve better speed in your circling. Avoid too tight turns. My favorite ploy is to sail an oblong circle, reaching for awhile on port tack to build speed before bearing off smartly into a jibe. If the other boat tries to turn inside you, she can't maintain speed and superior speed is very helpful. If you have better speed you can then make a quick jibe or sharp tack, cut inside your adversary, and gain the tailing position. Even if you don't, superior speed will keep you from getting tailed closely and blocked. To maintain speed, main and jib must be eased smoothly as you bear off to jibe and then trimmed furiously after jibing to rebuild speed as you sharpen up. It's an exhausting period for the crews and a mind-draining experience for the skipper and tactician. There are so many variables in this circling exercise, depending on how the other boat maneuvers, that you've got to be quick to change your game plan to fit the developing situation. Circles might be reversed, fakes initiated. If you are the trailing boat, it requires a fine sense of distance to tell whether you can swing and clear the leader's stern and thus continue to block her if she fakes a tack and instead bears off to jibe. If you touch you are out. If too far away you can't block her. The boat being tailed may try to build speed to get far enough ahead to be able to maneuver at will. Or she might kill way suddenly to force an overlap and hence be able to alter course without being blocked. In this case the tailed boat could well become the tailer. It's an exciting and deadly serious game with high stakes.

During all this maneuvering the skipper and tactician of both boats must always be thinking of how far they are from the line. If circling is not broken off at precisely the right time, the boat which appeared to have an advantage might lose out. Never should the tailing boat make one too many circles. If she does the other will come out of the circle nearer the line and in a great position to make the boat astern late for the line. You've got to break off when a bit early, but not too early. A book in itself could be written on all the variables that can occur at a match race start, but daring, judgment of time and distance, and the ability to adjust instantly to a fast changing situation, coupled with a complete knowledge of the right of way rules, are essential to be a good match race starter.

The best starters develop a killer instinct; not satisfied with just edging the other boat, once they get the upper hand, they use the time before crossing the line to widen the advantage they have gained. One should think ahead also as to which end to cross. Usually it is better to start with a safe leeward since this will force your adversary to tack into the wash of spectator boats after crossing and also, when the races were held off Newport, because more often than not the wind tends to back on the first leg of the America's Cup course (often hauling later in the day).

In prestart circling, Enterprise *(right) is close to getting on the tail of* Independence *but not close enough to block her from jibing.*

A comfort you can gain when about to engage in a match race start is the thought that the other skipper is probably as nervous about it as you are. That helps remove the butterflies and lets you think more clearly. Once the action starts you are too busy to feel nervous and, in fact, it can be great fun. It's certainly fun when you see your boat getting the upper hand.

We've devoted a great deal of space to starts because they are so important and also to give the reader a better understanding of what's going on during that period of apparently aimless circling. But important as the start is, there is so much more to match racing. Even if behind at the start in an even boat, there are still twenty-four miles to go, during which just one slip by the leading boat can turn the tables. All sailors know the axiom that in a match race the lead boat should cover. The trouble is they know it too well, because it simply isn't always true. It often isn't true if you are leading with a slower boat and sometimes isn't even if the two boats are equal in speed. Assume, for example, that the two boats are equal in speed or you are leading in a slower boat and you cross in the safe leeward position. The trailing boat *must* tack. If you tack with her you will be only one-half length ahead. If she is faster that lead is meaningless. If you see a better wind ahead or a favoring slant, or if you feel her tack takes her into unfavorable spectator wash, then *don't* tack to cover. If you are right you can build a really substantial lead. If you do get into a better slant or more wind, she will be forced to tack back and will have lost not only by taking two extra tacks, but also by not getting into the better wind as soon as you. Never in the race will you have such a golden opportunity to build a half length lead into a lead of five lengths *or sometimes a lot more.* And a five to ten length lead, even in a slower boat, is hard to overcome. Hence, *early in the race,* unless your boat is much faster, if you start with a slight lead and *you like where you are going, don't tack immediately to cover.* After all, if you're sailing for the America's Cup, you and your tactician can't be too stupid, and if you feel you're going the right way, the odds are greatly in your favor that you are. So trust your own judgment and don't cover until you've built a good lead. If it backfires and you lose the lead, the press will say how dumb you were, but it will seldom backfire. If, on the other hand, you like where the other boat is going after she tacks, you must go with her, looking for a later opportunity to build a lead. The important thing to remember is that a one length lead is far from safe early in the race and you as leader should look for an opportunity to build it by not covering when the boat astern tacks.

Courageous used this tactic in the first mile of each race against *Australia* in the 1977 match and quickly built large leads. These leads widened very little during the next twenty-three miles, proving that the two boats were more closely matched than most people realized. And also proving the merits of not always covering early in the race.

In the 1970 match, *Intrepid* beat the faster *Gretel* by almost always going where her skipper and tactician thought best, not just early in the race. That's an extreme example of the merits of not covering when

Weatherly *crossing* Gretel *in the second race in 1962. The two boats were this close throughout the race. By careful covering* Weatherly *stayed on top on the windward leg but was passed on the spinnaker reach to the finish.*

Courageous *is about to blanket* Independence. *Less than a minute after this photo was taken she swept by.*

ahead, but I don't think *Intrepid* would have won any other way. In Chapter X this fascinating match will be discussed in greater detail.

If you are ahead try to drive your opponent onto what you consider to be the unfavored tack. It is difficult to blanket the boat behind on both tacks but easy to sit right on her on one tack. Blanket her, therefore, when you feel she is on the preferred tack, thus forcing her onto the unfavored tack. And until you have a good lead, don't be too hasty to tack to cover. By delaying your cover you will increase your lead substantially, if in truth you are going the right way.

If you round the weather mark with a slight lead and the other boat sails high of the rhumb line, you can often build your lead by resisting the temptation of going up with her. Unless the wind increases in the latter part of the reach, she will lose as she comes down to the jibe mark.

After losing in light air to Columbia, *the crew of* Sceptre *(right) kept saying, "Just wait till we get a hard wind." But when it did blow they were annihilated. This photo was taken right after the start, which* Columbia *also won.*

Another time not to cover when leading is when you find you are losing in a tacking duel. In this instance break off the cover while still ahead and when you feel you are on the preferred tack. If you are right, the trailing boat will have to tack back and follow you, losing by two extra tacks and by being late getting to the favored side of the course. You'd better be good at determining which is the favored tack, but chances are you will be.

If ahead on a run, position yourself on the leeward bow of the other boat, on the very brink of being blanketed. You can always keep your wind clear by sharpening up and will increase speed as you sharpen up. But if you get dead ahead of the boat astern, when she jibes and you jibe to cover, she could well be right on your wind. That's why the position which seems precarious is actually much the safer. And if when slightly ahead on a run don't hesitate to jibe immediately if you get lifted. It's a golden opportunity to widen your lead, an opportunity which will be lost if you wait for the boat astern to jibe first. If the leader jibes when lifted and the boat astern elects not to jibe, the boat astern is almost certain to drop farther astern.

Don't be misled by all I've been saying about the merit of not always covering when leading in a match race. All of this applies only when you have a slight lead and hope to build it or if you know your boat is slower or, at best, even in speed. Once you have a substantial lead, unless your boat is much slower, it is imperative to cover the boat astern *even when you are quite certain she is going the wrong way.* That is when the axiom "when ahead cover" is absolutely true, simply because you could be wrong. Lowell North in *Enterprise* lost several races to *Courageous* in 1977 by not following this precept. I remember one race in particular (though there were a number of less extreme examples). *Enterprise* was about ten lengths ahead at the end of the run and when she rounded held port tack, heading towards a fine looking breeze to the south. With only one leg to go Turner had no option but to tack to starboard toward what appeared to be much lighter wind to the east. For awhile *Enterprise* gained, doubling her lead. Then the breeze to the south died and at the same time built in the east. *Courageous* got the new wind first and won by a distance of a full mile. Yes, I thought it looked better to the south. I'm sure Turner thought so too. But North was dead wrong in not covering and staying between his opponent and the mark when he had a big lead late in the race and had good boat speed. He picked the only possible way to lose. It matters not a whit how far you are ahead at the finish, just so long as you are ahead. Covering and taking extra tacks to ensure staying between your opponent and the mark is apt to reduce your lead, but when the lead is substantial or when nearing the finish, it *must be done even when you feel a different tack is better.*

Basic match racing tactics call for Intrepid *to tack on* Gretel II *in this situation. In the 1970 match, however, they did only when* Gretel *was on the favored tack.*

It is wise with a big lead to make somewhat of a loose cover to reduce the number of tacks and the possibility of an override, a torn sail, or other breakdown. But with a big lead this must never be done to such an extreme that you don't stay pretty much between the other boat and the mark.

What if you are behind in a match race? There it's smart to try a tacking duel, and if you see you are either holding your own or gaining, keep it up. Especially late in the race, keep tacking even if you aren't gaining because the more tacks you force on the boat ahead, the greater the chance she will suffer a breakdown which will let you through.

But early in the race, if you aren't gaining in a tacking duel, knock it off and try to get clear air on what you consider to be the favored tack. With the race still young it is vital to stay close, waiting for an opportunity to break through later rather than taking a flyer. Be particularly suspicious if the boat ahead lets you go off by yourself. She must be sure her tack is better, and unless you have a firm sound reason to believe yours is better, follow the boat ahead. In a twenty-four mile race there will be many opportunities to close ground. *So stay close.* This is particularly true if you have a faster boat. Remember that wishful thinking wins very few boat races. If *Gretel II* had followed this tactic of staying close and following *Intrepid* rather than blindly splitting when behind, I feel she would have won the 1970 match and the America's Cup. The only time to try to split or to continue a tacking duel which you are losing is late in the race when there is no other possible way to break through.

And when behind, avoid being driven to the lay line, thus allowing the leading boat to blanket you on a long last tack to the mark.

The boat astern can almost always gain by tacking in headers or jibing on lifts. The leader is apt to be thinking more about covering than he is about widening his lead, and this gives you a chance to close the gap and

Weetamoe *(left)* and Enterprise *in prestart maneuvering in the final 1930 trial. Compare* Weetamoe's *much larger wooden spreaders and her wooden spar with the trim metal mast on* Enterprise.

be in a position to gain the lead if you get a break or if your opponent goofs.

Initiating a jibing duel is also a sound tactic for the trailing boat on a run. Not only is she apt to blanket the leader at least momentarily as she crosses her stern, but there is also the possibility that the leader will make a poor jibe while you keep your chute full. It's easier for the boat astern to make a good jibe because the crew is forewarned as to the time of the jibe. Unless she gets headed as the boat astern jibes, the leader must jibe immediately after she sees the tailing boat bearing off to jibe, and hence she has a bit less time to get ready. America's Cup crews are so good that this isn't a great problem, but still it is a slight advantage for the boat astern to know in advance when she will jibe.

Once the jibe has been completed it is essential to head well high of course to rebuild the boat speed lost while jibing. This is particularly true in light air. Apparent wind must then be brought *forward of the beam,* even on a running leg, bearing off only after speed has been rebuilt. This is particularly true for the leading boat in order to keep her wind clear, but it applies also to the boat astern unless it is blowing so hard that little speed is lost while jibing and a high course isn't required to regain speed.

Match racing should be approached like a game of chess; think always about how you might thwart your opponent. It is a special and utterly fascinating type of sailing. To be good at it you've got to keep cool, be analytical, and avoid wishful thinking or flyers in hopes of catching the boat ahead of you. If you're ahead, don't be suckered into doing something foolish. One example of foolishness or wishful thinking on the part of a boat astern is a fake tack. It will *never* work in America's Cup competition because the tactician on the leading boat will be watching all through the tack and will see you abort yours. All that will happen is that you will drop farther astern.

There are so many variables to match racing that this single chapter can't begin to cover all of them. I hope only that it has given the reader a little better insight as to what goes on out there. And for those who partake in match racing and in the America's Cup itself, one parting shot of advice. Have fun doing it. I can guarantee you will sail better if you do!

Chapter IV
Why the Early Leader Often Loses

No bigger error can be made than to assume that the American boat with the best record in the June and/or July trials will surely become the eventual defender. There have been too many instances when the early leader has fallen flat in the final selection trials in August. Sometimes it has been close in the early races between two or more contenders: *Columbia, Vim,* and *Weatherly* in 1958; *Weatherly* and *Nefertiti* in 1962; *Intrepid* and *Valiant* in 1970; and *Courageous* and *Intrepid* in 1974. Eventually the first named in each instance came through in August.

Only thrice in the past fifty years has the early leader dominated all three sets of trials: *Ranger* in 1937, *Intrepid* thirty years later and *Freedom* in 1980. In 1977 *Courageous* did well in June, faltered a bit in July, but then came on strong in the final trials of August.

But in three other years the early leader failed dramatically when selection was on the line. In 1930 *Weetamoe* won the majority of the early races but *Enterprise* overtook her at the end. In 1934 *Yankee* appeared to have a lock on selection but then *Rainbow* nosed her out, winning the climactic race by a scant one second! An equally big turnaround (I am happy to say) came in 1964. *American Eagle* won the first fourteen races, being undefeated in both the June and July trials. At that stage *Constellation* had a rather dismal seven win, eight loss score. In the New York Yacht Club cruise, *Constellation* began turning things around by winning four and losing two while *American Eagle* was winning two and losing four. In the final trials *Constellation* won nine races and lost but one, while *Eagle* won four and lost six, all six losses being to *Constellation*. *American Eagle* never lost a race except to *Constellation* all year long but despite her sensational early showing, when the summer was over *Eagle*'s record in races sailed against *Constellation* was eight wins and ten losses and in the final trials, one win and six losses.

How were these dramatic turnarounds possible, and how, even when there is no big turnaround, does it happen so often that the eventual winner doesn't take charge until the final trials in August? There were different reasons for the three most dramatic comebacks, reasons we will delve into soon. But certain basic aspects in every campaign make the early races somewhat unindicative of what is to come. The June trials are not unlike spring training games in baseball or exhibition games in other sports. It is a time to experiment, to learn, and to test—a time when you would like to win but also a time when you don't feel you have to. The June trials are called "preliminary trials," and contenders are told by the Selection Committee that the results count very little in making the eventual choice. The July trials are called "observation trials," and as the name implies, the Selection Committee is watching with more care and making at least initial judgments. The trials in August are the "selection trials," the ones you *must* win to be selected to defend the America's Cup.

The June trials are frequently used for testing new sails. In 1974 on *Courageous* we persisted with a Kevlar mainsail all through June. It was a real dog to start with, and even after lots of recutting, it remained a dog. We stuck with it, though, hoping it could be recut into a breakthrough sail and knowing that a poor record in June would not hurt our chances. It did, however, hurt my confidence, even though I knew the main was poor. It hurt in another way because it was not until August that we had our final sail inventory, and even in August we were not sure which sails were best for each condition. Too much experimenting early can be harmful because the summer passes all too rapidly and everything must be sorted out prior to August.

Thus far we have been talking about trials for the American defenders and the references to June, July, and August refer to the dates of those trials. With *Australia II*'s dramatic win, we Americans are now challengers and can gain the challenger's berth only by beating the other aspirants. If they are as smart as I think they are, the Aussies will use a selection series similar to ours. It gives the defender an edge to choose the best boat, which *may* not be the boat with the best overall record.

The Aussies in 1982 and 1983 also demonstrated that the early races are not all that conclusive. In Australia, *Challenge 12* gave *Australia II* a real run for her money and remained a threat in the early elimination races in the U.S. Then she seemed to fall apart.

On some boats the early races are used to help in crew selection. Each boat has several alternate crew members and in some cases these are given a chance in June to prove their ability. The boats which do not rotate but instead use the "first team" in June are apt to be handled more smoothly in the early going.

But none of the above can explain fully the dramatic come-from-behind victories of *Enterprise* in 1930, *Rainbow* in 1934, or *Constellation* in 1964.

In 1930 many magazine covers pictured *Weetamoe* as the likely defender. Although *Enterprise* was generally sailed better throughout the summer, she simply did not match *Weetamoe*'s speed. Drastic action had to be taken and it came in the form of replacing her spruce mast with an aluminum one. The mast was first used on 3 June and at once she seemed like a different (and far better) boat. The designer, Starling Burgess, however, wanted to make some rigging changes and hence the lighter of her two wooden spars was restepped. This may have lulled *Weetamoe* (which also had an aluminum spar in reserve) into believing that *Enterprise*'s metal spar was a flop. In any event, they stuck with their wooden one on the basis that it would be foolish to change a winning combination.

When *Enterprise* restepped her metal spar for the observation trials, she encountered more rigging problems, but by the time the final trials began all the bugs had been ironed out. The new spar weighed only 4,000 pounds, 600 pounds less than the lighter of her two spruce spars. The wood spreaders were replaced by steel ones for an additional saving of 384 pounds aloft. The importance of this weight saving is dramatized by the fact that the center of gravity of her rig was 65 feet above the metacenter (which is 3 feet above the waterline). The lead keel was 14.5 feet below the metacenter, a ratio of 4.5 to 1. Hence for every pound saved aloft they could dispense with 4.5 pounds of ballast without affecting stability. Or if the ballast remained constant, stability and hence heavy weather performance would be improved. There is also much less tendency to hobbyhorse with a light rig.

Not only was the aluminum spar lighter, it also was a more efficient shape and dimension. The aluminum mast was 18 inches in diameter at deck, tapering to 8 inches aloft. The wooden was of elliptical shape 27 inches by 20 inches at deck, tapering to a circular shape of 9¾ inches diameter at the head.

While the new mast was the dominant change and biggest reason for improvement, other important modifications were made to *Enterprise* prior to the final trials. Her original boom was replaced by a Park Avenue boom, so named because its upper surface was four feet wide one-third of the way back from the mast. Two men could walk down it abreast. It weighed 2,330 pounds, 365 pounds more than the original rectangular boom, but it permitted a more efficient sail shape. Transverse tracks allowed the main to assume an efficient camber, and by adjusting the stops on the slides, the camber could be modified to suit the wind conditions—more curve for light air, less for heavy air.

The main was recut to fit the new boom. A smaller rudder was installed, reducing wetted surface by one percent. They also installed a new jib topsail winch. And to demonstrate Mike Vanderbilt's thoroughness, the compass was reswung to ensure the new boom had not affected its accuracy (it had not). When the final trials began *Enterprise* was as ready as a boat could be and ready with a lot of new tricks up her sleeve.

The most vital races were against *Weetamoe,* and *Enterprise* with her new lease on life won both of them, the first over a light leeward-windward course, the second in a twenty-five knot nor'easter. The latter was the one where the new mast brought her into her own, but few people know how close she came to losing the spar in that one. A fitting designed to keep her spreaders locked in position failed, and the after-guard was horrified to see them swinging badly out of line. They debated dropping out until Starling Burgess thought of hooking ends of the spinnaker halyard to the spreaders to keep them in line. It worked!

In writing about the incident in his book *Enterprise,* Mike said: "Every country, every individual, every boat has a high spot, a point of climax in his or its history, which often spells the difference between success or failure. I consider this the high spot of *Enterprise's* career. Had Starling Burgess failed to find the right answer, had we either withdrawn or lost our mast, I do not believe we would ever have defended the Cup. Little things often determine momentous questions."

The Selection Committee attempted more races, but the weather failed to cooperate. On two successive days there was virtually no wind. On the third day, 27 August, there was enough to start, with *Weetamoe* paired with *Whirlwind* and *Enterprise* with *Yankee.* This one was called when there was no chance of finishing within the time limit.

That night the announcement was made that *Enterprise* had been selected to defend the America's Cup. When the chips were down she had made the key moves to be able to defeat her main rival. Although they met in just two races in the final trials, one was in light air, the other in heavy, and she was impressive in both. An editorial in *Yachting* concluded with the words "No unbiased person will cavil at the ultimate selection."

Four years later Mike Vanderbilt had an even tougher uphill battle sailing *Rainbow* against *Yankee. Yankee* was improved in the four years since her launching and proceeded to beat the new boat in the first ten races they had against each other. The margins varied from twelve seconds to more than fifteen minutes but from 24 June through 15 August it was always *Yankee* first, *Rainbow* second. To make matters worse *Rainbow* lost both in light air and heavy.

Weetamoe had also been modified, but for the worse and never was in contention even with the seemingly outclassed *Rainbow.*

Prior to the Astor Cup Race on 16 August with the final trials just a week away, Vanderbilt decided something drastic had to be done. What he did was add a full five tons of ballast to *Rainbow.* Whether or not the additional ballast was the sole reason, the improvement was electrifying. *Rainbow* beat her arch rival by six minutes thirty-nine seconds and the next day won the King's Cup by three minutes twenty-two seconds.

She still entered the final trials on 22 August with a two win, ten loss record against *Yankee,* but momentum was on her side and *Rainbow*'s afterguard thought that despite the lopsided score their chances were roughly even.

The euphoria did not last long. After beating *Weetamoe* by a sound margin in the first race, *Rainbow* met *Yankee* on 23 August and got clobbered by more than six minutes. A note in Rainbow's log read "5:09 *Yankee* finishes. Good night. 5:15 we finished, licked by 6'20". This will come near finishing our hash." The only encouraging aspect was the fact that *Rainbow* lost partly by setting a quadrilateral jib instead of the genoa *Yankee* had used. This was a mistake they would not repeat. Still *Yankee* had now improved her record to eleven to two, and time was running out.

The next two days *Yankee* and *Rainbow* took turns beating *Weetamoe* which was then excused from further competition. On 27 August the *final* final races began. *Rainbow* rebounded to beat *Yankee* by more than three minutes in winds between six and nine miles per hour.

The next day in a thirteen mile breeze *Rainbow* led narrowly at the first mark, and then *Yankee* broke a strut on her mast and had to retire. Although the Committee then canceled the race, *Yankee*'s breakdown was a black mark. A blacker mark was administered on the next race day, 30 August. In winds ranging from sixteen miles per hour at the start to fourteen at the finish *Rainbow* led at every mark to win by over two minutes.

What proved to be the clincher occurred the next day over a thirty mile windward-leeward race, starting in ten knots, finishing in fourteen. *Rainbow* led at the weather mark by one minute twenty-eight seconds. On the run home with Frank Paine calling the spinnaker trim, *Yankee* kept closing. At the finish the two yachts were bow to bow. When the gun went no one on either vessel or on the spectator boats knew who won. Only the man on the line did. The official time difference was one second but it was less than that. *Rainbow* was three feet ahead!

By that slim margin she was selected to defend the America's Cup, and to defend it masterfully against the faster *Endeavour*.

While *Enterprise* and *Rainbow* came with a rush at the end by making changes to the boat, *Constellation*'s come-from-behind victory over *American Eagle* was achieved by making personnel changes. It is awkward for me to have to credit myself for part of the turnaround, but the fact is that when Eric Ridder was steering he never beat *American Eagle* and after I became helmsman we beat her in all but one trial race (losing two other fleet races on the New York Yacht Club cruise, in one of which we lost our mast). The other key crew change was getting Rod Stephens aboard as tactician and crew boss. He made the whole operation gel.

The only reason crew changes could make a difference was the fact that *Constellation* and *American Eagle* were quite evenly matched. *Eagle* won the first fourteen races because Bill Cox was sailing her superlatively well. I am convinced, however, that *Constellation* was slightly faster, certainly to windward and on a run. *Eagle* maybe had a slight edge on a reach. With *Connie* (as we often referred to her) being faster upwind, all we needed was to be close at the start with clear air. I found her an easy boat to feel, and by settling her into her groove and letting her do her stuff, we were usually in command of the race within two miles. Thereafter it was a matter of avoiding mistakes. It is pretty easy to seem smart if your boat is faster, even a slight bit faster.

I feel that *Constellation*'s last surge was due also to perfection of our sails. We did not have a large inventory (much smaller than *American Eagle*'s) but Ted Hood kept recutting the few we did have until they were perfect. *American Eagle* also had Hood sails and they were good, but whereas we never told Ted what to do on recutting and left everything up to his judgment, Bill Cox kept urging certain modifications.

During the final trials, when *Constellation*'s main looked like a fine piece of sculpture, I asked Ted if *Eagle* had one as good. "They used to" was his terse reply. Cox is a lot more scientific than I am, but our philosophy of giving the sailmaker a free hand without input from us worked better.

There is one other factor, perhaps the most important one of all, which works to the advantage of a boat which is behind in the early going. I refer to the pressure which builds on the early leader. If you are winning big like *Ranger* did in 1937 or *Intrepid* in 1967 your confidence grows and all the pressure is on the tailenders who know that only a miracle can save them. But if you are winning by small margins just the reverse is true. This is particularly true if you feel the boat you are beating is as fast or faster than yours. You keep wondering if you can keep on edging them and you worry because you know that all the wins you are racking up won't mean a damn if you do not win in the final trials.

I know that Bill Cox was running scared all through his winning streak of fourteen straight. His crew thought they had it made but Bill was too smart for that. He knew *Constellation* had latent speed and he worried about the time we would get it out of her. Bill kept sailing well, but I sensed that he did his most masterful sailing in the early races. Once we started to win, he did not sail quite as well as he had earlier.

Much the same happened to me ten years later. *Courageous* was the early favorite and in the early going I think I sailed well. But when we failed to live up to our favorite's role and had only an even record against *Intrepid,* I started to press, thought less clearly, and did not sail as well. Those sailing the underdog boat or the early loser which shows good speed can keep loose because they know that matters cannot get worse and might very well get better. It is the same as being close behind in an individual race and gaining. All your thoughts are on gaining the lead while the leader's thoughts are on how to maintain it. There is much more pressure on the leader. The trailing boat calls the moves, thinks positively, and feels there is a real chance to get past while the leader cannot help but worry about losing the lead. His tacks are apt to be hurried and in general it is harder for him to keep a cool head.

An America's Cup summer is a long one and the stakes are so high that it is almost impossible to stay relaxed. And relaxed sailors who are having fun are sure to sail to their best ability. Believe me, it is easier to stay relaxed when you are losing because any change has to be for the better. The only time I felt any pressure once I started sailing *Constellation* was after we had won a number of races but still had not been selected. I began to wonder if we could keep on beating that formidable opponent, Bill Cox. Finally we lost a final trial race on a flukey day. We lost only because of a drastic wind shift which I had called wrong, and I realized that we were not apt to do that again. The next day, with our winning streak broken, we went out full of confidence, led throughout, and gave *Eagle* one of the worst trouncings of the entire summer. That night we were selected as defender.

Chapter V
The Role of Computers

Maybe it's my unscientific mind. Maybe it's because I'm an instinctive, seat of the pants sailor. Maybe it's because I feel that in 1974 overattention to the role of a computer helped do me in. Maybe it is for some other reason. But let me say loud and clear that the supposed benefit from computers is grossly exaggerated, especially in America's Cup competition.

Don't get me wrong. They are wonderfully efficient and I take my hat off to smart people like Rich McCurdy who have developed them to help sailors get the most out of their boats. They *do* give a reading on when a boat is making her best speed made good to windward. They *do* tell you whether a fast tack or a slow tack gets you closer to the weather mark. They *do,* in the absence of a trial horse, give you a reading on how fast your boat is. They *are* a superlative navigational tool in helping you find the weather mark if a thick fog sets in. They *are* superb in telling you the precise apparent wind angle to expect on the next leg and hence a guide to chute selection. They *are* great in determining the most efficient apparent wind angle and hence course to sail on a running leg to get to the leeward mark faster. In short, as developed by Rich, they do everything they are supposed to do. Yet in America's Cup competition their value is exaggerated.

In the twelve years since I last raced in America's Cup competition, computers have become even more advanced. I used to feel they were not worth a damn for this type of sailing but I now know that it would be silly not to utilize them. It would also be silly to become too dependent on them.

If you cannot figure all of those things out either instinctively or with the assistance of a simple polar plot, dead reckoning navigation, or a pocket calculator, you should not be sailing for the America's Cup. The trouble with computers in connection with top-level sailing is that they are never wrong in a technical sense but, smart as they are, *they do not think,* do not forecast anything beyond the input that thinking people put into them. And because of their technical virtuosity and efficiency they are apt also to become a crutch and inhibit thinking. The batteries used to power them are heavy and their weight cannot be placed in an optimum position. Moreover, they need constant care to keep them running, and the time thus spent can be better utilized.

Despite their navigational ability, in the one trial race of 1977 sailed in heavy fog no boats found the weather mark and the race was canceled. Whenever fog becomes so thick that you cannot find the mark by dead reckoning the race is apt to be canceled and hence that supposed advantage of a computer is negated. And commencing in 1980 Loran was allowed, which makes it easy to find a mark even in thick fog. On a distance race where no boats are nearby or where boats are of different rating, a computer could be of great benefit in determining whether a helmsman was sailing the best possible speed to windward. But in America's Cup competition you have got a far more efficient measuring device—the boat you are trying to beat. By taking constant bearings and distances on your adversary, you learn immediately whether or not you are gaining or losing—and focusing on the adversary is what match racing is all about.

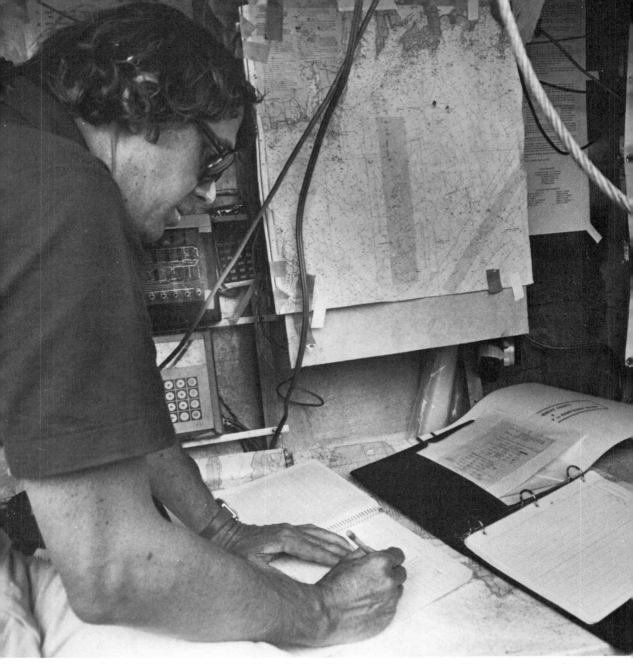

Partly hidden by Halsey Herreshoff is the ingenious computer Courageous *used in 1974, though not always to her benefit.*

As for tacking, the position of the other boat and the speed of her tack should govern whether you tack fast or slow. If a fast tack will allow you to sit on her wind, then that is the sort of tack to take, not the slower one which a computer says is better. Moreover, you do not need a mechanical device to prove the most efficient speed of tack when not in a position to blanket the other boat. You learn it pretty fast. In 1974 *Courageous* was beating *Intrepid* in the tacking duels of the June trials. Then I thought constantly of the position of the other boat in determining the optimum speed of tack. Between the June and July trials we practiced tacking for hours using the computer to determine the most efficient tacking speed. And in July we lost most of the tacking duels against *Intrepid*!

Computers are most efficient in determining the best sailing angle on a run. But this is easy to calculate almost as accurately by a pocket calculator, by a polar plot, or by simple observation of how you are doing against the other boat. *The other boat*—that is the thing to think about relative to your own. If she is sailing too broad for best speed downwind and you are ahead, it is tactically sound to sail a bit too broad yourself to better cover, just so long as you are gaining or holding even with a comfortable lead. Sailing higher and increasing your lead thereby will not work for long because your opponents will soon spot it and emulate you. Moreover, if they tend to sail too broad, why educate them? There may come a time when they are ahead, and if they sail too broad an angle, you will be able to close the gap before they catch on to why you are gaining.

As for predicting the apparent wind angle on an ensuing leg, computers are precisely accurate. And this, coupled with knowledge of what spinnaker is best for a given angle and weight of wind, should make them useful in this role. But their mere virtuosity in this respect can also do you in if you become overdependent on it and stop thinking of the tactical situation. This is precisely what happened in a 1974 final trial race against *Intrepid* where we lost a lead. We had a five-length lead at the weather mark and were preparing to set our three-quarter ounce tri-radial reaching chute for the ensuing leg. A check against the computer, however, told us that the half-ounce floater would be a shade faster since the wind had lightened and hauled a bit, making the reach slightly broader than usual. Since the computer was always right in such calculations, we stopped thinking and set it. The first stadimeter reading confirmed the computer's accuracy since we gained five yards against *Intrepid,* which was flying a three-quarter ounce radial. Then she started to gain. We lulled ourselves into believing she just had a puff, and by the time we woke up to what had happened she was nearly abeam. We switched to our three-quarter ounce spinnaker, but it was too late and she was by us.

Here is what happened. The wind came slightly ahead and increased almost imperceptibly and all of a sudden the floater was ineffective. Worst of all, it is suicide to try to luff with a floater, and hence to the surprise of unknowing spectators we held our course and must have appeared to have no fight in us. If we had not had such a blind faith in the computer, we would have thought ahead and realized that a slight header would ruin its effectiveness and also make us unable to defend ourselves. We would have deduced also that the probability was that *Intrepid* would not set a floater and in match racing it is basic that when ahead you match the opponent's weapons.

But what if we had set a three-quarter ounce chute and *Intrepid* a floater and the wind had remained constant, making the floater more effective? No big deal—we might have lost a length but certainly not our entire lead. All we would have had to do was sail a few degrees high to make the three-quarter ounce chute effective during the minute or two it took us to get the floater ready. If *Intrepid* followed us she would lose ground with her floater. If she sailed her own course she would be a length or two closer but on our leeward quarter—not a favorable position from which to pass on a reaching leg. That is the way sound sailors think and computers cannot reason like the human brain.

I asked Ted Turner a year ago what he thought of computers for America's Cup sailing. Without a moment's hesitation he replied, "Worthless." Lowell North is more sold on them, but remember who won in 1977. Lowell was probably the best fleet racer of the three at Newport in 1977. Despite my low opinion of computers, all the current Twelve Meters use them and I must admit that they have been vastly improved over the one I was using in 1974. My current opinion is that they are helpful, *provided* the input they give is not relied on slavishly and provided they do not become such a crutch as to stop the skipper and tactician from thinking and from observing how their boat is closing against the boat they are pitted against. It is important to always re-member that the America's Cup is a match race and that mastery of match race tactics is what is needed to come home first, not second. Do not count on a computer to do it for you.

Chapter VI
Why Twelve Meters?

For a number of years after World War II it appeared that the 1937 match between *Ranger* and *Endeavor II* would be the last one sailed for the America's Cup. Rising taxes and the enormous cost of building and campaigning a J-boat made them as extinct as a dinosaur. No challenges were forthcoming.

While no one knows for sure just what it would cost today to design, build, and campaign a J-boat for one year, a conservative estimate is ten million dollars, and it could well cost a great deal more. When one realizes that once a J-boat is no longer a winner, her resale value is nil (many were scrapped within a year or two of their building) it is no wonder that no one was interested. To complicate matters further the Deed of the Gift did not allow competition in smaller boats.

But there were feelers from abroad about the possibility of reviving the competition in smaller boats and, thus encouraged, the New York Yacht Club looked into the possibility of getting the deed altered. Commodore Henry Sears and past Commodore Harry Morgan were able to convince

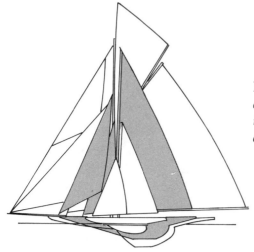

Reliance *was the largest defender, dwarfing the J-boats (shaded drawing). Both make the Twelve Meter, drawn to the same scale, look tiny.*

the courts that the deed should be changed, and it is only because of their efforts that the America's Cup races are alive and well.

Once the decision was made to go to smaller boats, it next had to be decided how small and of what type. There were those who felt it should be in boats as small as Six Meters to open the competition to a broader number. This was shot down on the basis that even though the competition would be keen it simply would not induce the same excitement. If nothing else, America's Cup boats have always been majestic and that fact contributes to the interest that not only yachtsmen but the general public has taken in the event.

A few people felt it should be sailed in a new one-design class but that is an aspect of the deed which I am sure will never be changed. The competition is intended to test not only the sailing ability of the challenger and defender but also the design capability and the technological savvy of the countries involved. This, incidentally, has had the beneficial effect of improving hardware, sails, and seagoing gadgets which then later have applications in the size and the type of boats more of us race.

A more responsible case can be made for sailing the America's Cup in ocean racing type yachts which could be converted to race and cruise after the match. Many people still feel this would make sense. I do not, for a number of basic reasons. The first is the fact that such a boat, if of comparable size to a Twelve Meter, would cost just as much to build. Yet the cost of a Cup boat itself is only about one-third the total cost of a year's campaign. True, such a boat would have a better resale value, but when one considers the cost of conversion, probably it would sell for only $100,000 more than a Twelve. While that is still a lot of money, it is only about one percent of the cost of a campaign.

Another flaw with using ocean racers is the fact that there already exist major events for that type boat—the Fastnet Race, Bermuda Race, the Transpac, the Admiral's Cup, etc. The America's Cup races might then become just another event.

An equally great problem would be the rating rule. Whether one picked the IOR, IMS, or any other rule for ocean racers, it would be far easier to design a boat which would be unbeatable if she happened to experience in the match the very weather she was designed for. This is true to some extent under the International Rule to which Meter boats are designed but to a far lesser degree. It would be a pity if the America's Cup was won or lost by an extreme boat which in effect lucked into it and this danger is minimized under the International Rule.

These lines of reasoning focused attention on Twelve Meters. In my view they are the ideal choice. The fact that they are out-and-out racing boats makes them logical for a closed course match race series. The fact that they are closer winded than other boats gives them appeal. The fact that they slice through a leftover slop or power to windward through a raging sea almost as if (except for the spray) it were not there makes them unique. The fact that in light air they will sail faster than the wind, despite their heavy displacement, gives them a feel which no other boat I have ever sailed can quite equal. Sure, a catamaran is much faster, faster even than a J-boat, but it is entirely different, a toy, albeit an impressive one, as compared to a majestic, powerful machine.

The mere impracticability of a Twelve gives it an allure and excitement. It is the type of boat any sailor would love to sail or to own if he lets his heart rule his head. And in America's Cup racing, despite all the cerebral

Models of all defenders and challengers for the America's Cup are on display in the New York Yacht Club. In the foreground is Intrepid *as of 1970, with* Gretel II *behind her. Behind* Gretel II *is* Intrepid *as she was in 1967, with far more lateral plane.*

shenanigans which go into it, emotion remains a vital part. Twelves are emotional boats. They are large enough to be majestic in today's yachting scene, and hence capture the public's fancy. Combine that with the practical aspect of a rule which provides for close competition in a variety of wind ranges and they emerge as an ideal choice. You may question that statement about close competition, but my guess is that the margin between two one-designs would be as great after twenty-four miles of racing as it has been in recent matches between the Twelves. Against *Intrepid* in the 1974 trials we won one race by two seconds, lost another by eleven.

But in the final analysis the Twelves are a better choice than an ocean racer primarily because they are exciting thoroughbreds. I am all for ocean racers, would far prefer to own one even if the cost of a Twelve were not out of my reach, but if you were either a jockey or a track nut, which would you rather have in the Kentucky Derby, a field of Percherons or those otherwise impractical animals—thoroughbred race horses?

Chapter VII
The Designers

No one has had a greater impact on the America's Cup than the small group of men who have designed the challengers and defenders. And great credit must go to the American designers for keeping the Cup in this country. George Steers, designer of *America* one hundred and thirty years ago, started our winning ways by giving her crew a superior boat. With few exceptions the Americans have been blessed with a "better mousetrap" in the matches. Superior sailing has helped us win the Cup but no more so than superior design.

Two American designers stand head and shoulders above all the rest in their influence on the Cup races—Nathanael G. Herreshoff and Olin Stephens. They are joined by two foreign designers who created the fastest boats in three matches, only to lose out to superior sailing by the American skippers and crews. I refer to Charles Nicholson of England and Alan Payne of Australia. They are joined also by Ben Lexcen, whose brilliant design of *Australia II* brought the Americans' long winning streak to an end.

Nathanael G. Herreshoff

I've elected to talk only about the years since 1930 but an exception must be made in the case of Herreshoff. Although I never knew him, I feel as though we are old friends. My first boat was a Herreshoff 12½ Bullseye sloop. My dad won the 1924 Bermuda Race in the converted N.Y. 40 *Memory* which Herreshoff designed. He also owned a Fishers Island 31 which excelled on the 1946 New York Yacht Club Cruise, despite being designed about 30 years before most of her competitors. And immediately after World War II I owned and raced a Herreshoff S-boat. All were lovely boats.

Nat's grandson Halsey Herreshoff crewed for me as navigator on *Courageous* in 1974 and was her navigator in the successful defense of the Cup. Nat Herreshoff, therefore, is close to me in many ways and it would be unthinkable even if he were not to exclude him from the list of America's Cup boat designers on the shallow premise that his era preceded the one covered by this book.

Nathanael Herreshoff was born in 1848 and died ninety years later. For most of his life he lived and worked in Bristol, Rhode Island, from which stemmed his appellation "The Wizard of Bristol." So great was his dominance in the field of designing and building of yachts that, as Bill Robinson points out in his book *The Great American Yacht Designers,* the period of 1890 to 1920 was known as "The Herreshoff Era."

He had equal success in designing both small boats and large, both power and sail. In power boats his 94-foot *Stilleto* set the unofficial but generally accepted speed record. Nat designed her engines too. With a beam of only 11'6" she could cruise effortlessly at 20 knots and in 1895 made an eight hour run at an average speed of 26½ knots. Herreshoff experimented also with sailing catamarans, the first of which was the 25-foot *Amaryllis*. He took great delight in reaching past the Fall River steamers, delight too in showing her heels to all the monohulls. He abandoned the type only when they were banned from open competition. It was seventy-five years before catamarans reemerged to any prominence, now being recognized as the fastest of all sailing types.

Nat Herreshoff, the "Wizard of Bristol," whose designs defended the America's Cup in five different matches. No designer has ever so dominated his profession.

Those who might consider fin keels and separate spade rudders as modern would be surprised to see models dating from 1890 in the model room of the New York Yacht Club, designed, of course, by Nat Herreshoff.

One of his most famous yachts was the 71½-foot *Gloriana,* built in 1891. Unlike other boats of the day which featured a deep sharp forefoot and short overhangs, *Gloriana* has a cutaway forefoot below the waterline and long ends protruding both fore and aft from her waterline of 45'4". Long diagonals enabled these ends to increase sailing length when heeled, length which was not then taxed under the rule. She bears more than a casual resemblance to the Twelve Meters of 1958 and 1962. In her initial year she was absolutely unbeatable.

We have just touched on the many famous yachts he designed, but his greatest fame came from designing the six successful America's Cup defenders between 1893 and 1920: *Vigilant, Defender, Columbia* (twice), *Reliance,* and *Resolute.*

Reliance was not only the biggest of the lot but best showed Nat's inventiveness. On a waterline length of 90 feet she was 149 feet overall and 201½ feet from the tip of her bowsprit to the end of her main boom. Her sail area of 15,000 square feet was more than twice that of the J-boat

Ranger and nearly eight times that of a Twelve Meter. On a reach she was surely the fastest Cup defender of all time, though *Ranger* would have probably beaten her around the course, largely because of her marconi rig which was more efficient to windward.

Reliance was a skimming dish with a very shallow hull to which was affixed an enormously deep keel. It is a wonder such a hull, light as it was, could hold up to the pounding she was subjected to when beating to windward in a hard thrash. But Herreshoff was as practical as he was inventive and devised ways such as laminated frames, and a number of small frames as opposed to the general custom of fewer, more massive ones. Most of her fittings were designed by Captain Nat himself. Nine of her winches, which he also designed, were below deck, including, as Bill Robinson points out in his book, two speed self-releasing ones for wire sheets and backstays. They also had worm gears, multiple speed clutches, and ball bearings, features previously unknown on yachts. These winches were so efficient that some were used on *Ranger* in 1937.

Herreshoff was a unique combination of artist and engineer. *Reliance* was designed from a model as opposed to the present practice of lofting a set of lines. It took him but two days from the very first model to develop her lines in this fashion. The term "an eye for a boat" applied to Nat Herreshoff better than anyone before or since. Only Bob Derecktor of the current top designers still works from models. Could this be one reason why Bob's boats are so sea-kindly as well as fast? Could it also be why when Bob was building *Valiant* for the 1970 Cup campaign he told me before launching that she did not look right to him? *Valiant* turned out to be one of Olin Stephens's few failures.

But Herreshoff was so much more than an artist. Like Derecktor three-quarters of a century later, he was a master builder. His Herreshoff Manufacturing Company, which built all his Cup defenders, was the premier yacht yard in the world. Herreshoff got his formal training at M.I.T. and maybe that's why all his inventive, even radical (for the day), ideas worked in practice. He was a master in figuring stresses and a genius in building hulls and fittings which, while lighter than those of competitors, stood up to the work they were asked to do.

The six challengers against *Vigilant, Defender, Columbia, Reliance* and *Resolute* were up against so much more than good skippers and crews. They were pitted against Nathanael Herreshoff. No wonder they were trounced!

Olin Stephens

The only other America's Cup defender designer to rival Herreshoff's dominance is Olin Stephens. Olin, with characteristic modesty, would insist that I refer to his firm name of Sparkman & Stephens, but Olin was the resident genius at S&S, with a notable assist from his brother Rod when it comes to the design of rigging, fittings, and making things work.

The brothers Stephens got their start with the success of *Dorade,* a breakthrough ocean racer which, though the smallest boat by far in the 1931 transatlantic fleet, finished two days ahead of the next finisher. From there followed such successful ocean racers as *Edlu, Stormy Weather, Baruna, Blitzen, Bolero, Gesture, Finisterre, Dyna, Bay Bea, Tenacious,* and a host of others. Their boats dominated ocean racing (*Finisterre* winning the famed Bermuda Race three straight times) for over thirty years; more than fifty years after their first design, *Obsession,* which came out in 1978, is one of the truly top offshore contenders.

Their successful one designs include the 13½-foot *Blue Jay,* and 19-foot *Lightning* plus a host of stock cruising/racing boats for such firms as Tartan Marine, Hinckley, and Nautor. While best known for designing sailboats, some of the most handsome and efficient power yachts and motor sailers have an S&S origin.

Olin was and is perhaps most at home and most successful with the deep narrow boats fostered by the International Rule of measurement. His six-meter *Goose,* designed in 1938, was a breakthrough for the class and forty years later was still winning an occasional race. His twelve-meter *Vim* designed in 1939 was so far ahead of her time that in 1958 she came close to being selected as defender of the America's Cup, the first

Olin Stephens has the record for designing successful defenders, six in his own right; Columbia *(1958),* Constellation *(1964),* Intrepid *(1967),* Courageous *(1974 and 1977), and* Freedom *(1980). When* Freedom *was designed, Bill Langan was project designer, but Olin, as head of the firm, provided input. In 1937, he collaborated with Starling Burgess on the design of* Ranger.

year it was sailed for by the Twelves. Of three new boats only *Columbia,* also designed by Olin, was able to beat her out.

Like Herreshoff, Olin Stephens's greatest fame came from his success in designing America's Cup defenders. In 1937 he teamed with Starling Burgess in the design of *Ranger,* the greatest of all J-boats. Olin also sailed on *Ranger* as did his brother Rod. The fact that both are crack sailors was of great help in perfecting their designs. Olin knew by feel, not only by calculation, what made a boat really go. In 1958, as already stated, his *Columbia,* sailed by Briggs Cunningham, beat his *Vim* with Bus Mosbacher at the helm. *Weatherly,* designed by Phil Rhodes, and Ray Hunt's *Easterner* were badly beaten.

In 1962 the only new American boat was *Nefertiti,* designed by Ted Hood, and a revamped *Weatherly,* sailed superbly by Bus Mosbacher, was the winner.

Olin was back in the winner's circle once again in 1964 with *Constellation,* which I had the privilege of sailing. She was clearly the cream of the crop. In 1967 he again designed the winning boat *Intrepid,* as close to a breakthrough design among Twelves as *Vim* had been in her day twenty-nine years earlier.

Olin proved himself to be only human by creating a bit of a turkey in the form of *Valiant* in 1970. *Intrepid,* redesigned by Britton Chance for the 1970 match, beat her out as defender. But his failure with *Valiant* showed one of Olin's greatest attributes—an ability to learn from his mistakes and to benefit thereby. *Valiant* did win the June trials by a narrow margin over *Intrepid.* I asked Olin how he felt. "Rotten," he said. "I'm afraid all of this year's boats are too heavy, too extreme in length and displacement. *Valiant* may be the worst of them all." He was perhaps too severe in criticizing *Valiant* which did wind up second but dead right in recognizing the weaknesses of all the American boats in that year.

He came back strong for the next challenge in 1974 by creating that great Twelve *Courageous* and also by redesigning *Intrepid* so effectively that she pushed *Courageous* right up to the final race before losing out.

In 1977 *Courageous* won again, only the third boat to defend twice (*Columbia* at the turn of the century and *Intrepid* in 1967 and 1970 being the others). Second to her, beaten largely because she was not as well sailed, was Olin's newest design, *Enterprise.*

Olin has more than matched Herreshoff's record of designing six America's Cup defenders. He has six in his own right (*Columbia* in 1958, *Constellation* in 1964, *Intrepid* in 1967, and *Courageous* in 1974 and 1977 and *Freedom* in 1980). In 1937 he had a major role in the design of *Ranger,* though he told me her basic hull design was one developed by Burgess. In 1970 he couldn't really claim credit for *Intrepid* (nor would he want to) because Britton Chance had reworked her design so much that she was in effect a Chance design. Langan did the lion's share of the work on *Freedom* but as head of S&S Olin deserves equal credit. He also spent the entire summer at Newport as advisor to *Freedom*'s crew.

While yacht design as practiced by Herreshoff was an art, backed up by an engineer's and builder's practicability, Olin's approach is perhaps more analytical and more scientific, backed up by a thorough knowledge and feel of boats. He was the first, together with Ken Davidson, of Stevens Institute, to use a towing tank to check a new design (originating with

Ranger). A tank does not create a design but if one is a past master at analyzing the input from towing a model (and Olin is!) it can tell you which of several models is apt to be faster.

While Herreshoff's full life was wrapped around designing and building (he often slept at the yard) Olin's interests are varied. He loves classical music and is most knowledgeable about it. I went to the London Symphony with him and between acts was astounded to hear him comment on how good the second violinist was. With anyone else I would have expected him to be showing off, but with Olin I'm sure he could detect said violinist's virtuosity. I have also accompanied Olin on a tour of London's art museums, and while I studied art appreciation in college, I felt like a babe in the woods. He paints for relaxation and this heightens his appreciation of the masters.

While Olin is a crack sailor, he has not raced or campaigned his own boat since 1934. He does still race from time to time with owners of his various designs and is always welcomed aboard. But most weekends are spent with his wife Suzie in a hideaway in Massachusetts and most recently Vermont. On the job he is all business and tireless. I have spent two summers with him in connection with the 1964 campaign on *Constellation* and ten years later on *Courageous*. Olin worked from dawn to after dark on perfecting each boat. He watched each race and each practice sail with intensity and shot many rolls of pictures. His comments and suggestions were most helpful, diplomatically presented, and were always listened to.

When around boats he thinks of nothing else. After the 1964 match as *Constellation* was sailing back to Newport in company with *Sovereign,* my wife Charlotte was on the bow of our tender along with Olin. Olin was saying hardly a word and kept his eyes glued on *Constellation.* Charlotte broke his reverie by asking Olin if he was mentally designing the next defender. Olin laughed and then admitted that that is exactly what he was thinking of and added something to the effect that he was watching the bow and stern overhangs and their minor contribution to sailing length. *Intrepid*'s ends three years later were distinctly different, and good as *Constellation* was, *Intrepid* was a definite improvement.

I've talked first about Herreshoff and Stephens since they were the two most dominant designers of Cup boats. The other great designers of America's Cup defenders and challengers will be considered in chronological order, commencing with 1930.

W. Starling Burgess

W. Starling Burgess was the designer of the three J-boat defenders: *Enterprise* in 1930, *Rainbow* in 1934, and *Ranger* in 1937. Were it not for his spectacular success with *Ranger* it would be all too easy to write him off as a good but uninspired designer. But, as Olin Stephens will verify, *Ranger* was primarily a Burgess design and she well deserved the often overused appellation "super boat." In her brief career she never lost a trial race and was the ultimate refinement of the type.

Burgess grew up in boats and the designing of them. His father Edward was a noted designer, including three Cup defenders: *Puritan* 1885, *Mayflower* 1886, and *Volunteer* 1887.

Like Herreshoff and Stephens, Burgess was a sailor as well as a designer and, as recounted in Chapter IV, it was his ingenuity which kept *Enterprise*'s rig in when a spreader swung loose in the climactic heavy weather race.

For both *Enterprise* and *Rainbow* it was an uphill battle for selection. *Weetamoe,* designed by Clinton Crane, was basically the fastest boat in 1930. Burgess's greatest contribution to the success of *Enterprise* was not only in the design of her aluminum spar but also in rigging it to stand properly. These were largely "uncharted waters" because heretofore all masts were of wood or steel, but Burgess did his calculations well.

In 1934 it was *Yankee* which was the apparent cream of the crop, but Burgess worked with Vanderbilt to perfect *Rainbow* for the final trials. Attention to detail is vital to bring a racing boat up to peak form and at this Burgess was a master.

Although he usually figured things most scientifically, he made one goof which, while amusing, did have its serious side. Burgess was of slight build and when he was hoisted aloft one day to check the sheave at

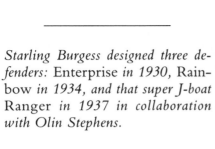

Starling Burgess designed three defenders: Enterprise *in 1930,* Rainbow *in 1934, and that super J-boat* Ranger *in 1937 in collaboration with Olin Stephens.*

Enterprise's masthead, he forgot to calculate the weight of *Enterprise*'s main halyard as opposed to his own. As he was nearing her masthead on a bosun's chair, he started to ascend at an ever increasing speed. Shouts to hoist more slowly were to no avail, and he shot up until coming to a jarring stop at the very top. What had happened was the fact that his own weight was so much less than that of the halyard that the halyard, with no one pulling on it, shot him aloft once he neared the top. This demonstrates the massive gear required by the J's. Burgess might still be up there if he hadn't figured out the problem and pulled himself down by means of the two-part halyard.

Burgess's masterpiece was *Ranger,* a personal achievement little less noteworthy because Olin had collaborated with him. *Ranger* was primarily Burgess's baby and a superb monument to a successful if not brilliant career as a yacht designer.

Burgess was in competition not only with noted American naval architects such as Clinton Crane *(Weetamoe),* Frank Paine *(Yankee),* and L. Francis Herreshoff *(Whirlwind)* but was also up against the great British designer Charles Nicholson.

Charles Nicholson

Nicholson was like Nat Herreshoff in being not only a naval architect but also a builder. Camper & Nicholson was to England what the Herreshoff Manufacturing Company was to America.

His 1930 challenger *Shamrock V* was a poor example of what was to come. *Enterprise* won with such ease that it is likely any one of the four American contenders could have defended the Cup successfully. I suspect, however, that the fault lay not with *Shamrock*'s hull but with her rig. Compared to the defender's, *Shamrock*'s rig was heavy and complicated, with crude fittings which increased windage and weight aloft. Bedecked with indifferent sails she was no match for *Enterprise*.

But Nicholson recognized these shortcomings and his *Endeavour* four years later sported a clean and efficient rig which one of her crew, Frank Murdock, helped design. She had the type of "Park Avenue" boom *Enterprise* had and her mast was not only of a small diameter but was also trimly stayed and equipped with clean fittings. Most significant, however, was the superb hull form of *Endeavour*. She was larger than *Rainbow* yet was so graceful as to appear smaller. Painted a lovely color blue which to this day bears her name, she was in my view the most beautiful J-boat of all time.

And how she could go! In light air and heavy, both upwind and down, she was a real flyer. In Chapter X we discuss how *Rainbow* managed to beat her after losing the first two races. But *Endeavour*'s loss was no fault of Nicholson. For the first time in the history of the America's Cup the challenger was faster and as *Yachting* reported at the time: "The only man to make no mistakes was *Endeavour*'s designer, Charles Nicholson."

As great as *Endeavour* was, Nicholson was able to improve on her three years later with *Endeavour II*. But the improvement was minor, while *Ranger,* the adversary in 1937, was a quantum leap forward. Had Nicholson had the benefit of tank testing, like Burgess and Stephens, he might have fared better. *Endeavour II* was no slouch, however, and put up a good fight. She was clearly the second fastest J-boat ever built.

Nicholson's reputation as a great designer was made in *Endeavour,* the boat that everyone knew could have and should have lifted the Cup. His

Charles Nicholson, designer of the British challengers Shamrock V *(1930),* Endeavour *(1934), and* Endeavour II *(1937).* Endeavour *should have beaten* Rainbow, *and only* Ranger *could have beaten* Endeavour II.

reputation as a gentleman was solidified by the fact at no time did he ever blame anyone for failure to win with *Endeavour*. He didn't have to because the yachting world knew *Endeavour* was the best J-boat in the world in 1934, but a lesser man than Charles Nicholson would still have complained, especially when the prize was so great and so obviously within his grasp.

When the America's Cup shifted to Twelve Meters thirty-one years later there were, with the exception of Olin Stephens, a new generation of designers. We've already talked about Olin's resounding successes with a series of Twelves, but who were his adversaries?

David Boyd

In 1958 and 1964 the designer of the challenger was a Scotchman, David Boyd. His credentials were some quite good Six Meter designs, particularly *Circe,* plus a sprinkling of ocean racers and local one designs. There were British designers such as Arthur Robb of greater renown but Boyd was given the nod.

His *Sceptre,* created in 1958, had trouble beating some ancient British Twelves in early brushes but improved with tuning. She was best identified by a round barrel-chested forefoot. When Olin Stephens first viewed her hauled out at Newport, he was heard to remark: "Either David or I are awfully wrong." It soon became apparent that it was not Olin who was wrong.

In the 1958 match *Columbia* won easily in light air. Perhaps to keep their hopes up the British kept saying: "Wait till we get a real breeze." But when the strong wind they had been waiting for did arrive, *Sceptre* lost by an equally wide margin. She simply would not go in any kind of seaway and at Newport, in light air as well as heavy, there is always a sea.

In Boyd's defense it should be noted that *Sceptre* had inferior sails and was hurt especially by her crew's predisposition to flying huge oversized spinnakers which simply do not work off Newport, with the possible exception of running in fresh air. Still *Sceptre* was a sure loser even with the finest sails.

She did have one clever and efficient feature, in the form of a large crew cockpit which allowed both winches and crew weight to be lower. Such a cockpit was subsequently barred but I suspect it was a good idea and that without it *Sceptre* would have been still slower.

Six years later Boyd was commissioned to design the British challenger *Sovereign* on the flimsy pretense that he now had experience with the type. In *Sovereign* he replaced *Sceptre's* barrel bow with a fine one, designed to slice better through a sea. The trouble was that above the waterline *Sovereign* had a great deal of flare and as a result she lifted to each sea and hobbyhorsed to a disgraceful extent. Again it was the wrong way to cope with a sea. She was hindered also by sails which were no match for *Constellation's* and by crude and heavy rigging and fittings aloft, reminiscent of the cumbersome gear *Shamrock* was festooned with thirty-four years earlier. It made you wonder if the British would ever learn and was a real step backward from the beautiful and efficient *Endeavour.*

David Boyd, designer of the British challengers Sceptre *and* Sovereign, *which were annihilated by* Columbia *and* Constellation.

Even though *Sovereign* lost by the greatest margins in America's Cup history, I do not think she was intrinsically as bad as her record and certainly an improvement on *Sceptre*. I base this largely on the fact that I raced *Constellation* against her two years later off of Marseilles. *Sovereign* was then outfitted with Hood sails, and I got the impression that though we beat her in four straight races there was little to choose between the two boats as long as there was not much sea running. This was confirmed when I was persuaded to skipper *Sovereign* for one race after the series was over. True, we got the start, and true, a sea never did build up and this helped me. Still, we gave *Constellation* a real licking. When I later reported our win to David Boyd he was beside himself with relief, accepting the fact that he and *Sovereign* were now vindicated. The truth of the matter was that *Sovereign* was still outclassed whenever the sea built and it always builds at Newport, if not by the wind then from the wash of spectator boats. David Boyd was a charming, diffident and modest man but, based on *Sceptre* and *Sovereign,* far from an inspired designer. I am sure that with equal sails and sailed equally, *Constellation* would beat *Sovereign* even in smooth water and kill her as the seas increased. *Sovereign* can best be characterized as an average Twelve, better than the dog that *Sceptre* was, but no match for the likes of her good contemporaries such as *Constellation, American Eagle, Gretel, Weatherly,* or *Nefertiti.*

Phil Rhodes and Bill Luders

I am lumping Phil Rhodes and Bill Luders together simply because they both deserve credit for *Weatherly,* the successful defender in 1962. Rhodes designed her in 1958, and although well sailed that year by Artie Knapp, she was beaten not only by *Columbia* but also by the aged *Vim.* She was in there in many races, won quite a few of them, particularly in light air and showed a great deal of promise. You just have to be the slightest bit slower to lose in a match race and *Weatherly* was a question of being close but no cigar. Rhodes was a successful designer of a number of fine ocean racers such as *Caribbee, Escapade,* and the Bermuda Race winner, *Kirawan.* He was, however, inexperienced with the International Rule and had never designed a Twelve prior to *Weatherly.* That she came so close, despite being third best, is to his credit.

Bus Mosbacher, who beat her with *Vim* in 1958, saw enough in *Weatherly* to accept the role of skipper of her for the 1962 campaign.

For 1962 she remained basically a Rhodes design but Luders was brought in to advise on modification. It will never be completely clear how much Luders did contribute. Her stern was shortened, weight was saved in other ways, and her keel shape was modified. Rhodes was in on these modifications but so was Luders, and to whom the greatest credit should go for her improvement the world will never know, though it is known that the change in her keel shape came as the result of tank testing conducted by Luders.

But no one will argue that she was improved. The fact that Bus Mosbacher was now at her helm certainly helped. A great skipper always makes a designer seem smart. But in any event, *Weatherly* prevailed not only over the 1958 defender *Columbia* but also over the one new boat, Ted Hood's *Nefertiti. Neffie* could beat her in a breeze but *Weatherly* was the cream of the crop in light to moderate and vastly improved in a breeze over her form four years earlier. She had to be improved, had to be well sailed in the match itself to prevail over a design by a new designer of Twelve Meters, Alan Payne of Australia. Phil Rhodes doesn't rank at or near the top of America's Cup designers, but he was a designer of great

Phil Rhodes designed only one Twelve Meter but Weatherly *was a close contender in 1958 and was the successful defender in 1962 against* Gretel.

talent, especially at home with beamy, fast ocean racers. In an era where deep narrow ocean racers were in vogue he developed extremely fast broad centerboarders. He also was the leading motor sailer designer of his era and had a number of outstanding motor yachts to his credit. He hardly ever designed a slow boat and never an ugly one. *Weatherly* was the first International Rule boat he ever designed and to come so close on the first crack shows his ability. He was at a disadvantage in not being an active sailor or racing man, but he knew how to design boats for others to enjoy and do well in.

Bill Luders, on the other hand, was one of the country's outstanding skippers. When the International One Design Class was in its heyday with such luminaries as Cornie Shields, Artie Knapp, Bill Cox, Bus Mosbacher, George Hinman, my dad and myself all competing, Bill

Luders was always up there and won as many races as any. Moreover, he did not race as seriously or intensely, having other interests such as tennis at which he was very good. Though a sound designer, I suspect the changes he recommended to *Weatherly* were of the sort a keen sailor would suggest, a sailor who had an instinctive feel of what makes a boat go.

In 1964 he proved his ability as a designer in creating *American Eagle,* the apparent shoo-in for selection until *Constellation's* late surge.

Alan Payne

Of all the designers of America's Cup challengers until Ben Lexcen created *Australia II* and won the Cup, only Charles Nicholson and Alan Payne had designed boats faster than the defender. Payne really exceeded Nicholson since he designed one boat that was surely faster, *Gretel II* in 1970 and prior to her, *Gretel* which in 1962 was better than *Weatherly* in a breeze and perhaps her equal in light to moderate.

Alan Payne, designer of Gretel *(1962) and* Gretel II *(1970). The former could have won and the latter should have.*

Payne was unfortunate in 1962 in having his boat up against Bus Mosbacher who surely got the very most out of *Weatherly*. He was unfortunate too in that *Gretel*'s owner Frank Packer mucked up the works by changing *Gretel*'s navigator at the last moment and in deciding only at the eleventh hour that Jock Sturrock was to be her skipper. Jock was a fine sailor but, as I know from firsthand experience, it is distracting to have an owner looking over your shoulder and second-guessing your every move. Jock sailed well but Bus and his crew sailed better, and better sailing decided the issue, although *Gretel* did win one race. *Gretel* was a fine Twelve and in at least one respect was a step ahead of any other. She was the first to have her coffee-grinder winches cross-connected so that by shifting a clutch those grinding on the windward winch could give power to the leeward one. This permitted four men instead of two to grind in the genoa, a great edge in a heavy weather tacking duel. They put this to good use in the second race of the match, the race which *Gretel* eventually won.

In 1970 *Intrepid,* as revamped by Britton Chance, was faster than *Gretel II* in hard going but everyone but Chance feels she was slower in light air and equal at best in moderate going. In Chapter X we describe how *Gretel* managed to lose. It surely was not Alan Payne who was at fault. He had designed but two Twelve Meters but each one in her maiden year was probably the fastest in the world.

In 1974 in *Courageous* we brushed against *Gretel II.* Until *Courageous's* sails got perfected the two boats were locked in. I am not implying that *Gretel* was as fast as *Courageous* but even when she was four years old she was very, very close.

Alan Payne is not only an extremely competent designer but one of the nicest people you could hope to meet. He loves boats, has an instinctive feel about them to supplement his technical savvy, and loves to talk about them. While not shy in the sense of Herreshoff and Stephens, he is quiet (except when talking about boats), is unassuming and so modest about his own ability that one has to find out for oneself that he is one of the world's finest yacht designers. He has the valuable asset of not feeling he knows it all and, like Olin, is always eager to learn. On top of it all, he is a warm and thoroughly pleasant human being. It is a sad commentary about the profession, at least in Australia, that this superlative designer is unable to pursue yacht design as a sole profession, though he will make time available if an inviting design opportunity presents itself. For the 1983 challenge he designed *Advance,* a Twelve that failed to live up to her name. His reputation as a fine designer, however, was already secure.

Warwick Hood

Warwick Hood, designer of the Australian challenger *Dame Pattie* for the 1967 match, is an unlucky man. He was unlucky first of all for his boat to have to meet Bus Mosbacher sailing *Intrepid* in the year when *Intrepid* demolished everything before her. *Intrepid* lost only one race that year and that one only because her navigator went to the wrong mark in an early trial race on Long Island Sound. In every other race all summer long she

Warwick Hood, designer of the unlucky 1967 Australian challenger, Dame Pattie.

took *Weatherly, American Eagle, Columbia,* and *Constellation* into camp, usually by wide margins. She won convincingly in light air but was even more impressive on the few days there was heavy air.

Hood was unlucky also that the gamble he made in designing *Dame Pattie* to be at her best in light air backfired. It was a logical, perhaps even sensible gamble but there were fresh winds, though not really strong ones, in all four races of the match, and *Dame Pattie* was overpowered. In the heaviest weather, which came in the first race which started in eighteen knots of wind, she lost by five minutes fifty-eight seconds, but in the other three the margins were all about three and a half minutes. In the last race when the wind died from twelve knots at the start to eight at the finish *Dame Pattie* actually gained on one leg and held virtually even on another. If it had been an all light air series, I still do not think she could have handled *Intrepid* but she would surely have been closer. As it was, in weather generally not to her liking, *Dame Pattie* lost to *Intrepid* by slightly lesser margins than the other American contenders had throughout the summer. Without question Hood had designed a good Twelve, capable of beating any Twelve Meter then afloat except the one she had to beat in the match.

Warwick Hood, who was 35 years old when he designed *Dame Pattie,* is a quiet, modest, almost self-effacing man. He will not go down in history as one of the great America's Cup designers, but he deserves to be remembered as a far better one than *Dame Pattie*'s record might lead one to conclude.

Britton Chance

Britton Chance deserves inclusion among the list of designers of boats which raced for the America's Cup because his redesign of *Intrepid* for the 1970 match was so complete that, though originally an Olin Stephens design, when Brit got through with her she was truly his own. Something in the neighborhood of $300,000 was spent modifying the lovely *Intrepid* of 1967. Her keel was replaced with a much shorter one to reduce wetted surface. Her stern sections were filled out and displacement increased. And her deck layout was changed drastically.

Brit should not be too heavily criticized for the fact that these changes probably slowed *Intrepid* down. This was the year that all the American designers went too far in exploring the upper limits of the International Rule. Olin Stephens started with a new design after extensive tank testing, as did Charley Morgan, designer of *Heritage*. Yet, Brit Chance's redesign was clearly the cream of a rather sour lot. The handwriting was on the wall when the venerable *Weatherly* pressed them in several races and even won a few. All the new boats accelerated slowly, made leeway in light air until speed was built up and required a real breeze before they began to feel lively. But Brit Chance had designed a faster boat than Olin, with both of them having explored the same type of design. In the final trials, *Intrepid* beat *Valiant* in six out of the seven races they sailed against each other. She was the only American boat of that year that could have beaten *Gretel*.

Chance's weakness, however, was his lack of objectivity in recognizing that while *Intrepid* was the best of the American boats she was no great shakes. With his already boundless self-confidence buoyed by this suc-

Britton Chance, designer of the successful defender Intrepid *in 1970 and the disastrous contender* Mariner *in 1974.*

cess, he must have believed himself infallible because four years later he created in *Mariner* one of the most radical (and disastrous) Twelves of all time.

While Olin recognized that he had goofed in 1970 and got back on the track by creating the more conventional but superlative *Courageous* and revamping *Intrepid* to an even higher standard than that achieved in her initial year, Chance plowed off boldly into uncharted waters. The most unusual feature of *Mariner* was a squared-off flat section at the after end of her run below the waterline. Tank tests had indicated to Chance that this increased sailing length and that, contrary to what one might have expected, it did not increase drag. What he had overlooked was the scale effect which made it efficient on a small model but which did not work on a full-sized Twelve. At a speed of twenty knots it might work, but in light air it was disastrous, disastrous also at a Twelve's top speed of eleven knots. Brit was so sure of himself that the same type "fastback" stern was affixed to *Valiant,* which was serving as *Mariner*'s trial horse. As a result they lost their yardstick and by beating *Valiant* in early brushes developed false confidence. I remember viewing her afterbody with horror on the day *Mariner* was christened. It just did not seem possible to me that such a shape could do anything but create turbulence and drag. Early trial sails revealed her causing all sorts of fuss and pulling a stern wave, instead of leaving a smooth wake. *Mariner*'s skipper, Ted Turner, was customarily outspoken (and correct) in evaluating this radical design feature by exclaiming: "My God, Brit, don't you know that even turds are tapered."

Through it all Brit maintained an air of supreme confidence. He even seemed unconvinced after *Courageous* annihilated *Mariner* in the N.Y.Y.C. spring regatta June 1 and 2. I couldn't believe how much faster we were than both *Mariner* and *Valiant* with their "fastback" sterns. It was obvious to us that *Mariner* was so much slower that nothing but drastic surgery could make her a contender. Chance, however, blamed her losses on the fact that Turner was sailing poorly, wiggling too much, and not keeping her in the groove. This did not make him very popular with *Mariner*'s skipper or crew but more important it prevented them from making modifications. Instead, *Mariner* went to Newport unmodified to participate in the preliminary trials commencing 24 June. It was only after she got trounced in that series that she went back to the builder's yard where at great expense her "fastback" was removed and a new underbody designed. This caused her to miss the July trials and the valuable experience they provide. When *Mariner* returned for the final trials in August she was improved, but by that time *Courageous* and *Intrepid* were in fine tune; *Mariner* never won a single race except when paired against *Valiant.*

Three weeks were lost while Chance was too stubborn or too blind to admit after those two early races in June that *Mariner* and not her crew was hopelessly outclassed. Had she been modified immediately she could have shaken down in the July trials and have been far more ready for the final trials in August. I do not feel that, even as modified, she could have ever been the equal of either *Courageous* or *Intrepid* but the delay in making changes made her cause completely hopeless.

Britton Chance is in many respects a fine designer, as well as a good sailor. His father was an Olympic gold medalist and Brit has also been a highly successful skipper in keen competition. He designed a number of outstanding 5.5 Meters and more than a few fine ocean racers. His Achilles heel is an inability to recognize or to admit his mistakes when he makes them. In consequence he pursues blind alleys too long. I remember a discussion about boats with Brit when we were flying back home from London following the I.Y.R.U. meetings. I admit to being no designer and to not having Brit's scientific mind, but I will not admit to not knowing something about boats. Whenever I expressed an opinion different from his, Brit gave me the Word as if from On High. I feel Britton Chance is a highly intelligent, perhaps even a brilliant man. Should he ever learn that he is not always right, he could still develop into a brilliant designer. He is plenty smart. All he needs are some "street smarts." He will have another opportunity to prove himself in 1987, since he is one of the three designers for Dennis Conner's *Stars and Stripes* syndicate.

Ben Lexcen

Ben Lexcen, designer of *Southern Cross* in 1974 and co-designer with Johan Valentijn of *Australia,* the 1977 challenger, is one of the finest sailors ever to design an America's Cup challenger. He has been Australian Champion in the Soling class (and twice on Australia's Olympic team) and he has raced everything from dinghies to ocean racers. It is his instinctive feel for boats, his constant involvement with boats, and not book learning that has made him a great designer. His formal education stopped at an early stage; he hated school and was bad at math, and so he quit. He feels this is perhaps an advantage because it forced him to learn yacht design by looking at boats, sailing good boats, and instinctively concluding what features make them go. In so many respects he is like that great American sailor and designer, the late C. Raymond Hunt. Both Lexcen and Hunt had little book learning, both made mistakes occasionally, but both had great empathy with the sea. They are both innovative and both have created some outstanding designs.

Ben Lexcen, né Bob Miller, designer of Southern Cross. *After changing his name, he designed* Australia *in collaboration with Johan Valentijn. Both boats were fast but* Courageous *beat both of them 4–0. Then in 1983, he insured his immortality by designing* Australia II *and her winged keel to win the America's Cup, ending the Americans' 132-year winning streak.*

I first met Ben when I was in England for the 1973 Admiral's Cup series when his name was Bob Miller. For somewhat obscure reasons, he later changed his name to Ben Lexcen. Miller's designs, *Apollo II* and *Ginkho,* were members of the Australian team and in my book were the two fastest boats there. He is a fun guy to be with. He is big, warm, good humored, amusing, and not a bit stuck on himself. But you know immediately that he knows what he is talking about.

He first got into the business by becoming a sailmaker and a very good one and then became a designer. One of his more recent designs is the maxi-ocean racer *Ballyhoo* which beat the great *Kialoa* in the races for the California Cup and the San Francisco Perpetual Trophy. She also won the China Seas Race and took fourteen hours off the previous record in the Around the State Race, a circumnavigation of the Hawaiian Islands.

In *Southern Cross* he came up with a fine Twelve, probably the fastest Twelve ever on a reach. She was innovative in having an articulated rudder, a feature which may or may not have helped her. Out of water she looked fast and on the race course she lived up to her looks.

She had the misfortune of sailing against *Courageous*, the misfortune also of trying to best Dennis Conner at the start. Still, in both of the first two races she was leading halfway up the first weather leg. Tactical errors did her in each time and she rounded the first mark behind. In the second race, which she lost by only one minute eleven seconds, she had her best chance. Had she not overstood, she could have rounded first and on the reaches she proved faster.

After two losses, at least one of which could have been a win, the brain trust on *Southern Cross* panicked and made a number of unfortunate changes in the sails they used. She then lost the next two by wide margins, but it is my feeling that with everything right *Southern Cross* was very nearly the equal of *Courageous* and capable of beating *Courageous* had she been the better sailed boat.

For the 1977 challenge Lexcen teamed with Johan Valentijn in the design of *Australia*.

In the match, *Australia* proved fast. She gained on the downwind legs but was always behind at the start and at the first mark. Thereafter she lost little ground. It is my feeling that if the crews and jibs had been swapped the Americans could have defended successfully sailing *Australia*. I do not mean to imply she is inherently faster than *Courageous* (I doubt it but I am not sure) but I do know her jibs were god–awful and she was not sailed as well as *Courageous*.

In 1980, Lexcen and Valentijn went their separate ways. Lexcen not only crewed aboard *Australia* but also designed her flexible rig and her sophisticated, hydraulically operated spreaders. They made a good boat so much better that she would almost surely have beaten either *Courageous* or *Clipper*. As discussed in Chapter X, they also gave her a real crack at beating *Freedom*.

Lexcen's crowning achievement was the design of *Australia II* in 1983. She was a smaller, lighter Twelve than any that had ever raced for the

Cup. Yet she excelled in heavy air, as well as light. Only in the intermediate wind ranges was *Liberty* her equal. The now famous winged keel was to a large degree responsible for her performance. In Chapter XII we discuss the questionable legality of this keel under the International Rule and the America's Cup Deed of Gift. But there is no question it was a brilliant concept. It enabled the ballast to be lower than ever before. It increased *Australia*'s draft as she heeled, instead of decreasing it as in all other boats. It bit against the water so effectively that leeway was minimized even though her keel was small.

The fact that the keel was so small did two things. First, the reduction in wetted surface contributed to straight-line speed, and second, the small fore and aft dimension made *Australia II* extremely maneuverable, a great advantage in prestart sparring and in tacking duels. Even without the creation of this innovative keel, Lexcen would be recognized as a fine designer. Creating the keel and an overall design that won the America's Cup insured his immortality as a designer.

The unique keel was a breakthrough in a rule that was believed incapable of breakthroughs. This, following on Lexcen's development of the flexible rig on *Australia* three years before, demonstrated his innovative genius. The rig was abandoned in subsequent boats only because the rule was modified to penalize it. The keel could easily have suffered the same fate but the IYRU keel boat committee decided that the America's Cup races were the proper venue for innovative ideas and decided not to tax the unquestioned speed factors of the keel. Will Lexcen come up with another breakthrough in years ahead? It doesn't seem possible in the strict confinements of the International Rule of measurements. But that's what we thought before *Australia II* was conceived. In any event, Lexcen will go down in history as a truly great designer.

Johan Valentijn

Johan Valentijn, already mentioned briefly as teaming with Ben Lexcen in 1977 to design *Australia,* is as nimble in changing nationalities as he is adept at designing fast boats. The America's Cup Deed of Gift requires

Johan Valentijn teamed with Ben Lexcen to design that formidable challenger Australia II, *in 1977.* Australia *was back in 1980 but Valentjin had switched camps as designer of* France III. *In 1983, he designed* Magic *and* Liberty, *the latter proving the best American Twelve but not quite the equal of* Australia II.

that a designer must be a citizen of the country his boat represents. Valentijn was originally Dutch and graduated in naval architecture and marine engineering from the Technical Academy at Haarlem, The Netherlands. For five years he was employed at Sparkman & Stephens and was familiar with the lines of *Courageous.* It was to his credit (and Lexcen's) that *Australia* was far from a copy of *Courageous.* While there was a family resemblance below the waterline (albeit with changes), above the waterline she was distinctly different. Her freeboard was a full six inches lower. That in itself would make her faster because low freeboard imposes a penalty under the Rule that can be offset only by reduction in waterline length and/or sail area. In *Australia*'s case the waterline length was reduced. It is interesting to note that *Freedom,* three years later, had low freeboard, too, almost the same as *Australia*'s.

In 1980, Valentijn became a Frenchman and designed *France III.* He did such a good job that she got into the finals of the four challengers. She then won one race against *Australia.* Many at Newport felt that had she had better sails, she could have gotten into the match against *Freedom*. If she then had a bendy rig, she could have given *Freedom* fits. You do not pay off on "ifs" and I mention this only to indicate that Valentijn knows how to design a fine Twelve.

Three years later, now an American, he designed two boats. The first was *Magic,* which explored the possibilities of a truly small, light Twelve. Had she had a winged keel, *Magic* would have been a real factor, but without it she was outclassed. In *Liberty,* however, he designed the fastest conventional Twelve of all time, conventional meaning she had a traditional keel. She was, in fact, faster than *Australia II* on reaches and her equal around the course in moderate wind strengths. In short, a very fine Twelve Meter.

For the 1987 match, Valentijn (still an American and I hope he will remain so) is the designer of the Eagle Syndicate's boat representing the Los Angeles Yacht Club. Little is known at this writing of this new boat, but you can rest assured that she will be faster than *Liberty.* Whether that is enough to prevail remains to be seen. When I talked to Johan a year after the 1983 match I asked him if he felt a winged keel was essential. Not necessarily so, he said. This indicates a mature approach. Valentijn will surely try a winged keel and I suspect his new boat has one, but great yacht designers retain an open mind, learning from the past but hoping to conceive a new approach. I consider Valentijn a great designer. It was unfortunate that *Liberty* had to run afoul of *Australia II,* but this didn't mean she wasn't a great boat, surely the best of the U.S. contenders.

Valentijn is a studious, quiet type, almost professorial in demeanor. He has an open mind and is not unafraid to explore uncharted waters in design. I'm glad he is on the U.S. team because I wouldn't be at all surprised to see a Valentijn design win the America's Cup, very possibly in 1987.

Bill Langan

Bill Langan was only twenty-three years old when he started to work on the design of *Freedom* in late 1978, and hence ranks as the youngest of all

Bill Langan is far more than a nice young guy. He is a brilliant yacht designer.

America's Cup designers. He is now chief designer of Sparkman & Stephens, which fairly shouts the esteem that prestigious firm has for him. In the best S&S tradition Bill emphasizes that the design of *Freedom* was a team effort. He points out that while he was working on *Freedom*'s design, Olin Stephens remained as chief designer, Mario Tarabaccia was the chief draftsman and Alan Gilbert the engineer. One has to almost drag out of Langan the fact that he was the project designer, was responsible for the plan and aided Olin in the design decisions. While Olin was overseeing the work and had the final OK, it was Bill Langan who did most of the work, who lived with the project and who was responsible for many of the new ideas.

Freedom was a *development,* as opposed to a *departure,* from the previous great Twelves designed by S&S. But she is far from a copy. She was designed more to encourage tacking efficiency as opposed to straight line speed. The forward end of the keel and underwater sections are therefore more rounded and less V-shaped on the premise that you would not put a V shape on an airfoil. The bottom of the keel has less V to get the ballast lower for increased stability. She has less freeboard, once again to increase stability and decrease windage. Her clean run is reminiscent of *Intrepid*'s, but is broader to increase reaching speed.

All of these modifications worked out as expected, and I feel it is safe to say that in 1980 *Freedom*'s hull was the fastest of all the Twelves. Langan feels that the bendy rig originally on *Lionheart* and developed on *Australia* was a bona fide breakthrough and a concept he wished they had thought of. He feels that with the injection of girth measurements in the future it will remain obsolete but that in 1980 it was brilliant. Had *Freedom* had such a rig, I suspect the 1980 match would have been a rout in her favor instead of the real cliff-hanger it developed into.

For the 1987 match, Langan has the enviable opportunity of designing the boats for the America II Syndicate representing the New York Yacht Club. He has created three new designs. The first did creditably in the 1986 World Championship, finishing third behind *Australia III* and *New Zealand,* despite some untimely breakdowns and snafus. If the next two boats are an improvement, as one would expect them to be, it will be tough to beat them. Now if he can prove his brilliance, he can recapture the America's Cup.

Bill Langan has everything going for him as a designer. He is, first of all, a fine small boat sailor (Lightnings, 470s, Solings, etc.) and has since proven himself as a good ocean-racing skipper. He has been sailing since he was ten years old and he has the bug as well as the ability. Since he was good in math and the sciences he latched onto yacht design as a great way to combine his two loves. While studying at Webb he worked for S&S between terms. Upon graduation he wanted to do yacht design but not seeing how it could pay off he went into ship design, working with Hank Tiedeman, a relatively lucrative but to him boring aspect of naval architecture. When Olin asked him to join S&S, with the assurance he would be given real responsibility for creating fine yacht designs, he leapt at the chance. Do not be misled by Bill Langan's quiet, unassuming manner. He is sharp as a knife, technically sound, has an eye and feel for boats and is one hell of a fine sailor. What else do you need to be a great designer?

Chapter VIII
The Famous Protests

The long history of the America's Cup has been marred by few protests but there were zingers in both of the two closest matches. Had they been decided in favor of the challenger the Cup could have gone overseas.

In the fourth race of the 1934 match *Endeavour* protested *Rainbow* for two alleged violations, one after the preparatory signal, the other on the second leg. In the first incident Sopwith claimed that *Rainbow* "while overtaking yacht" balked *Endeavour* and forced her to bear away to avoid a collision. The second incident occurred after rounding the first mark, Sopwith claiming that as *Rainbow* was passing *Endeavour* to windward she failed to respond to *Endeavour*'s luff and that *Endeavour* was forced to bear away to avoid a very serious collision.

Unfortunately, neither protest was heard by the New York Yacht Club Race Committee, which was also the protest committee. They were not, for the good and proper reason that the rules then as now specified that "a protest on the score of breach of rules occurring during a race must be signified by *showing a flag conspicuously* in the main rigging of the protesting yacht *at the first reasonable opportunity* and when passing the sailing committee unless the competitor has no knowledge of the facts justifying the protest until after the conclusion of the race. Failure to observe this rule will debar a competing yacht from bringing the incident to the notice of the committee."

Note particularly the words *"at the first reasonable opportunity."* You might not like this rule. In fact I do not, since it prevents a guilty yacht from being disqualified if the innocent one is tardy in flying a protest flag. BUT IT IS A RULE, IT IS SPECIFIC AND WHETHER THEY LIKE IT OR NOT A PROTEST COMMITTEE MUST BE BOUND BY IT.

It is a matter of uncontested fact that *Endeavour*'s flag was not displayed until about three hours after the occurrence of the first alleged foul and nearly two hours after the occurrence of the second alleged foul. Sopwith was tardy because the frequent practice abroad was to display a flag only when next passing the Committee boat. Their rule specified that the flag must be displayed "at the earliest possible moment and when next passing the Committee boat." They often sailed a course two or three times around and tended to neglect the "and" in their requirement and considered that they had fulfilled the requirement of the rule if the flag was displayed when next passing the Committee boat.

Sopwith, in learning that the committee would not hear his protest, wrote as follows: "I regret to note that your committee refuses to hear *Endeavour*'s protest of yesterday owing to my not having complied with a very trivial technical formality regarding the time my protest flag was flying." I sympathize with his point of view but I do not agree with it. The rule under which he was racing was specific and he did not comply with it.

The general public and the press, however, were all on Sopwith's side and felt that the New York Yacht Club had acted in a high-handed manner.

What they did not know, or chose to overlook, was the fact that the Race Committee had seen the first incident at close hand, had made notes on it, and subsequently had the added evidence of a series of photos and were convinced that in the first incident *Endeavour* was dead wrong. They expected *Rainbow* to hoist a protest flag but Mike Vanderbilt chose not to. In its own account, printed later in the club's records for that year's racing, the committee stated:

> We are reliably informed that the international character of the race alone prevented *Rainbow* from protesting at the start, it having been agreed between Harold S. Vanderbilt and the America's Cup Committee, prior to the commencement of the races, that as a matter of policy protests should be avoided.
>
> Your committee were unanimously of the opinion that in the event of a hearing held by them they would have had to disqualify *Endeavour* for having failed to observe the Racing Rule which reads: "When both yachts have the wind free on different sides, and neither can claim the rights of a yacht being overtaken, the yacht which has the wind on the port side shall keep out of the way of the other."

They did not buy Sopwith's claim that *Rainbow* was overtaking and anyone studying the photos of the incident, as I have, would have to agree. The committee also stated that: "It seemed impossible to your Committee that the taking of evidence at a hearing could cause us to materially modify the views formed as a result of our own very clear observation and now substantiated by photographs of the incident."

It is for the above reason that the committee decided not to institute an investigation of its own into the incidents covered by the protests. They had the power to do so under the rule of the era which read: "Should it come to the knowledge of the Race Committee, or should they have reasonable grounds to believe that a competitor in a race has in any way infringed these rules, they shall have the power to disqualify such competitor without protest . . . after a hearing."

They did not utilize this power simply because had they done so they would have had to disqualify *Endeavour* for the incident, which occurred before the start.

None of this explanation was given at the time nor did it appear until months later. Instead the committee suffered in silence and based their case solely on the fact that Sopwith had flown his flag too late, which in fact he had. I am certain, however, that had the committee not viewed the first incident so clearly and been so sure that *Endeavour* was wrong it would have instituted an investigation of its own into the second incident. Nowadays if they did so and *Endeavour* had been found to be in the right, *Rainbow* would have been disqualified under the second incident, *Endeavour* under the first one, and the race would have been resailed. But under the rules in force in 1934 if a yacht was disqualified for an incident early in a race, it was impossible to disqualify the other yacht for committing a foul later in the same race. That is not the way it is now but that was the law of the sea in those days. In the committee's own words, published months later:

> *Endeavour*'s second protest, covering the luffing incident which occurred after rounding the first mark, could never have come before your committee since we would have had to disqualify one of the yachts prior to the start (see case of *Lena* versus *Countess,* Report of the New York Yacht Club Race Committee, 1924).

The committee then went on to write for posterity:

> Your committee believed it would serve no useful purposes to hold a hearing which, in its opinion, could only have resulted in the disqualification of *Endeavour* and furthermore that to institute a proceeding on its own initiative where in the language of the rule it had "reasonable grounds to believe" that the challenger had fouled the defender and not the defender the challenger, and the defender had not protested, would be regarded by many as indicating an advocacy of the *Rainbow* on the part of a committee whose sole duty was to enforce impartially the agreed rules of the Race.

These words may sound self-serving but when one considers that the rules of that day would not have allowed a consideration of the second incident, since by then one of the yachts would have been already disqualified, they must be accepted as an honest and accurate statement. I feel this also because I know the chairman of the committee, Edmund Lang, and my dad knew him intimately. He was one straight guy!

But even though the committee could not look into it, what was the story on the second incident? Was Sopwith right or wrong? While we will never know for sure, I am inclined to feel he was right. What is known is that when *Rainbow* was passing *Endeavour* on a reach, *Endeavour* luffed and *Rainbow* did not respond. What is also known is that *Endeavour* then bore off to avoid a serious collision.

There was no mast-line rule in those days to determine when luffing rights were lost. Instead a leeward yacht maintained luffing rights as long as her luff would result in her boat striking the windward yacht forward of her leeward shrouds. To be sure who was right a collision would have had to occur—a pretty risky business in boats the size of J-boats.

Knowing Mike Vanderbilt as I do, I am convinced he felt *Rainbow* was far enough past by the time *Endeavour* luffed so that she would have struck *Rainbow* abaft the shrouds. Most of his afterguard felt the same way, but remember that those on the windward boat in such a situation are apt to indulge in a bit of wishful thinking. They want so much for the leeward yacht to have lost luffing rights that they are apt to talk themselves into truly believing that she has, even though in fact she has not lost them. Just the reverse is true of those on the leeward yacht.

But one member of *Rainbow*'s afterguard felt differently. That was Sherman Hoyt, who was stationed at the leeward shrouds. He shouted in vain for Mike to come up. In his book, *Sherman Hoyt's Memoirs,* published many years later, Sherman is vague on this point, perhaps out of loyalty to Vanderbilt. But he was not vague in talking to me about it. He told me point blank that he believed that if *Endeavour* had pursued her luff she would have struck *Rainbow* right at the shrouds, perhaps even a bit forward of them. This was expressed to me even more definitely by Frank Murdoch, one of *Endeavour*'s crew members, some twenty years after the incident. Frank is convinced that *Endeavour* had not lost luffing rights and would have hit *Rainbow* forward of the shrouds.

Sir Ralph Gore, the British observer on *Rainbow,* was of the opinion that *Endeavour* probably had lost luffing rights though he was not sure. What he was sure of was that the proper course of action on *Rainbow*'s part would have been to respond to the luff and then protest if she felt *Endeavour* had luffed too late. With this I agree.

It is risky to surmise who was right and who was wrong without the benefit of a full hearing to determine all the facts, and such a hearing (quite properly under the rules of that day) was never held. But even though it is risky, I am of the view that if a hearing had been held *Rainbow* would have been found in the wrong. The facts would have been inconclusive, with everyone on *Endeavour* claiming that she never lost luffing rights and those on *Rainbow* claiming she had. The committee, faced with this difference of opinion, would then be apt to disqualify *Rainbow* for not responding, one fact that all agree with. As stated earlier, it would not have mattered in any case since prior to that, one boat (almost certainly *Endeavour*) would have been disqualified under the prestart incident. But if they had then been sailing under the rules in effect in 1980, my guess is that the committee would have initiated action on both alleged violations, and would have thrown out *Endeavour* under the first incident and *Rainbow* under the second one. Had that been the case the race would have to be resailed and the score would have remained two races to one in favor of *Endeavour* instead of being two to two. In that event *Endeavour* might still have pulled out the match because she was the faster boat and even after losing the next two races might have come back to win two more and take the Cup.

It is a pity that all this had to happen in the closest match in America's Cup history but it did happen. Still, the protest committee acted in the only way it possibly could and forty-six years later Tom Sopwith bore no grudge and instead remembered the 1934 match as one of the great experiences of his life.

One good thing did come out of these protests. I am confident they had a big bearing on getting the luffing rule changed to today's far better version and also in sparking the rule change which retained a yacht's rights after she has committed a foul earlier in the race, including the right to protest the other yacht and have her disqualified for a later violation in the same race.

The other big protest occurred thirty-six years later in the 1970 match between *Gretel II* and *Intrepid*. This one did come to a hearing and did result in the disqualification of *Gretel II* from the second race after she had won it on the race course.

There has never been a more significant protest yet never one in which the facts were easier to determine since it happened right at the start, in full view of the committee. The facts were further corroborated by a series of aerial and sea-level photos.

Here is what happened. Both yachts were approaching the weather end of the starting line with *Gretel II* to leeward and attempting to close the gap between herself and the Committee boat. *Intrepid* was in a barging situation on *Gretel II*'s weather quarter and had no right to ask for room. But if there was room for her to pass between *Gretel II* and the Committee boat without illegally forcing *Gretel II* to bear off to provide it, then she would commit no foul. There is nothing illegal about barging if there is sufficient room but it is a ticklish situation. Until the starting gun fired *Gretel II* could sail as high as she wanted, including luffing head to wind and, knowing this, Ficker held back and waited to see if there would be sufficient room. He knew that once the starting gun fired *Gretel II* could no longer sail above a close-hauled course to close the gap between her and the Committee boat. With a few seconds still to go he determined that when *Gretel II* did bear off to such a course after the starting gun fired there would be sufficient room between *Gretel II* and the Committee boat for *Intrepid* to sail through without fouling either and without forcing *Gretel II* to bear off below a close-hauled course. Hence he trimmed in, built speed, and charged for the narrow gap, feeling it would become just wide enough once *Gretel II* bore off to a close-hauled course with the starting gun. It was a gutsy call but faint heart never won a boat race and he was confident that enough room (but just enough) would be there.

As the gun fired *Gretel II* was just under two lengths short of the line with *Intrepid* almost overlapped on her weather quarter and traveling almost twice as fast. To Ficker's astonishment, when the gun fired, *Gretel II,* instead of bearing off to a close-hauled course, continued to luff. I was 200 feet away on one of the privileged vessels allowed inside the spectator fleet and I exclaimed to a keen sailing friend I was standing next to: "The gun has gone and *Gretel* is luffing higher instead of bearing off." He agreed and we could both see her sails, both main and jib, luffing badly even though they were trimmed in tight. *Intrepid* was now committed; she kept going, swept past *Gretel II* and all the time she did so (and this was some fifteen seconds after the gun) *Gretel's* sails kept shaking and we could see no alteration of her course to leeward. Finally as they passed the Committee boat, with *Gretel II* well above close-hauled and *Intrepid* tight reaching, *Gretel's* stem struck *Intrepid's* leeward quarter.

Gretel II was now nearly dead in the water because she had been luffing so long and *Intrepid* sped out to a huge early lead. *Gretel II* proved so fast and sailed such a masterful race thereafter that despite the early deficit she went on to win. I remember, even though I wanted *Intrepid* to win, feeling sorry for Hardy for losing a race through a silly foul which he otherwise deserved to win. There was no question in my mind, based on what I had seen from close hand, that *Gretel II* had fouled and would lose the protest.

The pertinent rule reads as follows:

SECTION E—Rules of Exception and Special Application
42.1(e)When overlapped when approaching the starting line to start, a leeward yacht shall be under no obligation to give any windward yacht room to pass to leeward of a starting mark surrounded by navigable water; but, after the starting signal, a leeward yacht shall not deprive a windward yacht of room at such a mark by sailing either above the first mark or above closehauled.

I was at *Gretel's* dock when she came in, both to congratulate Jim Hardy for a well sailed race and at the same time to commiserate with him about the unfortunate foul.

This sequence of photos shows why Gretel II *was disqualified. In photo #1, the starting signal has just been hoisted (see smoke from starting gun). Hereafter* Gretel II *can sail no higher than close-hauled to deprive* Intrepid *of room between her and the Committee boat.*

In photo #2, Gretel *is luffing almost head to wind. Note how much her sails are luffing.* Intrepid, *having expected* Gretel II *to bear off, keeps going for the line.*

Photo #3 shows the moment of contact with Gretel II *still sailing well above a close-hauled course. Note the committee looking closely at the action.*

In photo #4, Gretel II, *her speed spent by luffing and from being blanketed, is almost dead in the water.* Intrepid *appears home free but* Gretel II *gained on the fifth leg and finished more than a minute ahead, only to lose through disqualification for the foul of the century.*

I was one of the first people to talk to him and was surprised to find him without a care in the world and ebullient about his victory. When I lamented the foul, he replied instantly, "No problem, we will win that too." I was so surprised by his confidence that I asked if he had luffed after the starting gun had fired. "Sure," he replied, "we kept luffing to squeeze Ficker out." To be absolutely sure, I repeated the question. "Did you luff after the gun had fired?" Again he said, "Yes, we kept luffing." Then he added something to the effect, "We wanted to nail him good and prove he was barging."

I have kept this conversation in confidence for ten years, and especially during the ensuing day that the race committee was deliberating the protest. The chairman, Dev Barker, was a good friend of mine and I was fearful he might ask my view of the incident and I wanted no part of supplying information I had gained from Jim Hardy in a friendly and casual conversation. I realized it would cook his goose, and while I knew it should be cooked, I did not relish the idea of being the master chef. Dev could have asked my opinion because I was a member of the International Yacht Racing Union's Racing Rules Committee, had written a book on the interpretation of the racing rules, and was considered somewhat of an authority.

Actually the committee needed to consult no one since they had seen the incident at close hand and they knew the rules cold. But to leave no stones unturned they did confirm their own judgment by talking to Gregg Bemis, chairman of the I.Y.R.U. Racing Rules Committee. It was overkill to check in this manner, but they wanted to be absolutely sure before rendering a decision.

After the most careful deliberation they rendered their decision, disqualifying *Gretel II*. The pertinent part of their decision read as follows:

> Both yachts were approaching the starting line to start within the context of Rule 42.1(e). Prior to the starting signal, *Gretel II* was under no obligation to give *Intrepid* room to pass to leeward of the Committee boat. After the starting signal, however, *Gretel II* acquired an obligation, as soon as the yachts were

overlapped, not to deprive *Intrepid* of room to pass on the required side of the Committee boat by sailing above close-hauled.

Had *Gretel II* fulfilled her obligation to fall off to a close-hauled course under Rule 42.1(e), *Intrepid* would have had room to pass between *Gretel II* and the Committee boat.

Therefore, *Gretel II* is disqualified for infringement of Rule 42.1(e).

That succinct and accurate decision should have ended the matter but it did not. The Yacht Club was deluged with telegrams and phone calls from people who knew little of the racing rules but who still accused the Club of foul play. One such came from the Princeton University football coach, who did not know the bow of a boat from her stern but who like many others still felt emboldened to castigate the Club.

Press conferences are an integral part of the America's Cup. This one, in which I am serving as M.C., shows Dev Barker reading the fateful decision disqualifying Gretel II *in the second race of 1970.*

And the Aussies, or rather Frank Packer, chairman of the *Gretel II* syndicate, did not take the decision lying down. Instead Packer attempted to reopen the case, citing rules which had no bearing on the case in hand. All such attempts were listened to carefully and then dismissed on logical ground. Still the furor continued.

At this time, after another race had been sailed I asked Bill Fesq, navigator of *Gretel II,* how he felt about the disqualification. He told me they then knew they were wrong. "Will you so state at a post-race press conference?" I asked. "Sure," he replied, "but not until the end of the series." He indicated that to do so sooner would tend to undermine Martin Visser, their starting helmsman, who was at *Gretel II*'s wheel when the foul occurred.

Yet at the end of the series neither Hardy nor Fesq did make such a statement. They did compliment the Yacht Club for behaving in a gentlemanly fashion but they never did admit they were wrong.

Strangely, in all the years since, neither Hardy nor Fesq has so admitted. In fact, a number of years later they appear to have talked themselves into believing they had a case after all. Both are honorable and forthright men and I can conclude only that they wanted so very much to be right that they convinced themselves, albeit with no logical reason, that they were right. The fact of the matter is that at the time of the foul they were ignorant of the right-of-way rule which required *Gretel* to fall off to a close-hauled course as soon as the starting gun had gone! That ignorance cost them the race and even conceivably the Cup itself.

Sixteen years later, in January 1986, I had lunch with John Bertrand, skipper of *Australia II* when she won the America's Cup in 1983. In 1970, he was port jib sheet trimmer on *Gretel II,* the best possible position to determine whether she had sailed above close-hauled. I asked him how he viewed the situation. Without a moment's hesitation he said, "We were dead wrong. We kept luffing after the starting gun fired. The plain fact is that we simply did not know the rules."

I was pleased to read in Bertrand's book the following, 16 years after the event:

"Martin was so involved emotionally that he literally had blood in his eyes. He struggled desperately to block *Intrepid*'s way, but he went too far and luffed the sails to beyond close-hauled. This meant he was no longer in control or even sailing on a proper course. He was just hoping to drift into his opponent and ram her like a renegade from the Spanish Main— which is against the rules. You must stay close-hauled and keep sailing a course. Anyway, we hit *Intrepid* with an almighty thump and smashed our bow. The artificial coaming, the whole front section, just fell off— like Salmon and Forbes had done the day before. There were protest flags all over the place, and then, amazingly, we went on to win the race.

"The American protest was upheld, and *Gretel II* was disqualified. The Australian press went berserk. There were headlines screaming outrage: 'We Was Robbed' and 'Home-Town Decision Robs Australia.' But I remember what it was like. I was holding the genoa, and I was the one who had to let it go because we were going above close-hauled and it was backwinding. Then, when we crossed the finish line, Bill Fesq, the navigator, got out the rule book and read the relevant passage. Among the crew there was a thunderous, stunned silence as the full significance became apparent. Our afterguard did not know the rules any better than we had known them in race one."

Nice to have an admission in writing from the Australians that they were wrong.

The pity of it all, from their standpoint, is that if they had just sailed their own boat instead of trying to make *Intrepid* commit a foul they would have won that race and perhaps the series. They protested in race one also, claiming that *Intrepid* had been guilty of an opposite tack violation. In truth, it appeared more likely that *Gretel II* was guilty of balking in an attempt to nail *Intrepid* while she was on port tack, but taking every proper action to keep clear. Since no collision occurred neither yacht was disqualified, but had there been one, *Gretel II*, on starboard tack, might well have been thrown out for balking *Intrepid* while the latter was fulfilling her obligation to keep clear. The handwriting was on the wall that Visser was out for blood. The same type of aggressive tactics in the second race proved to be his undoing.

There is one other anecdote regarding *Gretel*'s disqualification which now with the passage of time is, I feel, appropriate to tell. It was after another race had been sailed but before the series had concluded. I was viewing the match from the same boat as the America's Cup Committee. I noticed a meeting going on between the committee, the then commodore of the club, and several immediate past commodores. About ten minutes after the meeting had been in progress I was invited to join the group. I was then President of the North American Yacht Racing Union and it was in this official capacity that my advice was sought. Without indicating their own view on the matter, they informed me that they had been discussing the advisability of canceling the second race and ordering it resailed. They did say they agreed with the Race Committee decision to disqualify *Gretel II* but then asked how I felt about canceling the race in the interest of harmony and future good relations between nations competing for the America's Cup. It took me all of five seconds to blurt out that such might promote goodwill but that it would also make it appear that the Yacht Club had erred in the first place, whereas in fact it had made the only possible decision under the racing rules. I further stated that it would make a mockery of rule enforcement and would establish a very bad precedent. They thanked me for my opinion and then opined that they had come to precisely the same conclusion but wanted the view of the head of the national governing body on yacht racing. I mention this only to demonstrate how far the New York Yacht Club bent over backwards in the interest of being fair and impartial. They actually were considering nullifying a decision they knew to be right. I hope these gentlemen do not take exception to my divulging this conversation ten years after the event. It is a story which I feel needs to be told to offset all the unwarranted vilification the Club had received from a number of bleeding hearts who knew nothing about what really had happened or the pertinent rule which governed the situation.

One most fortunate thing evolved from this unfortunate protest. After the 1970 match and for all future matches the protest committee has been and will continue to be composed of an international jury, with no members from the same nation as the defender or the challenger. Beppe Croce, president of the International Yacht Racing Union, was chairman of the jury for the 1974, 1977, and 1980 matches. In 1983, Livius

Sherwood, Canadian member of the IYRU Racing Rules Committee, chaired the jury. The result was fair decisions more quickly arrived at, and decisions which were accepted with less criticism than heretofore. Not better decisions, not worse ones. Just the same correct ones, but fairer to both parties and *far less subject to criticism.* In the past the New York Yacht Club has leaned over backwards to be fair, leaned so very far as to risk being unfair to their own boat. For example, prior to the start of the first race for the 1934 match the New York Yacht Club Race Committee noticed that *Endeavour* was having difficulty hoisting her mainsail after the course signals had been set. Despite the fact that the conditions of the match called for yachts to be ready to start at the agreed-upon time, they postponed the start long enough for *Endeavour* to be ready. I approve of their action but it certainly gave *Endeavour* a break. And you can bet your bottom dollar that if it had been *Rainbow* which was having difficulty getting ready for the start, *the starting time would not have been postponed.* Or if it had been, the Club would still be hearing repercussions of favoritism. Far better to have an international body make such decisions and render decisions on protests. The same decisions will be rendered. The only difference will be in their more ready acceptance by the competitors, by yachtsmen everywhere, and by the public at large which becomes an overnight expert on things it knows nothing about when the America's Cup is on the line. The only thing which I criticize the New York Yacht Club about is why they took so long to realize how vital it is to have an international jury rather than their own Race Committee to decide protests. It took the *Gretel–Intrepid* protest and the ensuing hue and cry from their perfectly correct decision to wake them up.

There was a protest in 1983 lodged by *Australia II,* accusing *Liberty* of tacking too close while covering on the windward leg of a race eventually won by *Liberty.* It was a tight situation and the burden of proof was on *Liberty* to satisfy the committee that she had not tacked too close. It took six hours for the committee to decide. While a close call, I believe the decision was correct. I'm also sure that a New York Yacht Club committee would have thrown its own boat out as the sporting thing to do in a close situation.

One of the witnesses the committee called was none other than yours truly. I had seen it all from the blimp. Telephoto pictures taken from the blimp made it appear that there was a foul, but that's not what I saw. I pointed out that telephoto shots make things seem closer than they really are, closer than what one sees with one's eyes.

I later found out that John Bertrand didn't like my testifying, believing I was prejudiced. I don't see it that way. I merely reported what I had a ringside seat to see—*Liberty* making a tack very close in front of *Australia—but not too close.*

Chapter IX
The Role of the
Selection Committee

William H. "Bill" Taylor wrote in the September, 1930 issue of *Yachting:* "There is probably no less enviable a task connected with the defense of the America's Cup than that of the Selection Committee." Bill is probably the most noted yachting reporter of all time, having received a Pulitzer Prize for his reporting on the 1934 match, the only sports writer to receive this award. And in this statement he was as usual dead right. The Selection Committee, otherwise known as the America's Cup Committee, has an awesome burden to select the yacht which in their opinion has the best chance to defend the Cup successfully. Sometimes it is easy, as in the case of *Ranger* in 1937, *Intrepid* in 1967 and *Freedom* in 1980. These three so dominated the trial races that the Committee's job was superfluous. No other selection was conceivably possible.

In the majority of years the winning yacht selects herself by dominating the final trials. But on a few occasions it comes right down to the wire. In that instance only those on the selected yacht are happy; the losers feel that with just a few more races they could turn the tide. And it is a sobering and difficult task to tell a skipper and his crew who have been in close contention for several months that a decision has been made to select an opponent which has only a slightly better record, or conceivably a worse record over the course of the full summer of racing.

I know the feeling because I was privileged to be a member of the 1977 America's Cup Committee and it was not easy to tell the crews of *Enterprise* and *Independence* that they were through and that *Courageous* had been selected. *Enterprise* in particular took it hard, believing that with just a bit more time they could turn the tide, this despite the fact that *Courageous* had dominated not only the final selection trial races but most of the prior races. In 1980 our job was even easier, because *Freedom* was so dominant. Even so, the crew of *Clipper* would have liked a few more races before getting the axe. I can thus imagine how very hard it would be in a really tight series.

I was once again a member of the Cup Committee in 1983, and hence had the dubious distinction of helping pick the loser of the America's Cup. Actually, our selection was not a difficult one. *Liberty* dominated the trials to such an extent that we had no other real choice. *Defender* was a real factor in light air, probably the fastest of all the American contenders. But as soon as the wind built, *Defender* folded and hence was the first one eliminated. *Courageous* seemed almost equal in speed to *Liberty* in all conditions and had her sails and organization been equal to *Liberty*'s she just might have prevailed. I remember finding this a bit disquieting. *Courageous* was then nine years old but still very close in speed to the boat we were selecting to defend.

There is a feeling which has persisted for many years that the Selection Committee is partial to a New York area boat. I know that in the Boston, Marblehead area there at least used to be a feeling that the decks were stacked against them, a feeling which perhaps was engendered by the selection of *Rainbow* over *Yankee* in 1934, despite the fact that *Yankee* won far more races through the course of the summer.

I suspect also that the crew of *Intrepid* in 1974 felt that the Selection Committee was partial to *Courageous* as a home town favorite. But having served on the Committee, and having learned how they reason

The 1977 America's Cup Committee, which selected Courageous *to defend. Left to right: Jim Michael, Bob Bavier, Harry Anderson, chairman George Hinman, Clayton Ewing, Briggs Cunningham, and Bus Mosbacher. Bob McCullough was absent when the photo was taken. The 1980 Committee was the same, except for George Hinman, who resigned to lead the* Courageous *syndicate. Vic Romagna replaced him and Bob McCullough became chairman.*

and the criteria for selection, I can state most categorically that the only thing they are concerned with is finding the boat which in their view will make the strongest possible defense. She can come from Boston, Seattle, California, or Timbuktoo and her chances are precisely even with a boat hailing, say, from Long Island Sound.

The Committee might hate one skipper's guts but if he can win the trials, especially the final trials, and if his boat shows the all-around ability deemed so essential for a defender, he will be selected. The Cup Committee feels an awesome responsibility to pick the right boat, and logic, not emotion, is the only criterion they use.

I knew and liked all three skippers in 1977, 1980, and 1983. Still each year I had a particular skipper I was rooting for. Other members of the Committee, I am sure, had their favorite but none of us tipped our hand. All deliberations were based on race results and results in various wind strengths and never did I detect any member arguing in a partial way for some skipper who I suspected was his personal favorite or against some other he might have been less keen for in a personal sense. Keep in mind that no Committee member wanted to be the first to select a loser of the America's Cup.

The selection, in my view, is based on a few key points. First, the defender must prove to be a well-rounded boat which is not going to lie down and die in either light or heavy air. One boat might win almost all the time in heavy air, and if the trials have a predominance of strong winds she could well have the best record. Let's say, however, that in light air this boat is a real dog, while there is another boat which loses very narrowly in a breeze but dominates in light. The latter boat is much the best bet. Challengers might go all out and gamble with a one weather boat and then hope that the match is sailed in that weather. It could be a way to beat us, but the Selection Committee prefers not to gamble and instead to select a well-rounded boat.

For example, in 1962 Ted Hood's *Nefertiti* had a record of eleven wins, one loss in the July trials. She beat *Weatherly* in three out of the four times they met. But all but one of these races were sailed in winds over eleven knots, most of them over fifteen knots. Her one light air win was over *Easterner,* the weak boat of the group. Although *Weatherly*'s record in these trials was six wins and five losses, one of her wins was against *Nefertiti* in fourteen knots and she had a close loss against *Columbia* in nineteen knots. In short, she proved to be no dog in fresh air.

In the final trials seven of the nine races were in winds under eleven knots, and *Weatherly*'s record was eight wins and one loss. Furthermore, she beat *Nefertiti* in four of the five races they met. Of equal importance was a win over *Columbia* in twenty knots, again proving she was no slouch in a fresh breeze. *Nefertiti*'s only win over *Weatherly* in the final trials was in a twenty-five knot wind.

Weatherly did two things to earn selection. She peaked in the final trials which are the most important ones. Secondly, she won big in light air,

The Selection Committee got this close to the action during the 1977 trials. We are on the power boat to the right, watching Enterprise, *followed closely by her tender.*

148

won several medium air races, one heavy air race and was never completely out of it. For the summer her record was fourteen wins, six losses while *Nefertiti*'s was fifteen wins and six losses. Still, it was not a difficult decision to pick *Weatherly.*

And it is fortunate that she was picked! In the match against *Gretel,* four of the races were in light to moderate air (ten knots, nine to twelve knots, and two in winds of eight to ten knots). *Weatherly* won these four but one of them by a scant twenty-six seconds. The only race she lost was the second one in winds ranging from twenty to twenty-five knots. Even in that one she came close, leading at the first mark by twelve seconds, at the second one by fourteen, until *Gretel* swept by on the last reach to win by forty-seven seconds. Had *Nefertiti* been the defender she probably would have won the second race, but she could very possibly have lost the other four.

The toughest and most debatable selection was that of *Rainbow* over *Yankee* in 1934. Throughout the summer *Yankee* won eleven of the seventeen races between the two yachts. She beat *Rainbow* in the one race between them in the preliminary trials. She then beat her in all four meetings in the observation trials. The New York Yacht Club cruise saw *Yankee* beating *Rainbow* in the first five races, making her record against her arch rival at that point ten to zero.

Just when *Rainbow*'s cause seemed hopeless she beat *Yankee* in the last two races on the cruise. Then after losing badly to *Yankee* in their first meeting in the final trials *Rainbow* took the second one by 3:07 and was leading by 37 seconds in the next one when *Yankee* broke a strut and had to retire. *Rainbow* won the ensuing race by 2:21 and the final one by one second. Charlie Adams felt the trials should continue but the Committee felt otherwise. They were impressed by the fact that in the last seven meetings *Rainbow* had won five and was leading in a sixth when *Yankee* broke down. The fact that *Yankee* won only once in the final trials counted more heavily in the Selection Committee's minds than the previous ten straight wins by *Yankee. Rainbow* had come through when she had to. The record in the final trials is the one which really counts.

This is not to mean that the record in the preliminary and observation trials has no bearing on selection. In the event that the final trials were sailed in one weather condition, either all light or all heavy air, even though one boat might dominate she would probably not be selected if she had proved in earlier races to be slow in other conditions. To be selected a boat has to prove her versatility and then, having proved that, she must come through in the final trials.

Despite *Yankee*'s superior summer-long record I feel *Rainbow*'s selection was a sound one. She won when she had to and she kept on improving right through the match against *Endeavour*. Maybe *Yankee* would have beaten *Endeavour,* maybe not. All we know is that *Rainbow* did and I do not buy the garbage that her selection as defender was influenced by the fact that she was the New York boat and *Yankee* the outlander. If *Yankee* had won the last race by one second I am sure there would have been another one. Had she won that one too, my guess is she would have been selected and would have assumed the awesome burden of trying to beat *Endeavour.*

I was personally involved in the other real squeaker confronting the Selection Committee. In the summer of 1974 I was skipper of *Courageous* and we were having a battle royal against *Intrepid.* We split the races between us in the preliminary trials at two apiece but *Intrepid*'s record was slightly better than ours in July—four for her and three for us. In the final trials, after losing the first race to *Intrepid, Courageous* won the next four. We were looking good and a few people even had kind remarks for her skipper, Bob Bavier. Then we lost the next three to put us all even at four races each and by then I was a bum. By this time it seemed apparent that *Courageous* was very slightly faster than *Intrepid* but that most observers and in particular the Selection Committee felt that *Intrepid* was being sailed better. The logical move in such a situation is to boot the skipper. It was a hard pill for me to swallow after months of racing but I could not quarrel with the wisdom of letting Ted Hood take over.

Several more races were planned but on the ensuing two days the races were postponed for lack of wind. Finally on 2 September, with time for selection absolutely at hand, there was a beautiful eighteen to twenty knot wind. While it was not officially announced ahead of time, everyone

The 1974 Selection Committee congratulates Courageous *crew on their selection.*
Bob McCullough, head of the Courageous *syndicate, greets them.*

knew that the winner of the race would be named as defender. With Ted
Hood driving, *Courageous* led at every mark to win by one minute forty-
seven seconds and that evening was selected to defend the America's Cup.
The two boats had nearly identical records for the summer. Over the
course of the three sets of trials *Intrepid* beat us one more time than we
beat her. On the other hand, we never lost a single race to either *Valiant* or
Mariner, the other two contenders, but *Valiant* did manage one win over
Intrepid. Therefore the record of the two boats in the trial races was
identical and selection was determined on the basis that *Courageous*
seemed a slight bit faster and in the hands of Ted Hood was therefore
deemed to be a somewhat better bet as defender. Had *Intrepid* won the last

race she would have been the only boat ever to defend the Cup in three matches and I have no doubt that she would have defended successfully against *Southern Cross.*

This series of elimination trials probably set a record for personal anguish. Ted Turner was replaced as skipper of the real turkey, *Mariner.* I was replaced as skipper of *Courageous* with but one race to go and Gerry Driscoll, skipper of *Intrepid,* came within one race of skippering an America's Cup defender. If you cannot stand up to disappointment then stay out of the America's Cup. This game is for keeps and the Selection Committee, quite properly, does not consider people's feelings in selecting a defender. They want only to keep the Cup here.

For the 1987 match, only the Australians will have a selection committee. All the U.S. boats will vie against each other and against those from other countries to see who will compete against the Aussies. It will be decided on a mathematical basis.

In theory, at least, this should favor the Australians. They can choose a boat best suited for the winds expected to prevail at the time of the match in January and February. The consensus has been that it blows hard at that time, but in 1985 and 1986, the winds were quite moderate. It would be dangerous, therefore, for the Australians to pick anything but a well-rounded boat. Still, being able to select is an advantage.

On the other hand, the eventual challenger will have a real advantage, too. There are more challengers (a lot more) than ever before. The successful one will have survived a long, hard series of races, will be battle-tested, and will be a very hard boat to beat.

Chapter X
The Matches We Nearly Lost: 1920, 1934, 1970

On the afternoon of Thursday, 20 September, 1934, Mike Vanderbilt went below in *Rainbow* to drown his sorrows with coffee and sandwiches. In the preceding few days he had lost two races to the British challenger, *Endeavour,* by comfortable margins and minutes before had rounded the leeward mark of the third race six minutes thirty-nine seconds behind the blue British boat, which by then had proven she was faster than the defender. To make matters even worse the wind had shifted to make the leg to the finish a near fetch. Following the leader at such a hopeless distance is hardly a time for optimism, and being three races down with just one to go against a faster opponent made Mike conclude that at long last the America's Cup would go overseas. With him was the British observer Sir Ralph Gore, who tried to make Mike feel better by pointing out that it was a faster boat which had done him in and not poor sailing on his part. They also ruminated on the possible benefit to the sport from a victorious challenge. Being honest, objective men they agreed that *Rainbow*'s cause was hopeless. What happened thereafter proved more eloquently than ever before or since in the history of yacht racing the old adage that "a race is never over till the finish," or, as Yogi Berra put it, "It's not over till it's over."

Up on deck Sherman Hoyt was at *Rainbow*'s wheel, acting for all the world like a race was still on. Up ahead he could see *Endeavour* in a bit of a flat spot and not quite fetching, while *Rainbow* had been lifted so that she could more than fetch. He held as high as possible, even a bit above the finish in hopes of getting into different sailing conditions than the leader. It was still a pretty hopeless situation because when *Endeavour* got the lift she too could fetch or at worst would have to make one small hitch for the finish. With her big lead that was all she required. But Sherman kept holding high in the quite forlorn hope that *Endeavour* might not know exactly where the finish was, would get nervous, and would tack to cover. It was a real long shot but it was the only card they had to play and certainly better than following *Endeavour* directly.

Just as Mike Vanderbilt got back on deck the hoped-for opening happened. Up ahead they could see *Endeavour* slowly coming about! What had been a completely hopeless situation was now just a very bad one and for the first time in the race there was a glimmer of hope. If *Endeavour* tacked on *Rainbow*'s leeward bow she would still win, though by a smaller margin than originally expected. But, if by some miracle *Endeavour* actually elected to cross *Rainbow*'s bow before tacking, not realizing that *Rainbow* was fetching, then there was a real chance.

Mike let Sherman keep the wheel, as was his wont in light air beating, and also because he did not want to disturb a fast improving situation. Sherman kept a full head of steam on *Rainbow* but held as high as he could so as not to tip his hand that she was fetching. It was agonizing as the two boats converged, *Endeavour* actually sailing slightly *away* from the line as she became headed entering *Rainbow*'s lift. It was evident that she could cross by several lengths, but the question was whether she would elect to or would instead tack short in a safe leeward position which would again make *Rainbow*'s cause hopeless.

Not a word was said on *Rainbow* as the two yachts converged. Instead, the crew lay on the leeward deck as though their only thought was how

Endeavour leading Rainbow *in the 1934 match, a match she should have won.*

to get *Rainbow* as far to windward as possible just as though they were on a true windward leg. As the time neared when *Endeavour* would have to tack to assume a safe leeward the suspense was almost unbearable. On she came and now it was too late to tack without crossing!

When she did tack finally, she was directly on *Rainbow*'s wind. Sherman bore off slightly, got clear air, and in a matter of minutes had broken through and ahead into a safe leeward position. J-boats can maintain quite astounding speed in light air, traveling several knots faster than the true wind speed once they have built up headway. The resulting apparent wind strength is sufficient to keep them going. But when they tack in light air, boat speed and hence apparent wind strength is reduced and it takes many minutes for them to build their speed back up. That is what happened to *Endeavour.* Although she tacked right on *Rainbow*'s wind, she took so long to rebuild speed in the light air that she could not stay there and could not prevent *Rainbow* from charging through. A few minutes later *Endeavour* had sagged off into *Rainbow*'s backwind and tacked again to clear her air. It was a futile and desperate move which merely put her further behind. *Rainbow* let her go, kept driving for the finish and finally won by three minutes twenty-six seconds. *Rainbow,* making no tacks on the final leg as opposed to *Endeavour*'s four, had gained ten minutes, five seconds.

In Tom Sopwith's defense one can understand his anxiety when he saw *Rainbow* lifted and gaining. A short tack and then a tack back on *Rainbow*'s leeward bow as soon as she was headed would have reduced the lead. But it would have put her in the same wind conditions as *Rainbow,* would have put her in the safe leeward position, and would have retained a victory, albeit a narrow one. But crossing *Rainbow* when *Rainbow* was fetching was an inexcusable error in navigation and tactical judgment.

Now down two races to one, *Rainbow*'s prospects were still dim but not as desperate as the 3–0 score that should have been. Just as important as the mathematical improvement was the psychological one. *Rainbow*'s afterguard and crew got a tremendous lift, while *Endeavour*'s were shaken. Sopwith had sailed well in the first two races as well as the third until making his monumental goof but thereafter everything seemed to go wrong. After the third race *Rainbow* added 4000 pounds of ballast. After the second one *Endeavour* had removed 3360 pounds, a surprising move since she had won the first two quite handily and had shown good speed. Vanderbilt made another and more important move. He added Frank Paine to his afterguard. Paine had been sail trimming officer on *Yankee* and had made *Yankee* excel whenever her parachute spinnaker was up. Paine not only came aboard but brought *Yankee*'s chute with him. He and the sail were so helpful that Mike magnanimously referred to Paine after the match as the "saviour of the America's Cup."

The fourth race was a thriller marred by a protest on the second leg of the triangular course, a protest discussed at length in Chapter VIII. On the opening beat by careful covering *Rainbow* maintained the slight lead she had achieved at the start. Approaching the mark, however, *Endeavour* was so close on *Rainbow*'s weather quarter that *Rainbow* couldn't tack without fouling. *Endeavour* rounded first by thirty-three seconds but was so slow in setting her genoa that *Rainbow* drove by to windward. As she was passing, *Endeavour* luffed and the protest evolved around Sopwith's claim that Vanderbilt did not respond properly. In any event *Rainbow* swept past, rounded the second mark a minute ahead, and gained another fifteen seconds on the reach to the finish. Frank Paine's sail trimming was credited for her improved reaching ability. The added ballast might well have helped also.

With the score now even and *Rainbow*'s confidence building, she poured it on in the fifth race over a leeward-windward course. The two boats were even at the start but *Rainbow*'s spinnaker broke out smartly while *Endeavour*'s crew seemed to take ages. With Frank Paine calling the spinnaker trim, *Rainbow* kept moving out ahead, gaining so rapidly that even though it ripped halfway down the leg and had to be replaced *Rainbow* still led by four minutes thirty-eight seconds at the leeward mark. *Rainbow*'s lead was gained partly because Sopwith failed to jibe when lifted, while *Rainbow* jibed prior to setting the replacement chute. Still *Rainbow* came close to losing her lead when her boatswain Ben Bruntwith was knocked overboard while releasing the backstay while jibing. Fortunately, Ben had the backstay tail in his hand and although largely underwater for 30 seconds hung on for dear life until the crew could haul him back aboard. Had he lost his grip, *Rainbow* would surely have lost the race as she went back to recover him. On the beat home, *Endeavour* gained thirty-seven seconds but still lost by over four minutes.

In what turned out to be the final race, *Endeavour* should have won but managed to make enough mistakes to more than offset her superior boat speed. It was a triangular race starting with a reach, then a beat and finally

Endeavour leading Rainbow at a start in the 1934 match. Rainbow's spinnaker was broken out so much faster, however, that she soon gained the lead.

a ten-mile reach to the finish. *Endeavour* led by one minute eight seconds at the first mark but then made a fatal error by starting upwind with her genoa despite the fact that her afterguard could see *Rainbow* was switching to a quadrilateral jib. It is an axiom of successful match racing to duplicate the sail selection of the other boat whenever you have a good lead.

When *Rainbow* tacked after rounding, *Endeavour* tacked to cover but when Vanderbilt tacked back Sopwith let him go. He realized that in a tacking duel *Rainbow* would be more efficient with her smaller jib but this is only a partial excuse. He should have covered until he saw he was losing, he should have changed jibs while still ahead, or (and this is a bit of Monday morning quarterbacking) he should have left *Rainbow* only when he felt she was on the unfavored tack. Instead, he let her go for a full forty minutes (belatedly shifting to doublehead rig), and when the weather mark was reached, *Rainbow* had a handsome lead of two minutes forty-seven seconds. On the run to the finish *Endeavour* came to life, but it was too late. She closed to within fifty-five seconds—a gallant but futile last try.

There is no question that the faster boat lost. She lost by sloppier sail handling, by a schoolboy mistake in the third race, by the inexperience of her gallant but raw, amateur crew, by less effective trimming and poorer sail selection, and in general by not playing heads-up ball. As Herb Stone wrote in the October, 1934, issue of *Yachting:* "During the series it can truthfully be said that everyone made mistakes but Charles E. Nicholson—and he designed *Endeavour,* the best yacht that has ever come in quest of the America's Cup."

Three years later Sopwith sailed *Endeavour II* with consummate skill but was trounced by that super J-boat *Ranger.* Had he sailed in 1934 like he sailed in 1937, the Cup would have been his!

While the 1934 match was the biggest threat to the Americans' long-lasting reign, there were two other squeakers. Since I was not there I will not talk much about the 1920 match when *Resolute* so nearly lost to *Shamrock IV,* aside from reciting the bare statistics. In those days the match was a best of five series with the first boat to win three races being the winner. In the first race *Resolute* was leading comfortably when she lost her mainsail when the throat halyard parted. When her cause became hopeless she elected not to finish. No great cause for alarm since *Resolute* had been leading at the time. Since *Shamrock* gave her approximately seven minutes time allowance *Resolute* still looked golden for the series.

The second race was something else. Despite sloppy sail handling *Shamrock* showed great speed in the light going and after being behind early swept into the lead. Thereafter she got the better of several shifts in the flukey wind and crossed ten minutes five seconds in the lead, saving her time by two minutes twenty-six seconds.

One more win and Sir Thomas Lipton's dream of winning the Cup would have been realized. In the third race the two yachts had identical elapsed times in a good sailing breeze with *Resolute* winning handily on corrected.

The series was squared in the fourth race, a flukey affair in which *Resolute* was usually in the right place at the right time to win by over three minutes on elapsed time and approximately ten minutes on corrected.

On the day scheduled for the fifth race there was a puffy twenty-three to twenty-five knot sou'wester blowing as they sailed about the starting area. Both skippers agreed with the race committee's decision to postpone. One can only wonder what would have happened if William Burton, skipper of *Shamrock IV,* had not agreed and the race had been sailed.

But it is known that on the ensuing day a fickle four knot wind was blowing. *Shamrock* got the start by forty seconds but that was her last hurrah. *Resolute* led at the windward mark of the thirty mile windward-leeward race and on the run home kept widening out to cross thirteen minutes ahead, winning by the handsome margin of nearly twenty minutes.

It had been a close series only in the fact that *Resolute* had been down by two races and one more slip would have spelled disaster. But under the conditions that prevailed for the series she proved to be the faster yacht. This coupled with better sailing gave her the wins she required when her fate was in the balance.

A still closer shave and one almost equaling *Rainbow*'s squeaker over

Twelves can't plane but they can surf if they catch a big sea just right. Here (top left) Gretel *does! Her bow is rising as a big sea sweeps by. A moment later an even bigger sea lifts her stern and in the photo above she rides it to sweep by* Weatherly, *picking up several lengths in a matter of seconds. She went on to win this second race in the 1962 match by 17 seconds, the largest margin between the two boats throughout this closest race in the history of the America's Cup.*

Endeavour came in the 1970 series sailed in Twelve Meters. Do not be misled by the fact that *Intrepid* beat *Gretel II* four races to one. The score could have been and should have been exactly reversed! By the time the series was over most knowledgeable sailors concluded that *Intrepid* was faster in wind strengths over sixteen knots. There seemed little to choose between them in winds of twelve to fifteen except for the fact that *Gretel* accelerated faster after tacks and hence should fare better in a tacking duel. But in twelve knots and under it was all *Gretel*, not only in acceleration but in pure boat speed, especially upwind. When one then considers that only one race was sailed in a strong breeze you begin to recognize the magnitude of *Intrepid*'s achievement. In the first race there was twenty knots of wind at the start and twelve to fifteen at the finish. In race two it was six knots at the start and nine at the finish, race three ten and eighteen respectively, race four ten at the start, dropping to four to six at the finish and race five nine to ten at the start and only five at the finish—all these wind strengths being official N.Y.Y.C. recordings.

How then did skipper Bill Ficker, his tactician Steve Van Dyke, navigator Peter Wilson, and the rest of *Intrepid*'s crew do it? It is a long and fascinating story, but in essence they pulled it off by recognizing the situation early and applying unorthodox match racing tactics, aided and abetted by failure on the part of *Gretel*'s brain trust to realize soon enough just how good their boat was. They also made some pretty bad errors in judgment and revealed ignorance of a couple of key racing rules.

The first race, sailed in heavy air, was all *Intrepid*. She had an edge at the start to weather of *Gretel* and throughout the leg favored the right hand side of the course to take best advantage of a clocking wind. *Intrepid* rounded the weather mark one minute three seconds ahead, a comfortable margin, but the fact that she had the better of the start and had sailed a better course also proved that *Gretel* was no pushover even in a breeze. On the first reach, although *Gretel* got a horrendous spinnaker wrap which took six minutes to unravel, she lost only five seconds. But when she lost a crew member overboard on the second reach and had to go back to recover him her goose was cooked. American supporters were lulled into complacency but on *Intrepid* they realized that *Gretel* was no slouch even in the sort of weather *Intrepid* reveled in.

The second race, started in nine knots of wind, revealed to all that *Gretel* was for real. She led at the first two marks and was close behind at the third, after which the race was abandoned due to thickening fog which made for an unsafe situation considering the huge spectator fleet. Imagine the howls of favoritism which would have ensued if the New York Yacht Club had canceled with *Gretel* in the lead!

Most people feel that in 1970 Gretel II *was the fastest Twelve Meter in the world, a boat that could, and in fact should, have won the America's Cup for Australia.*

In the real second race *Gretel* showed her class and at the same time showed the shortcomings of her crew. In the most famous protest situation of America's Cup history she fouled at the start and got off almost dead in the water in *Intrepid*'s wake. The protest was discussed in Chapter VIII, but let it be said here that *Gretel*'s starting helmsman, Martin Visser, seemed more intent on sucking *Intrepid* into a foul than on getting a good start. He could have gotten a lovely safe leeward start. Instead, he forced a collision, and to further compound the error, he did not know the pertinent right-of-way rule and hence instead of throwing *Intrepid* out, it was *Gretel* which got the axe in the subsequent hearing.

After starting with a huge deficit, *Gretel* got going on the first beat and nearly caught *Intrepid* in a tacking duel until the latter broke it off when she was in light air letting *Gretel* tack away all by herself into a header. This enabled *Intrepid* to round the first mark 42 seconds ahead. Reaching is *Intrepid*'s strong point and this, coupled with more efficient chutes and smarter sail handling, enabled her to build her lead to 1:42 starting upwind the second time. On that beat she lost 30 seconds but still started the run with what appeared to be a safe margin.

But it was not safe for long! *Gretel* did everything right on this leg and was aided also by bringing up a fresher wind early in the leg. She slacked her backstays well off, tacked downwind at sharper angles than *Intrepid,* and ghosted into a fifty second lead at the leeward mark. There was no stopping *Gretel* now and she opened up on the last beat to a one minute seven second lead at the finish.

The score should have been one to one but even though the protest hearing quite rightly made it two to zero in *Intrepid*'s favor, Ficker and his gang knew they were in for the fight of their lives, especially if the wind stayed light. It was not too light in the third race, ten knots at the start building to eighteen at the finish. Still *Intrepid* had no easy victory. Ficker forced Visser over at the start, and although he was also over, he was able to dip back first, getting away to a commanding lead. If *Gretel* had had the same initial advantage it is unlikely she could have been caught. The

Snafus like this are one of the reasons Gretel II *lost the 1970 match to* Intrepid. *Later in this race they lost a man overboard.*

margins at the first four marks remained virtually constant and all under one minute. On the run to the fifth mark, *Gretel* again began closing but just as it appeared that she might actually gain the lead, *Intrepid* jibed away after being lifted and *Gretel* did not follow. Visibility was poor and Peter Wilson had calculated that their new course would take them directly to the mark. He was right and by not following, *Gretel* sailed lots of extra distance. It was blowing hard enough so that tacking down wind at the wide angle she was sailing did not increase her speed nearly enough to offset the added mileage, and she started the last beat 1:16 behind, losing only two seconds more on the last leg. Had *Gretel* gotten the start, and had she jibed at the right time, she would almost surely have won, this despite the fine sailing breeze which was close to suiting *Intrepid*.

The fourth race was *Gretel* weather, yet for five legs *Intrepid* stayed ahead. She did so by getting a nice jump at the start and thereafter eschewing standard match racing tactics. Instead of applying a close cover she sailed her own race. Van Dyke and Wilson had figured the cycle of the wind phases and they kept tacking in them almost irrespective of *Gretel*. Whenever *Gretel* did not follow she lost ground. Whenever she did she gained and finally they wised up and started following. On the second reach, *Intrepid* gained by setting a ballooner instead of matching *Gretel*'s selection of a chute. *Intrepid* had lost five seconds on the preceding reach and started the third leg a scant twenty-four seconds ahead. The ballooner did its trick, however, stretching the lead to forty seconds as they started upwind the second time. Sailing pretty much her own race on the second beat and ensuing run and making no mistakes, *Intrepid* built her lead to one minute two seconds at the start of the final windward leg.

Finally the law of averages plus a bit of overconfidence caught up with her. This was probably enough of a lead for *Intrepid* to stay ahead through careful covering. But they let *Gretel* get out on their quarter where she got a nice lift. When *Intrepid* finally tacked to cover it was too late and *Gretel* steamed by to win by 1:02, picking up over two minutes on the last leg.

With the score now three to one (remember that without the disqualification it would have been two to two) *Intrepid* was still in the driver's seat but running scared. The fifth race was the most exciting of all, and if Bill Ficker ever sailed a better race I would have to see it to believe it. I did see this one (as I had all the others) and I rate it as the best sailed race in Twelve Meter history, a race where the slower boat won despite great odds. It was nine to ten knots at the start dropping to five at the finish—*Gretel* weather! It was also a fickle northerly which provided an opportunity for tactics to offset pure boat speed.

Hardy got the start to windward of Ficker and with a one second jump. And to windward was just the place to be since there was better breeze to the east, coupled with a tendency for the wind to haul. Ficker, Van Dyke, and Wilson suspected this and hence a few minutes after crossing the line, they tacked close under *Gretel*'s stern. If Hardy had tacked with them instead of crossing he could have kept Ficker from the favored side of the course. Once given the opening Ficker kept always a bit east of *Gretel* and despite inferior boat speed his position let him close the gap. The clincher came when *Intrepid* was approaching the mark on starboard tack and not quite fetching. It appeared that *Gretel* could cross by the narrowest of margins but instead Hardy elected to tack short in a safe leeward position. The tactic backfired when *Intrepid* got a lift a few seconds later, a lift which just enabled her to fetch while *Gretel* had to make two extra tacks just short of the mark to get around it.

Intrepid rounded forty-four seconds ahead. On the first reach she lost four seconds, on the second one she lost one more to start upwind the second time thirty-nine seconds ahead.

On the ensuing windward leg Ficker kept tacking on *Gretel* whenever he and his brain trust thought she was going the right way and then delaying her cover. Sometimes *Gretel* would tack back losing by the two extra tacks but utilizing her better speed to once again get close. Several times she nearly broke through, particularly late in the leg when she was on *Intrepid*'s lee bow on port tack and already on the starboard lay line for the mark. But she was so close to *Intrepid* that she could not tack and gain starboard tack rights without *Intrepid* having to alter course to avoid a collision prior to the tack's completion. Ficker kept driving Hardy ever farther past the lay line, waiting for a puff, and when it came he tacked in it and reached for the mark. Hardy waited a few seconds before following

Gretel II *shown finishing ahead of* Intrepid *in the fourth race of the 1970 match. The margin isn't as close as it seems. She won by 1 minute 02 seconds, picking up more than two minutes on the last leg.*

suit and by this time Ficker was riding the puff on a tight reach for the mark.

While they had been just seconds apart a few minutes before *Intrepid* had a fifty-one second lead as the run started.

She needed every bit of it. The wind had now lightened still more and both boats tacked downwind at radical angles, *Intrepid* jibing on the lifts and never letting *Gretel* get on her wind. Still *Gretel* kept coming and was less than two boat lengths and a scant twenty seconds behind at the leeward mark.

Here Ficker made his final key move. The wind had hauled to make it a near fetch to the finish on starboard tack. Instead of waiting for *Gretel* to tack before covering, he tacked immediately, figuring that this was the most direct course home and detecting what he thought was better air to the north instead of the east as in the two prior windward legs. Again he was right and built a more comfortable lead within a few minutes after rounding. Thereafter it was a question of staying always between *Gretel* and the finish yet making as few tacks as possible to thus negate *Gretel*'s better ability to accelerate.

The eventual margin at the finish of one minute forty-four seconds was misleading. It was one of the closest races in Cup history, a race which Ficker would have lost if he had made a single mistake. His support boats owned by members of the syndicate had flags rading "Ficker is Quicker." Right on! Particularly in this race but also throughout most of the match it was Ficker and his crew who had prevailed over a boat which was usually going faster than *Intrepid*.

There was another close match ten years later when *Freedom* beat *Australia,* 4–1. Once again the score is misleading because *Australia* could have won the first three races, all sailed in light air. Her bendy mast made her faster in such conditions but better starts and better tactics enabled *Freedom* to win two of them. I do not list this match as one we nearly lost because *Freedom* was ahead early on and so promptly in control that the issue was not really in doubt. Still the apparent ease of her victory was misleading.

This twenty-fourth match is described in detail in Chapter XI.

Chapter XI
The 1980 Match

While the Twenty-fourth Match for the America's Cup was not quite one we nearly lost, it was one we *could* have lost. I think of it as the bendy rig match, after an innovation on the challenger, *Australia,* which could have done our *Freedom* in. In fact, if *Freedom* had not been such a fine basic design with excellent sails, and if she had not clearly outsailed *Australia,* the Aussies with their bendy mast could very well have won all the marbles. *Australia* very likely would have beaten *Courageous* and *Clipper.*

Never before had there been such a concerted effort to lift the Cup. For the first time in sixteen years the British were back, with a brand-new boat created by a bright young designer named Ian Howlett. His charger had the stirring name of *Lionheart,* but far more important than her name was that she was being sailed by John Oakley—a world-class helmsman. In 1979, *Lionheart* had annihilated both *Sverige* and *Gretel II.* She looked like a good one, and when she arrived in Newport with a radical bendy mast which permitted a ten percent increase in unmeasured sail area, she looked better still. However, when Oakley got bounced as skipper, her chances went with him.

This is Australia *with the rig she used to win the trial races and before she switched to her bendy rig for the match. With her straight spar, she was a good Twelve, but she was not nearly as fast as with the bendy one.*

France III, *with her tricolor spinnaker, is more than a striking boat. She was fast enough to push* Australia *to the limit and with better sails (note the old-fashioned straight roach mainsail) might have become the challenger. That's Baron Bich at her wheel.*

Baron Bich was back for his fourth attempt, but this time with a promising new design by Johan Valentijn named *France III.* Her skipper was Bruno Troublé, the European Soling Champion and certainly one of the best sailors in France.

Pelle Peterson returned with *Sverige,* which had been unsuccessful in 1977 but which he had modified somewhat along the lines of his 1979 Six Meter World Cup champion, *Irene.*

Lionheart *was so much faster with her bendy rig (which was often bent much more than is shown here) that Aus-tralia was encouraged to try such a rig in the match against* Freedom.

Clipper, *despite getting her campaign underway late, beat* Courageous *to wind up second to* Freedom *among the American defense candidates. She proved to be a fine Twelve.*

Pre-race favorite among the challengers was *Australia*. She proved to be a fast Twelve in 1977 and since then Ben Lexcen had modified her to improve her light air performance. Jim Hardy, who had come close in 1970 with *Gretel II,* was her skipper. The best thing the challengers had going for them was that a long series of elimination races had been scheduled, so that the eventual challenger would be just as battle-tested as the defender.

To meet this quite formidable challenge the Americans had three boats.

Ted Turner and the entirety of his crew that had won in 1977 were back with *Courageous,* hoping to make her the first three-time defender. She had only minor modifications, and they were pinning their hopes on experience to bring her through.

Pitted against *Courageous* were two new boats. One was *Freedom,* the latest creation of Sparkman & Stephens. She was sailed by Dennis Conner and a superlative crew that had been training almost every day in the summer and fall of '79 off Newport and then through the winter of 1980 in California. Never before had there been such intense preparation.

The third contender among the defenders was *Clipper,* a brand-new design by Dave Pedrick. Her skipper was young Russell Long, a recent graduate of Harvard, where he had excelled in intercollegiate competition.

From the outset in the challenger trials, *Australia* was the cream of the crop. Despite losing some races, mostly through breakdowns, she swept quite easily into the final round. Also making the finals was *France III,* giving the Baron much his best showing in four campaigns. *Sverige* was outclassed except in a strong breeze and *Lionheart* performed poorly in all but light air. Still, it was *Lionheart* which was responsible for the greatest excitement because of her innovative rig. The top third of her mast was fiberglass and was capable of an extreme bend. This provided her with a great deal of extra unmeasured sail area along her leech (since there were no girth measurements used in measuring the sail area of the main). Despite ill-fitting sails, she showed bursts of speed and it was this which prompted the Aussies to work in secret on a similar rig to be used in the match itself should *Australia* win the trials with her conventional rig.

In the final round *Australia* beat *France III* handily, losing only one of the five races sailed and that one only because of a huge wind shift. She looked like a formidable opponent as she stood, but the Australians, noticing how *Freedom* was demolishing the other American boats, figured drastic action was needed. Hence, once selected, they stepped the new bendy rig they had been building in apparent secrecy and started feverishly to build new sails to accommodate it. What they did not know was that the Americans were aware of their plans even before the final

Courageous, *sporting her new snubbed bow and sliced transom, was still no match for* Freedom *or even* Clipper *and failed in her attempt to be the first three-time winner.*

challenger trials began but felt it was then too late to perfect such a rig. Had the Aussies unmasked their secret weapon a few weeks earlier, we still would not have emulated them but the challengers would have had a few more invaluable weeks to perfect their clever innovation, which proves once again that overly striving for secrecy can backfire.

Throughout the summer *Freedom* annihilated the other American boats. *Courageous* managed to beat her in the very first race they met, in June, but *not once* thereafter. *Clipper* beat *Freedom* there a couple of times

Sverige *was a fast* Twelve *in heavy air, beating* Australia *twice in the trials, but she was badly outclassed in light and moderate going.*

and was closing the gap at the end, but when *Freedom* was finally selected she had lost only four races of the more than forty sailed. Never since *Ranger* in 1937 and *Intrepid* in 1967 had a defender appeared so invulnerable. All the smart money was on *Freedom* and a real rout was quite generally anticipated.

Immediately prior to the match I talked to Jim Hardy and Dennis Conner. Jim felt buoyed up by what he had seen of their new rig and felt that if they got light air he had a real chance. Dennis, while guardedly optimistic, feared the bendy rig. He expected to win and was confident that he and his crew would not beat themselves, but he recognized the significance of *Australia*'s bendy mast and what it might do for her, especially in light air. It turned out that both Jim and Dennis had it sized up better than the general public, and to this day few yachtsmen, even many who were there, realize what a great opportunity the Australians

This photo tells the story of the 1980 match. Freedom *is in this enviable position right after the start of the final race, but* Australia's *bendy rig is providing tremendous power. With better starts, the challenger might have won the Cup.*

Bill Luders created the drawing at right to show the sail area gained by the bendy rig. The gray area is 240 feet, the white area lost in the triangle above the bent spar and along the luff of the jib totals 75 square feet, for a net gain of 165 square feet. This gain, however, doesn't take the roach into account. Yet even when the large roach to the mains of the American Twelves is added, the approximate gain in area achieved by such a rig is approximately 90 square feet; this was very nearly enough to give Australia *the Cup.*

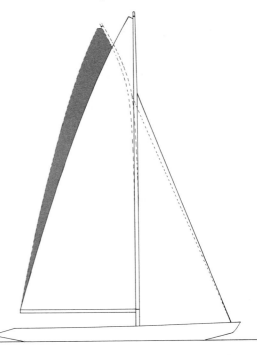

had to win the Cup. I honestly believe that if Hardy had sailed as well as Conner and had Conner sailed as indifferently as Hardy and his crew, *Australia* would have won. While I feel *Freedom* was basically the fastest Twelve of 1980, I feel also that *Australia's* bendy rig and the extra sail area it provided made her faster in light and moderate air, and in a match race the faster boat should win. An analysis of the five races makes the magnitude of *Freedom's* victory come into proper focus.

The first race looked like a yawner, with *Freedom* winning by one minute, 52 seconds. But in truth that should not have been. This light-air race was decided right at the start. Dennis Conner was on top of Hardy approaching the leeward end of the line. Instead of camping on him, he tacked away with about a minute to go. Dennis is not one to let an opponent go unmolested, but he tacked away in order to ensure being on the right side of the course in a wind he expected to clock. The wind *did* clock, and on top of that *Freedom* sailed into a stronger wind before tacking back to starboard shortly after the start. When *Australia* tacked eleven minutes after the start *Freedom* had a ten length lead.

I cannot remember a greater lead established so early in a Cup race, *but it was not gained on boat speed.* Thereafter on the first beat, *Australia* closed the gap to round 52 seconds behind. That is an awesome lead in a match race, but *Australia* made it even more so on the first reach by staying in the spectator wash instead of jibing away from it as *Freedom* did. She thereby lost 40 seconds on that leg and another 20 on the second reach by a sloppy spinnaker change. By now the race was over, though *Australia* showed her potential by gaining 25 seconds on the final beat.

The first attempt at a second race failed to finish within the time limit but *Australia's* potential was further demonstrated by her huge lead when time expired.

In the real second race, sailed in light air throughout, the serious nature of the Aussies' challenge was demonstrated even more vividly. In this one both skippers sailed superb races. *Australia* was on *Freedom's* leeward bow at the start, though not yet in a safe leeward position. Some ten minutes later, she *was,* and *Freedom* had to tack—the first time all summer any boat had been successful in squeezing up on her. Thereafter *Australia*

179

retained her lead at the first four marks by margins of 28, 15, 47 and 46 seconds.

Starting the run, however, *Australia* went off on a bear-away set while *Freedom* did a jibe set. When *Freedom* obtained a better angle, coupled with a stronger wind, she surged ahead to round the last mark with a lead of 21 seconds. She stretched that lead early in the beat, but once *Australia* got clear air she went well. When she got a wind shift and a slightly stronger wind it was all she needed to sweep into the lead, accompanied by wild cheers from her tender and the support vessel Alan Bond and the other Aussies were riding on. She covered carefully thereafter but still had to worry about finishing within the time limit. By now it was nearly dark but she finally crossed with some seven minutes left on the clock, concluding the most exciting race in the long history of the Cup. Most exciting of all was the realization that when well-sailed and in conditions to her liking here was a boat that was thoroughly capable of winning not just a race but the America's Cup itself!

In the third race, *Australia* was fully capable of winning had she not been snookered at the start. Once again conditions were to her liking on all but the last leg, but early mistakes put *Australia* too far behind to be able to capitalize on mistakes that *Freedom* made later.

Dennis Conner started with a full head of steam on a port tack toward the Committee boat end of the line, with *Australia* on her weather quarter. With a minute and a half to go before the start and with both boats over the line, *Freedom* was in a position to block *Australia* from getting back on time and could have started with a sure safe leeward. Instead Dennis peeled off early to get as close as possible to the Committee boat end, eschewing the safe leeward. What was the motive behind this uncharacteristic generosity? Simply that he, his tactician, Dennis Durgan, and his navigator, Halsey Herreshoff, were so convinced that the

Freedom (to windward) was helped immeasurably by having Enterprise *as her trial horse. Every sailing day over a period of two years, the two worked together.* Enterprise *might have been the second-fastest American Twelve.*

right-hand side of the course was going to be favored that they wanted to get as far to that side as they could.

As usual, they were right. They sailed into the header they expected and thereafter protected the right-hand side of the course. This enabled them to round the first mark 45 seconds to the good.

They needed every bit of that lead to win because thereafter they made more mistakes than they had all summer. They lost 19 seconds on the first reach when their spinnaker split due to a tear while hoisting. They lost another five seconds on the third leg simply because *Australia* was going faster. Still, they had a 21-second lead starting upwind the second time, and with the wind now up to 14 knots *Freedom* took off. She opened up dramatically, but just when the race seemed on ice—about 500 yards short of the weather mark—her jib ripped. Instead of replacing it they nursed it along to round 48 seconds ahead.

That should have been enough but then *Freedom*'s great crew made it really exciting by hoisting their spinnaker inside the topping lift. When they lowered it to clear the foul-up the pole dropped into the water and it was more than two minutes before they could manhandle it back to its rightful place and get the spinnaker drawing properly. During this time *Australia* kept charging and was right on *Freedom*'s heels. The margin at the final mark was a scant eight seconds after 20 miles of sailing. (Who was it who said viewing a match race was like watching grass grow?) Since the breeze was now fresh, *Freedom* had superb boat speed and opened up to win by 53 seconds, yet it is unlikely she could have won without her big jump right after the start.

After three races the score was 2–1 in *Freedom*'s favor but it so easily could have been 3–0 for *Australia*. In the fourth and fifth races conditions were more to *Freedom*'s liking. In the fourth, *Australia* had too flat a main, expecting heavy air but getting only moderate. This made her perceptibly slower than *Freedom*. In the fresh air of the fifth and final race both boats had their best sails up and *Freedom* was clearly faster. Hence *Freedom*

Australia's *bendy rig and sharp sailing powered her to an exciting win over* Freedom *in the second race.*

won both races big. The margin of victory was enhanced, however, by virtue of getting both starts and sailing flawless races thereafter. While *Freedom* would have won both these tests even if she had not sailed superior races, the score at this stage could so easily have been 3–2 in *Australia*'s favor. Instead, the match was all over. When one realizes that in the days following this Twenty-fourth Match the wind was light and that in light to moderate air *Australia* with her bendy rig had an edge in speed, one begins to realize how close a shave we had.

This match demonstrates why for so many years we kept on winning the Cup. Usually we have the faster boat. But on the rare occasions when the American boat is slower, as *Freedom* was in light air, as *Rainbow* was in 1934 and as *Intrepid* was in 1970, the American sailors have always risen to the occasion. Maybe it is because we went into the series expecting to win and also fiercely determined not to lose. Whatever it is, it worked for 111 years.

I suspect also that the reason it stopped working in 1983 was because the Australians went into that series feeling *they* would win and the Americans were running scared. True, *Australia II* was a fine boat, a boat slightly faster than *Liberty*. But even more important, in my mind, was a reversal of confidence in the two camps. You have to feel like a winner to be a winner. In 1983, Dennis Conner and his crew felt before the series started that they might well lose. That hurt them, as we will see when the series is discussed in Chapter XIII.

Chapter XII
Shenanigans Over "The Keel"

A lot more than exciting boat racing was going on at Newport in the summer of 1983. In the American camp the trial races were going along pretty much as expected. Dennis Conner in *Liberty* was winning most of the races. John Kolius in *Courageous* appeared almost equal in speed but more often than not kept losing to *Liberty*. Tom Blackaller, who had no love for Dennis (and kept saying so), won some races convincingly in light air with *Defender*, but was slaughtered by both other boats as the wind built. It looked like *Liberty* would win selection, but the fact that the nine-year-old *Courageous* was pressing her, despite having sails that seemed inferior, did nothing to build confidence among the American sailors and the Selection Committee.

The cause for worry was compounded by the way *Australia II* was slaughtering the opposition in the challenger trials. She hardly ever lost a race no matter whether it was light, moderate, or heavy air, and when she did lose, her skipper, John Bertrand, blamed himself for having thrown the race away by poor sailing or faulty tactics. The image of *Australia II* as a super boat was fast emerging.

Australia II's owner, Alan Bond, contributed to unease in the American camp by always keeping her underbody covered by huge tarps whenever she was hauled and by having guards in place twenty-four hours a day. From the realization that *Australia II* had something very different about her came the question as to whether the difference was legal or, put another way, did she really rate Twelve Meters?

It was not an idle question. All evidence pointed to the fact that she did have a unique underbody, something quite different from any other Twelve and very likely a loophole not contemplated when the rating rule was drawn up. If a loophole that the framers of the Twelve Meter Rating Rule did not foresee, then Rule 27 specifies that if from any "peculiarity" in the build of the yacht the measurer feels that the Rule will not rate the yacht fairly, he must report it to the "National Authority," which will award an equitable rating, and that "the measurement shall be deemed incomplete until this has been done."

The America's Cup Committee, despite Bond's secrecy, had a pretty good idea of what *Australia*'s keel was like, and we felt it was most definitely a peculiarity. Never before did a Twelve Meter have wings on its keel and it is certain that the framers of the Rule never thought of them or of the effect they might have.

The fact that this keel was new—and beneficial—is borne out by the fact that Alan Bond filed a patent application for it (No. 8200457) in the Netherlands in the name of Ben Lexcen, citing the following benefits: (1) The fins increase the development of side force by the keel (thus reducing leeway) and they decrease the resistance of the keel; (2) The fins reduce keel vortexes (the separation of boundary layer from the body of the keel), which in turn reduces drag, and thereby increases lift; (3) This is most beneficial in the area near the tip of the keel; (4) The draft increases with heel and thus increases the aspect ratio of the keel; and (5) The fins

These two photos of Australia II'*s keel, taken the day after she won the Cup, illustrate how unusual and effective it is. The photo above is taken from aft and the one below from forward. Note the small lateral plane. It is easy to visualize how draft increases as the boat heels.*

lower the center of gravity of the ballast, which results in an increase in stability.

The most telling of these four benefit claims is the fourth, because an increase in effective draft can cause a major saving in induced drag. A brilliant way to increase effective draft without actually making a keel deeper in the water is to install endplates. So important is draft considered in the rule that any increase results in a severe rating penalty. Rating Rule 6 provides that if the maximum draft (calculated from the waterline length) is exceeded, then three times the excess is added to the rating. When measured in an upright position, *Australia II*'s draft is within prescribed limits and she receives no penalty. But as she heels, draft is increased instead of reduced as in all other boats. It has been estimated by experts that the amount of increased draft, if applied to her rating, would make her rate between 12.5 and 13 meters.

If that's not a peculiarity of design not contemplated by the framers of the Rule, then what is? And that is why the America's Cup Committee of the New York Yacht Club raised the question of whether *Australia II* was rated fairly. Taking nothing away from Ben Lexcen for his brilliant concept, I don't feel the rating was fair. But there was one rub. The measurers who had certified that she rated Twelve Meters did not think of the keel as a peculiarity. I can't fathom why they didn't—but they didn't. And here comes the crusher. Condition 22 of the America's Cup match, which the New York Yacht Club drafted, provides that the decision of the three-man measurement committee on questions of interpretation of the Twelve-Meter Rating Rule shall be final. Mark Vinbury, the American on the measurement committee, did not feel the rating was fair, but the other two did and hence she was certified as a Twelve Meter.

In my mind that should have ended the matter. But the majority of the Cup Committee felt such an injustice had been done that they pulled all sorts of ploys to get the matter reconsidered, even trying to overrule the measurers by having the IYRU Keel Boat Committee look into the matter and make a final decision.

Meanwhile, Alan Bond was having a field day, accusing us of doing anything in order to keep the Cup. The press, by and large, sided with

The America's Cup Committee often had worried looks in the summer of 1983.

Bond, partly because we presented our case clumsily, but largely because the fact remains that our own conditions specified that the decision of the measurers should be final.

The New York Yacht Club kept pursuing the matter, urging that IYRU make a final decision. Finally, on August 23rd, with time fast running out, the IYRU revealed that on August 17, 1982, three members of the IYRU Keel Boat Committee gave an interpretation to the British designer Ian Howlett that "winglets are permitted on the keel but they shall be fixed and not capable of being adjusted in trim or retracted." Sir Gordon Smith, chairman of the committee at that time, is now dead. James McGruer is now retired. The third member, Tony Watts, advised that the British ruling would apply to *Australia II*. I very much doubt whether that three-man body, when making their original ruling, had any idea of the benefits that might accrue. If so they would, I believe, have ruled that the wings on *Australia II* did constitute a peculiarity and would have assigned a rating penalty. A year later, with the America's Cup match about to start, Tony Watts was loath to upset the applecart.

The New York Yacht Club, when so advised by Watts, quickly withdrew their objection. This doesn't mean they felt the ruling was correct and the rating fair. But with good grace (finally), they dropped the matter.

Just when it seemed that we could all get down to focusing on the racing, a far more serious matter arose concerning *Australia II*'s legality.

One of the requirements of the Deed of Gift and the conditions of the match for the America's Cup was that each yacht must be designed by nationals of the country it represents. Ben Lexcen is very much an Australian, so no problem there. However, in 1982, the *Australia II* syndicate requested permission to use the Netherlands ship model basin to tank test their new boat. This permission was granted, provided that the tank tests were under the sole supervision of Australian nationals and provided also that the "designs were from the drawing board of Australian nationals." It was a sporting gesture on the part of the Americans to allow use of the Dutch tanks, since the Aussies had so such facility, but it was crystal clear that this use applied only to the physical facility and not to input from Dutch designers. As a precedent, a year before the British syndicate sought to hire Johan Valentijn as a consultant to the designer of the British Twelve-Meter. Valentijn was not British and in early 1981 the committee stated: "To have a foreign designer—however he is designated—participate in the design of a boat or sail would violate both the letter and spirit of the 1980 Resolution, and any boat or sail so designed would not be eligible for use in Cup competition." A copy of this ruling went to all challengers, including the *Australia II* syndicate. They knew and agreed to the rules of the game. But later, as you will soon see, they chose to break the rules.

It was quite sporting of the New York Yacht Club to allow the Aussies to use the Dutch facility. They didn't have to. You might ask, Why not? and might feel that it is contrary to good competition to insist that only nationals of each country challenging for or defending the America's Cup be allowed to work on the design. In fact I'm not altogether convinced myself that it is desirable. But that is beside the point. Those are the rules and conditions under which the America's Cup is sailed, *conditions agreed to by all participants.*

Imagine our concern when we heard representatives of the Netherlands aerospace laboratory (NLR) boasting on the docks of Newport and at seminars in Boston that *Australia II's* winged keel was their "brainchild." NLR, we found out, was a subcontractor to Netherlands Ship Model Basis (NSMB), where tank testing of *Australia II* had been conducted.

These reports were reinforced by Dutch newspaper articles with banner headlines proclaiming the role of Dutch designers in creating a "super yacht" in *Australia II.* It was true that Ben Lexcen was at NSMB while tests were underway and it appears also that the winged keel was his original concept. It is also crystal clear that the Dutch helped him. To determine the facts, the New York Yacht Club sent Dick Latham, a member of the Cup Committee, to Holland. The Dutch admitted that their role had been substantial, but since they were friends of Ben Lexcen they would sign no statements to that effect, even if true. In fact, even though agreeing orally that NSMB and NLR had contributed to the keel design of *Australia II,* they would sign nothing to that effect. Moreover, it was obvious that in any hearing before the IYRU they would deny their complicity. New York Yacht Club Commodore Robert G. Stone therefore issued a press release on August 26, which read in part: "Having completed such investigation as we felt necessary and proper, we have concluded that the evidence available to us to date is insufficient to press the matter further at this time."

Lest you question my objectivity in all this, let it be known that a year later Lexcen himself admitted getting help from the Dutch designers. He wondered, How could he turn a deaf ear when they made suggestions? A good point and one that points up the danger of using a foreign facility. But this doesn't change the fact that the conditions governing the America's Cup match had been violated.

Commodore Stone's press release wasn't the end of the matter. Right after the Aussies won the challenger trials we got word that *Australia II* had been using a mast that had been manufactured in the United States and that the design for the mast's taper and splice was not Lexcen's, but was American. The Australians were then asked by the New York Yacht Club to sign a certification covering each area of doubt concerning both keel and mast, assuring us that they had complied with each item. They refused to do so on the basis that the draft was insulting. Instead they made a general representation to the effect that they had complied with the Deed of Gift.

The day before the match was to be held, an extraordinary meeting was convened to determine whether or not to accept *Australia* as challenger. In attendance were all present flag officers of the New York Yacht Club, several past commodores, and the entire America's Cup Committee. Three of those present voted to cancel the match. That's how convinced they were that the Australians had not lived up to the rules. All the flag officers, the chairman of the Cup Committee, and a majority of its membership (including me) voted to race. By so doing we were not conceding that the Australians had complied with conditions. Instead we felt that to rule otherwise would be a question of winning the battle and losing the war and would do irreparable harm to the America's Cup and to the New York Yacht Club. The general public and the press would never understand and would merely conclude that in the face of certain defeat we would stoop to anything in order to keep the Cup here. The other reason I voted as I did, and I suspect the same applies to many others, was that I was looking forward to a battle royal on the race course.

The astounding thing is that the Australians who had at the very least stretched the conditions came out of that long summer as the "good guys," and the New York Yacht Club (which was only trying to insure compliance) as the villain. Part of the explanation was Alan Bond's effective way of going on the offensive and making us appear to be going to extreme ends to keep the Cup. Part has to be the fact that we were ponderous, self-righteous, and really quite stuffy in the way we presented our case. And it must be admitted that *Australia*'s compliance would in all likelihood never have been questioned if she hadn't seemed so bloody

Alan Bond was not one to be taken lightly. He outmaneuvered the New York Yacht Club at almost every turn.

fast. We needed a spokesman with a sense of humor and a flair for communication. But a large part of the reason is the fact that few people give a hoot about the detailed conditions. They just want to see a great boat race and may the better boat win. I admit to being close to that persuasion, even though with some reluctance I know deep down that a rule is a rule and even though adherence thereto might hurt, it should be done. That's why three people voted to cancel the match. But there are times when it's better to be technically wrong in the interests of furthering the sport, and especially the America's Cup. And that's why the overwhelming majority voted to sail the series. Isn't it ironic that having done so, and having then lost the America's Cup, the New York Yacht Club is still perceived by so many as the "bad guys" of the summer of '83?

Chapter XIII
How the Cup Was Lost

In the 1981 edition of this book there was a chapter titled "When We Lose the Cup." It was evident that the longest winning streak in sports couldn't continue forever. While the Americans remained the number-one sailing nation, their years of invincibility had passed. While I forecast a United States win in the 1983 match, I expected it to be a real cliff-hanger. A cliff-hanger it was, but with *Australia II* coming through instead of *Liberty*.

It might be more accurate to have called this chapter "How the Cup Was Won," because *Australia II* was a fast boat, and Bertrand sailed well and deserved to win. Still, it could have gone the other way if Dennis Conner hadn't gotten psyched into making uncharacteristic errors in each of the last three races, after being ahead three races to one and needing but one more to keep the Cup. In each of these races *Liberty* was ahead. In each I believe she could have stayed ahead if her skipper hadn't been so afraid of what he considered to be the blazing speed of *Australia II* that he abandoned normal match race tactics.

We will go into those three races shortly, but lest we appear too hard on Dennis Conner let it be said right now that *Australia II* could easily have won in four straight races. Only superior sailing by Dennis, and a bit of luck in the form of breakdowns on *Australia II* in races one and two, kept it from being a clean sweep. The point is, however, that after having victory within his grasp, Conner let it slip away.

There is no doubt that *Australia II* was the faster boat, but only by a slim margin. She simply wasn't the super boat Dennis believed. In very light air *Australia* had the edge. In very heavy air she also had an advantage over *Liberty*. In medium winds the two boats appeared to be an even match around the course.

Liberty proved to be faster on reaches, *Australia* faster on a run. Upwind, *Australia* had the edge in light or heavy going, with the two boats apparently equal going to windward in moderate air. *Australia II* had another edge that was helpful in match racing. She turned on a dime and hence had an edge in prestart maneuvering. One might use this edge to apply to tacking duels as well.

My estimation is that, all things considered, *Australia II* was the faster boat but not by as big a margin as *Endeavour* had over *Rainbow* in 1934. The big difference and the factor that brought *Australia II* home a winner was the fact that for the first time the challenger not only thought she could win but *expected* to win, and for the very first time the defender was not only afraid of losing but more than half expected to lose. Such an attitude is not conducive to winning, especially in the case of Dennis Conner.

In his book *Born to Win,* John Bertrand wrote, "Dennis only sails to his full potential when he is much better prepared than everyone else. He has to feel, mentally, that he has the advantage. That's what sets him up for the kill."

Bertrand characterizes himself as being somewhat like Dennis in that he has a methodical streak that goes with being a marine engineer, and that he, too, likes to be well prepared. He goes on to say that he asks for no more than "a boat that will compete on equal terms. But I want no more than that. Give me a fair chance and I will race anyone down to the wire, man-to-man, one-on-one."

John Bertrand knew Dennis well, having sailed with him in the 1978 SORC. Although he had great respect for Conner's ability as a skipper, he did not consider him unbeatable. He also felt that when Dennis did make an occasional error or when he lost his confidence he wasn't always absolutely certain what to do.

Since Bertrand expected to meet Conner in the match, he did all he could all summer long to worry him, realizing his vulnerability when he didn't feel the dice were stacked in his favor. Whenever *Australia II* lost a race, Bertrand took full blame. Whenever she won Bertrand was unbelievably (and uncharacteristically, I might add) modest. He gave full credit to *Australia II* and her blazing speed. Sure *Australia II* was fast. But she wasn't the super boat Bertrand pictured her as. Still, Dennis Conner didn't know that and hence he entered the match with trepidation and not the confidence that he usually felt and that he needed to do his best.

Even so, I feel Dennis Conner outsailed John Bertrand in the first four races and only because he did (assisted by breakdowns by *Australia II* in the first two races) was the score three to one in his favor.

In the first race, the lead changed five times over the first five legs, with the two boats always within two or three lengths of each other. On the fifth leg, *Australia II,* which had been twenty-eight seconds behind starting downwind, first demonstrated her awesome speed on a run, to draw even. She became overlapped with *Liberty* to leeward of her on port tack, with both boats having to jibe to fetch the leeward mark. It looked bad for *Liberty.* If *Australia II,* which was running faster, played her cards correctly, she would be right on top of *Liberty* when both boats jibed, would blanket her and almost surely round first. Secondly, it seemed impossible for *Liberty* to jibe first since she had to give *Australia II* room to respond. In short, *Liberty*'s chance at rounding ahead seemed hopeless.

But Dennis and his crew found a way. They sharpened up, gained an additional length of water between the two boats, and jibed suddenly. *Australia II,* caught flat-footed and not prepared to jibe, but obligated to keep clear, had to swing hard across *Liberty*'s stern to avoid a collision. In the process, a steering cable sheave failed and she became a wounded whale, steerable only with her trim tab for the next ten minutes. *Liberty* won by one minute ten seconds, but if *Australia II* had either sharpened up and kept close enough to *Liberty* to prevent her from jibing or had jibed with her, she would have rounded the fifth mark in the lead and almost certainly would have won the race. Score one for *Liberty* through superior sailing, coupled with the breakdown of *Australia II*.

Australia II would almost surely have lost the first race even without her breakdown, but race number two would just as surely have been hers were it not for a crippling accident. A few minutes before the start, her mainsail headboard car slipped from the halyard hook and the head of the main was a full foot below normal. There was no way to get it back up and you've never seen such a sorry looking main.

Instead of giving up, however, the Aussies sailed a great race and even led by forty-five seconds at the first mark.

Liberty ground her down on the ensuing two reaches, during which time one of *Australia II*'s crew was aloft trying to fix the damage. He couldn't reengage the car but was able to lash it so that it wouldn't drop

Liberty *tacking into a safe leeward position right after the gun in the second race.* Note Australia II*'s sick mainsail.*

Three minutes after the start of Race 2 Liberty *appears in command (above) but when both boats get headed (below) the crippled* Australia II *gains the lead.*

Australia II *was still ahead approaching the third mark in Race 2 but she was hurting. Note man aloft attempting repairs.*

farther. *Liberty* was only twenty-one seconds behind starting upwind the second time. She played the shifts well and was going fast enough that she led at the second weather mark by forty-eight seconds. Despite losing seventeen seconds on the run, *Liberty* was never really threatened, and won by more than a minute and a half.

She very nearly lost the race at the protest table, surviving a claim by *Australia II* that *Liberty* had tacked too close in front of her. It is rare to win a burden of proof protest such as this, but Dennis and his tactician Tom Whidden convinced the jury. I suspect my testimony helped. I saw the whole incident from almosty directly overhead in the blimp, and to

199

me it looked like *Liberty* had indeed tacked close—*but not too close*. The Aussies didn't like my testifying, feeling I was a prejudiced witness. What they don't know and probably still don't believe is that if I had seen it in *Australia*'s favor, I would have said so or would have refused to be a witness when Dennis asked me to.

The first attempt at race number three failed to conclude within the time limit when the wind died a mile from the finish. But *Australia II* had led all the way and was a whopping five minutes fifty-seven seconds ahead at the last mark. Dennis now knew that *Australia II* was very formidable in light air. Despite being ahead two races to none he wasn't all that confident.

The real third race did nothing to restore confidence. In winds ranging between seven to ten knots, *Australia II* won by three minutes fourteen seconds. *Liberty* was still ahead in the series by two races to one, but it could have been four to zero in favor of *Australia II*. Without clever sailing on *Liberty*'s part, coupled by a steering breakdown, *Australia II* would probably have won the first race. Without the headboard break-down, *Australia II* would surely have won race two. Without the wind collapsing at the first attempt at race three, *Australia II* could then have gone up by a score of three to nothing, and then in the third completed race the Aussies did win big.

You don't pay off on "withouts" or "ifs," however, and hence *Liberty* still had a shaky series lead. Her skipper and crew had reason to be running scared in the fourth race. Instead they kept their cool and in winds ranging from ten knots at the start and building to fifteen at the finish (the most favorable range of conditions for *Liberty*) they sailed a perfect race. An eleven-second jump at the start enabled them to go where they thought best. *Australia II,* recognizing they had good speed in all conditions, followed instead of attempting to split tacks. Still the closest they could come was thirty-five seconds at the end of the run (on which they gained eleven seconds). When *Liberty* won by forty-three seconds to go up by three to one, the Cup seemed reasonably safe. It seemed inconceivable that even against as fast a boat as *Australia II,* *Liberty* couldn't find a way to take at least one race in three tries. Dennis

Conner, however, didn't think it was inconceivable. He knew he had sailed brilliantly in race number four, had made no mistakes, and had won by less than a minute. He knew also that the other two races he won were tainted victories that could so easily have gone the other way. Therefore, he and his crew remained nervous. They were psyched out by *Australia II*'s speed, rated her even faster than she really was, and were convinced that only by deviating from normal match race tactics could they win. There is no other way to explain the moves they made in the next three races that caused them to lose all of them. Bertrand's summerlong buildup of *Australia II* as a super boat had taken its toll and the Americans were tight. They were tight also because the pressure is greatest when victory is so very close, which is when you start wondering if you can pull it off.

Prior to the fifth race, *Liberty*'s crew had a real reason to worry. The ram that actuated their jumper struts broke more than an hour before the start. They could race without it but the top of the mast would fall off to leeward and make their main less efficient. The spare part was rushed out to the race course and Tom Rich and Scott Vogel spent more than half an hour aloft attempting to make repairs. While they were still aloft, *Liberty* was towed to the starting line, casting off just before the ten-minute gun. With six minutes to go, the luff tape on the jib they planned to hoist broke and it was less than five minutes before the start that *Liberty* was ready.

Despite this pandemonium, *Liberty* got a super start, while *Australia II* was over early and started thirty-seven seconds behind. It was Dennis Conner's finest hour, and his last one for that race. An initial lead of thirty-seven seconds in a match race should ice it for the boat ahead, even against a faster boat. It probably would have if the jumper strut ram had not failed again soon after the start. Dennis then concluded that being somewhat crippled they could win only by going for better wind shifts. Therefore, they didn't cover closely, and when *Australia II* got a favoring slant she not only erased the thirty-seven second deficit but swept into the lead to round the first mark twenty-three seconds ahead.

It is true that the breakdown hampered *Liberty,* but only slightly. To

In the fifth race it was Liberty's turn to suffer an equipment failure. Tom Rich and Scott Vogel are aloft just prior to the warning gun, attempting to repair the jumper strut. The repair didn't last and this, plus Liberty's decision not to cover when she was well ahead, might well have been responsible for losing the Cup.

me, her main still looked pretty good, immeasurably better than *Australia II*'s had in the second race when her headboard slipped. She was, I feel, going fast enough to keep *Australia II* at bay by careful covering. I thought so at the time and John Bertrand corroborates it in his book. Describing the first leg of this race, starting at the point when *Australia II*, left to her own devices, had drawn even, he wrote as follows: "At this point in the race we have taken 37 seconds off the Americans. It's not totally because of a broken strut that we outsailed them. They made a mistake. They should never have let us go off on our own. They should have followed and covered us. They should have come after us and found a way to keep us from outspeeding them, no matter what."

Later in that chapter he wrote, "I can hardly believe it, but we have the Americans rattled. They just made a judgement error and they made it because they are intimidated by our boat. They went looking for wind when they should have been in a dog fight with us. This has to be the first time in history that a defending American crew has been intimidated by a foreign challenger. I have a predatory instinct in these matters, so I'm obliged to say that I smelled blood and weakness on that first upwind leg of Race 5."

Once ahead, *Australia II* used her superior speed to stay there, winning by one minute forty-seven seconds. We will never know if she could have won if *Liberty* had covered closely.

Following this win, *Australia*'s confidence had to be building and *Liberty*'s declining. This had a bearing in race six. Dennis once more got the start, this time by seven seconds. Ten minutes later *Liberty* had a four-length lead. She was moving well and covering closely and looking good. At this juncture *Australia II* tacked, *Liberty* tacked on her, but when *Australia II* tacked away before gaining headway, *Liberty* let her go. Not once all summer had I seen Dennis let an opponent go with such a lead. He quite obviously didn't want to get in a short tacking duel, fearing *Australia II*'s quick tacking ability and acceleration. It wasn't until the last leg of the last race, when *Liberty* was behind, that she got into a short tacking duel with *Australia* and actually *gained*. Conner had, as was so prevalent throughout the series, done a superb job to gain the lead, and then let his slippery opponent off the hook.

In this case it proved to be an absolute disaster. *Australia II* sailed into a huge header, coupled with a fresh breeze that never did get down to *Liberty*. *Liberty* was on the outside of the circle in a hopeless position. She was two minutes behind at the first mark. The important thing to recognize is that if she had not feared *Australia*'s tacking ability and had tacked on her and forced her once more to tack away, it could very easily have been *Liberty* instead of *Australia* on top, with an unbeatable lead and the series in her pocket. Instead, *Australia II* went on to win the race by more than three minutes.

The moment of truth. Australia II *rounds the last mark in Race 7 with a 21 second lead. Despite a furious tacking duel in which* Liberty *actually gained a bit it was all over but the shouting.*

With the score now three to three, the stage was set for what was billed as the race of the century. It turned out to be just that. The ten- to twelve-knot wind was the range that prior experience had indicated would give *Liberty* her best chance. She got the start by eight seconds but *Australia II* was moving well. Halfway up the weather leg she had the lead, but for some unfathomable reason failed to cover. If *Liberty* had gone on to win the race this failure by Bertrand would have been forever cited as the turning point that kept the Cup in America. Instead it is all but forgotten.

Once out from under a cover by *Australia II, Liberty* made the most of it, played a shift just right, and rounded the first mark with a twenty-nine second lead. It was a virtual standoff on the two reaches but *Liberty* played the second beat well and had good boat speed. That combined to give her a fifty-seven second lead starting the run. In the six previous races, *Australia* had gained on the run in all but one. Still, a lead of nearly a minute seemed pretty secure to everyone except Dennis Conner and his afterguard. They felt so threatened that they thought they had to be clever to stay ahead. After sailing for about half a mile on starboard tack with *Australia II* following, *Liberty* jibed away.

It was at this juncture that the Cup was lost. When *Liberty* jibed, I assumed they were going to jibe back in a minute or so to position themselves on *Australia II*'s leeward bow, between her and the mark, an ideal spot to insure clear air if *Australia II* gained and both boats then had to jibe for the mark. An ideal spot also to initiate a fierce luffing match if *Australia II* should gain an overlap. Instead, *Liberty* kept going until the boats were widely separated. The reasoning by her brain trust was as follows: *Australia II* had proven to be faster on a run and was gaining. On *Liberty* they were apprehensive that at the same rate of advance the lead would be all gone by the leeward mark and that therefore the best bet was to split and look for better shifts or stronger wind. All quite understand-able with a lead half of what she had, but fifty-seven seconds is a big margin—one that I doubt very much could have been erased with both boats sailing in the same water and same winds.

In short, I felt at the time (and still feel) as the two boats widened out that this was an unnecessary flyer. It appeared as though *Liberty*'s crew was psyched into believing they could remain ahead even with a big lead only by splitting. When *Liberty* was headed after the boats got widely separated, this gave her a poor sailing angle when she had to jibe for the mark, cooking her goose.

On *Australia II* they would have followed *Liberty* if they felt they were gaining fast enough to pass on that leg. They didn't follow because they thought the lead was too great and also because they liked the looks of the wind where they were going, as opposed to where *Liberty* was headed. Bertrand describes that leg in his book as follows: "As a matter of fact, on that fifth leg, theirs was a bit of a lame-duck performance, and they gave it to us on a plate. If it had been Race 1 instead of Race 7, it would have been a damned sight harder, of that I am certain. But by now the

Americans have psyched themselves into believing that we were so much faster than they were, and on their boat as we began to catch up, there was a feeling of 'Uh, oh here she comes' . . . what they did *not* know was that we were stretched to the limit—everyone working away, thinking, helping, trimming, searching out the wind, taking bearings, sailing the boat as she had *never* been sailed before. Our pulses were racing, our hearts were pounding, but I think the public thought we were all sitting there having a drink and laughing as we rolled inevitably by on our winged keel."

He goes on to recount one of his crew reporting: "Their heads are swiveling, John! We're giving them the heebie-jeebies!"

We will never know whether *Liberty* could have remained ahead had she not jibed away. But history will record that she lost one minute eighteen seconds—a huge amount. Moreover, *Liberty* jibed eleven times on that leg and *Australia* only five. In light air a Twelve loses between thirty to fifty feet each time she jibes, which accounts for thirty to fifty seconds of the lead. *Liberty* also missed both of the major wind shifts. Perhaps most important is the fact that when *Australia II* did go by the two boats were so separated that *Liberty* could not luff her.

Bertrand attributes their success on this leg to panic on the Americans' part, panic caused by the fact that they were psyched out and sailing with an inferiority complex. I agree with him to a large extent, and that is exactly what I wrote in the January 1984 issue of *Yachting* (prior to reading his book or even talking to him after that fateful seventh race).

What I don't agree with is his feeling that the Aussies sailed a better series. A better fifth leg in the final race, yes. Cooler performances in races five and six after they were behind. But let's not forget that it was *Liberty*'s skipper and crew that *put* them behind. And let's not forget either that *Australia II* was a very fast Twelve Meter. Having a fast boat under you breeds confidence and makes you look smart.

In conclusion, however, I feel that the Cup need not have been lost. This was borne out in the last leg of the final race. *Liberty* had no alternative to engaging in a short tacking duel. In race number five, they avoided such a duel when ahead in the strong belief that in a short tacking

Bertrand, Lexcen and Bond, the trio which brought the longest winning streak in all sport to an end, savor the moment at the awards ceremony at Marble House.

situation *Australia II* was sure to gain. Yet in the last race it was *Liberty* that *gained* so much in this situation that *Australia II* had to break it off to maintain her lead.

Hindsight is, I well know, a marvelous way to look smart. Acknowledging that, let me say that after having sailed well, after having had several good breaks, the skipper and crew of *Liberty* could have held the Cup if they hadn't been so very afraid of losing it.

Chapter XIV
Sailing for the America's Cup

0930, September 15, 1964—The dock at Newport Shipyard was jammed with shipyard workers, syndicate members, crew wives, girl friends, and anyone else who could scrounge a pass to what was at that moment the most exclusive piece of waterfront in Newport, Rhode Island. As I kissed Charlotte goodby, she said with calm conviction, "You can do it, Bob." I waved to my oldest son Rob, my daughters Louise and Anne, hopped aboard *Constellation* as the dock lines from *Chaperone* were cast off precisely at 0930. We had developed the habit of leaving at the exact moment we had decided we would leave, not a minute earlier or later, and the fact that we were on our way to tow out for the first race of the 18th match for the America's Cup made it seem even more vital to be punctual.

As the last line was cast off and our tender *Chaperone* surged ahead, with *Constellation* nestled alongside her, the crowd ashore shouted, whistled, waved, clapped, blew kisses (the females that is) and exhorted us into battle with the usual inanities. From the yachts still at the pier, and from a swarm of others milling around just off it, air horns and deep

208

throated ship's whistles raised a discordant and deafening chorus. Just as our stern cleared the dock, the cannon manned by the shipyard workers thundered their own special salute. Theirs was the most fervent exhortation because to a man they had bet up to a month's wages on *Constellation,* often at big odds or even money for a clean sweep. It crossed my mind that if we did not win it might be aimed at us, and loaded with more than blanks upon our return.

Once clear of the dock we cast off the bow, stern and spring lines from *Chaperone* while she surged ahead with the towing line sucking out astern of her. As Rod Stephens put our large American ensign in our stern socket, I was swept with an inexplicable shortness of breath. "For God's sakes, Bob, don't be so corny," I muttered to myself but to no avail.

From the Williams & Manchester dock we saw *Sovereign* getting underway and now it was their turn to receive an equally loud send-off. "Well, we're ahead of them already," someone remarked, and everyone laughed as though they had just heard the best joke of their lives.

As we passed Fort Adams, towing now at nine knots, the throngs ashore waved like madmen. I perceived one family holding what looked like a bedsheet with a message written on it. I grabbed the binoculars, and was really moved to read the words, "Good luck, *Connie*." I did not know who they were but I have wished ever since that I could tell them how much I appreciated that message, referring to *Constellation* by the nickname we so often used for her.

As we passed Castle Hill, the entire staff of our summer home was on the lawn waving towels as though they were shipwrecked sailors trying to attract the first ship they had seen in months. One of them dipped the American flag, another manned their signal cannon, firing in rapid sequence.

Then we were clear of the land, but surrounded by a vast armada of spectator craft with hundreds more following us out from Newport and small planes and a Goodyear blimp overhead. Everyone seemed overcome with America's Cup fever and for us eleven, it was a send-off unlike others in a lifetime of sailing. We loved it and appreciated it. Instead of building my confidence it merely emphasized the importance of not blowing it, not letting these thousands of well-wishers down by sailing poorly.

Now the hard part. It was an hour's tow to the starting area with absolutely nothing to do. The sails had been selected, the weather checked. *Constellation* was as ready as a boat can be. Often I took a snooze on the tow out, but on this day I wanted to savor the excitement from watching the armada going out to watch us. It was heartwarming and exciting, but did nothing to still the butterflies which were doing a war dance in my stomach. "It's just another race," I told myself, but of course it wasn't. I did convince myself, however, that in all probability, *Sovereign* would be easier than *American Eagle,* but we couldn't be sure. And it was the America's Cup that was on the line.

0900, August 31, 1974—For some inexplicable reason I was feeling pretty good as I walked down the dock at Newport Shipyard to board *Courageous* for what could be the last race of the final trials to select the defender. I had little reason to be happy. After winning four straight races against *Intrepid* I had managed to lose three straight, and we now stood all even in the final trials at four wins apiece. In one of our losses, we were slightly ahead of *Intrepid* but elected not to cover because we expected a header which would give us a safe lead. When instead we got a lift it cooked our goose, and that evening I had to be polite when one of the crew wives started educating me on the importance of covering in a match race. And just the day before, in a race which was called because of an impending storm, I had blown a lead by setting a floater spinnaker on the reach instead of a three-quarter ounce tri-radial. That evening another wife asked me why I had just let *Intrepid* reach by without luffing her. She did not seem very convinced when I pointed out that it is suicide to luff with a floater against a boat with a reaching chute.

If the wives were concluding that Bob Bavier was pretty dumb, I was sure that the crew must be of the same persuasion.

Perhaps I was feeling better on this particular morning because I felt things could not get worse and hence might well get better. But there was another reason. The previous evening I had what I considered to be a good discussion with Ted Hood and Halsey Herreshoff. I pointed out that we had lost our lead the previous day by deferring too much to each other and having too many cooks, which had slowed our decision making.

It was decided that after Dennis Conner started and Ted Hood took over as helmsman on the windward leg, I would make the final decision on upwind tactics, with Halsey and Dennis giving me their thinking but only me advising Ted. Then when we rounded the windward mark, and I started steering, Ted was to concentrate on sail trim and sail selection, including when a spinnaker should be replaced. Halsey was to be the key tactician on the leeward legs, getting input from Dennis and Ted, but he alone communicating their thoughts to me. Earlier, I had made the mistake of not making it clear who was primarily responsible for what, with the end result that there was either too much talking or too little fast decision making. By clearing up the priorities and responsibilities, I felt we would operate more smoothly and decisively. Ted and Halsey seemed to agree.

Thus buoyed up, and encouraged also by the conviction that *Courageous* was now a slight bit faster than *Intrepid,* I felt surprisingly confident as I strode down the dock. Half way to *Courageous* was the imposing figure of Bob McCullough, head of our syndicate. He was all alone and apparently waiting for me. He didn't look happy. As I drew near, he stepped forward to meet me and with only a perfunctory "Good morning, Bob" instead of his customary hearty greeting, he then blurted out the fateful words—"The syndicate has had a meeting and we feel you should get off the boat." Those might not have been the exact words but they are close.

Suddenly it wasn't such a sparkling day. For a moment I thought that this might be the opening gambit of a discussion, rather than a decision. "Have you talked to Halsey?" I asked.

"Yes."

"How's he feel about it?" I asked.

"He approves."

"How about Ted?"

"Yes, he knows and is ready to take over, and some of the crew know too, and they are in favor."

All of a sudden, it was apparent that this was not a discussion Bob and I were having. It was an irrevocable decision.

Just at this time, Charlotte came down the dock to board *Escort* to watch the race. She took one look at Bob and me and with her usual good sense kept right on walking past us.

If I had still had any questions about whether or not a firm decision had been made, it was dispelled when Bob showed me a neatly typed press release. It commenced with the statement that Bob and I had been friends since we were kids, and that the previous evening we had had a long discussion about what was best for *Courageous,* and I had volunteered to get off and turn her over to Ted Hood. It had some other statements which made me look good. The rub was that aside from the statement of our being longtime friends (we still are) there was not a shred of truth to it. All of a sudden I wished there had been, but I simply had not become convinced that I couldn't pull it off. What's that saying about an athlete being the last to recognize that he has slipped a bit, lost that extra step? "OK, Bob, I'll go along with your decision," (as if I had a choice), "but that press release has to go. When they ask me, I'll tell them I was kicked off."

We left it at that and as Bob went to give the word to the crew, I gave Charlotte the bad word. She wasn't as surprised as I had been but she did her best to make me feel better. She was surprised, however, at the timing and she did not like the press release any more than I. "What are you going to do now?" she asked.

"Break in on the meeting Bob is having with the crew, wish them well and tell Ted and the others that I know they can pull it off. Then I'm going out on *Escort* and watch the race."

I not only went out and watched, but spent most of the time steering *Escort,* as if to prove to myself, if no one else, that at least I could handle a powerboat. To make things harder the wind never came up enough to permit a start, which allowed more than the usual time for everyone to see me in an unusual place. It was almost funny (though I did not think so at the time) to see the startled looks on the faces of friends, the press and spectators when they recognized me on *Escort*'s flying bridge instead of on *Courageous.* They did not seem to know whether to wave, or look away or whether or not to say anything. It wasn't easy to take, but was nothing compared to the look on the faces of my daughters, Louise and Anne, who had already embarked on a friend's boat to see their dad take on *Intrepid* in what could be the last race of the summer.

1224, September 15, 1964—After the long tow out to the America's Cup buoy we had a further delay because the Coast Guard had trouble clearing the vast spectator fleet from the starting area.

Finally, at 1215, course signals were hoisted. In 20 minutes the start would be history. We had decided to be aggressive at the first start even though we felt *Constellation* was faster than *Sovereign.* First of all, you could not be sure. Secondly, it seemed important to convince Peter Scott at the outset that he couldn't push us around, and that we enjoyed aggressive starts. If we proved faster, he would not be encouraged to be overly aggressive in subsequent starts. But most important was the matter of pride. With thousands of my peers watching, I wanted to prove I could get a good start.

With eleven minutes to go we were approaching *Sovereign,* reaching on a reciprocal course, us to leeward. "This time we hook up," I told the crew, "but make it look as though we won't." Now with something immediate to think about, something to do, the butterflies in my stomach went away. Or perhaps I was too busy concentrating to notice them.

As we neared *Sovereign* our crew was lounging on deck as if they were out for a Sunday sail. I tried to look casual too, looking at *Sovereign* only out of the corner of my eye. But just after we passed bow to bow I spun to windward, the crew leapt to their feet and trimmed furiously and before Peter knew what had happened and could bear off we were squarely on *Sovereign*'s tail. We had her where we wanted her. The question was, could we keep her there? As *Sovereign* jibed, tacked and jibed again we maintained our position just one length astern. I was pleased to note we could turn even sharper and maintain speed. There were a couple of instants when we might have turned inside of her, or held our starboard tack, and perhaps hit her when she jibed to port. But the last thing we wanted was to win the first start by inducing a foul. We

213

Favorite breakfast pastime was reading what the press had to say about yesterday's race. This is Constellation's *crew at Castle Hill in 1964.*

were content to follow like a dog on heel, knowing this position gave us the option of breaking off the circle at the time we thought best for us.

With two-and-a-half minutes to go and several lengths below the line, Peter jibed, then trimmed and headed toward the line to make still one more circle. We elected not to follow but instead reached off to leeward and then, with a minute-and-a-half remaining, tacked for the line, tight reaching for a spot a couple of lengths to leeward of the Committee boat, the end we preferred. This would enable us to hit the line with full headway, while *Sovereign,* being so close to the line and having to make an extra circle, would surely be going slower. But we could still lose the start if not timed perfectly. And we had to be wary of barging.

Peter played it perfectly, tacking on our bow to assume a safe leeward position. With our extra speed we could break through to leeward, provided we had it timed just right. But I preferred to go past to windward. The trouble with that was the proximity of the Committee boat. Peter could luff until the gun fired and, if he did, we could be squeezed out.

"Better drive through to leeward," I said to myself and shouted, "Trim for speed!" as I bore off a few degrees. Peter was watching and bore off with us, smack on our wind. But we were going nine and one half knots, at least three knots faster than *Sovereign,* and it looked like we could drive on through into a safe leeward.

Then a better opportunity dawned on me. As *Sovereign* bore off, the gap widened between her and the Committee boat. No longer was there any danger of being squeezed out. The trouble is that when I said "trim for speed" and bore off, everyone aboard surmised we were committed to going through to leeward. The bow man, Buddy Bombard, stopped calling distance between our bow and *Sovereign's* stern, quite rightly calling only distance from the line.

There was no time for discussion or for asking whether we could swing her stern. Instead, if I wanted to go by to windward, I had to chance it and swing up without a second's delay. A summer of sailing in close quarters gives you a pretty close eye. I knew our bow was not overlapped, but we were closing so much faster that it was going to be mighty close by the time we swung up.

I spun the wheel, said a silent prayer and as I did, our great crew trimmed for the new unexpected course without a word being spoken. There simply was not time to say anything. Buddy told me later that we cleared by twelve feet, close enough since we were going three knots faster.

As the gun went off, our bow was thirty feet in front and we were a full length to windward. Rod and Eric cheered in unison.

My mouth was suddenly very dry and I asked for a stick of gum. A few minutes later when we were several lengths ahead of *Sovereign* and right on her wind when she made her first tack I relaxed and thought to myself, "This racing for the America's Cup is fun."

1800, September 3, 1974—There were tears running down several of the faces of *Intrepid's* crew. Others seemed to be having trouble swallowing. Skipper Gerry Driscoll was dry-eyed and had a tight smile on his face as

215

he led the way onto the Newport Shipyard dock to congratulate Ted Hood and the crew of *Courageous*. Two hours before, *Courageous* had beaten *Intrepid* by a minute and a half in a heavy air race—the very wind that the press had kept referring to all summer as "*Intrepid* weather." The Selection Committee had paid their respective visits, first giving *Intrepid* the bad news, then notifying *Courageous* that she was to defend the cup, having won five, lost four to *Intrepid* in the final trials.

We had been whooping it up on *Courageous,* but a sudden hush fell as *Intrepid*'s crew arrived. They said kind words, and were congratulated in turn for putting up such a magnificent fight in an "old" 1967 wooden boat. Everyone had a swig or two of champagne, and smiles broke out all around. But half of the bunch was dying inside and the other half was acting embarrassed, knowing the pain their summer-long rivals were feeling.

Perhaps I could best read their thoughts. I had had my own disappointment a few days before, being kicked off as skipper, and the hurt still lingered. A yachting reporter friend of mine whispered to me, "This America's Cup racing is a damned meat grinder, a destroyer of men." "I know what you mean," I replied.

Intrepid's crew did not linger long. When they left, and even later back at Hammersmith Farm for our victory dinner, the celebrating was strangely subdued for a crew just notified that they had been selected to defend the America's Cup.

1810, August 30, 1977—I donned my traditional coconut hat, bedecked with the New York Yacht Club ribbon and joined the rest of the Selection Committee as we boarded our tender to pay the fateful call on *Enterprise*. *Courageous* had just beaten her by a minute twenty-six seconds, her sixth straight victory over her arch rival in the final trials. A thunderstorm was approaching, but we did not want to delay longer. We had seen enough.

That's me sailing Courageous *in one of the many close contests against* Intrepid *in 1974. In this situation we crossed with just enough to spare but it wasn't until the last race, with Ted Hood as skipper for the first time, that she finally got the better record in the final trials, to be selected as defender.*

The hardest job of the America's Cup Committee is notifying the losers that they are eliminated. In 1974 it was particularly hard to tell Intrepid *that she was out. Skipper Gerry Driscoll (kneeling) keeps up a brave front but the rest of his crew is close to tears.*

A few days earlier, Lowell North had been replaced by Malin Burnham as skipper of *Enterprise,* but to no avail. All it did, said Ted Turner to me as we got the word during a cocktail party, was add a distinguished new member to our "club"—the group of sailors who had been relieved as America's Cup skippers. Lowell had twice won the Star Worlds and was an Olympic gold medalist. "Our club's getting real class," exulted Ted.

As we approached the Williams & Manchester dock we could see the sudden turning of heads by the *Enterprise* crew and could almost lip read their remarks—"My God, they're coming." Malin seemed particularly stunned. He had lost by close margins in the races he sailed and in the last one had gained forty-two seconds on the last leg. Obviously he had not

All hail the conquering heroes as Courageous *heads home after beating* Southern Cross *4–0 in 1974.*

expected the axe so soon and in fact we interrupted them in the process of checking delivery of a new sail due the next day. The loser always feels the elimination series had been too short and, despite *Courageous*'s superb record, they had not given up hope. Once over their initial surprise, however, they took it well. It was not the emotional blockbuster of three years before when *Intrepid* was dismissed.

As soon as we arrived the storm hit, accompanied by torrential rain. We huddled inside *Enterprise*'s tender, fast running out of things to say and wishing the rain would quit. Finally it did and we scampered back aboard our tender and powered over to Newport Shipyard. Ted Turner and his crew were expecting us. They had watched us out of the corner of their

It wasn't long after Courageous's *final victory in 1974 before her entire crew as well as innocent bystanders were heaved overboard.*

eyes as we headed toward *Enterprise* and were lined up Navy-style as we came alongside *Courageous.* Just as we got there and just as George Hinman blurted the traditional words, "Captain Turner, I have the honor to inform you and the crew of *Courageous* that you have been selected to defend the America's Cup," the sun broke through. Talk about symbolism!

It was a happy visit, enlivened by champagne, which appeared on cue from the bilge of *Courageous.* It remained happy and little strained upon the arrival of the *Enterprise* crew, despite the flow of nasty words which had been exchanged by the two camps throughout the summer. The real shock only comes in a cliff-hanger elimination.

Seeing the exuberant faces on board made me reminisce on the excitement I had felt thirteen years earlier—the first time I had started against *American Eagle* and the first time we had beaten her, the race in the final trials when we trailed at all five marks only to sweep by a mile from the finish—a win which gave us the confidence to know we would eventually gain selection, and then finally the thrill of competing for the Cup itself against *Sovereign*. Lowell North joined the group and this made me think of other things, despite Lowell's brave front. We did not stay long. It was a joyous occasion but we knew full well that this crew would have even more fun when we left.

1600, September 21, 1964—A strange thing was happening. We had beaten *Sovereign* decisively in the first three races of the nineteenth match for the America's Cup and now on the last leg of the fourth race we had an absolutely unbeatable lead. We had rounded the last mark with a lead of twelve minutes twenty-six seconds, a margin of nearly two miles. The wind was steady, yet gentle enough so that a breakdown (the only possible way of being caught) was out of the question. We were staying between *Sovereign* and the finish, making a loose cover and we were opening up distance with every passing minute. If ever there were the

Peter Scott never won a race against Constellation *but such was his charm that he never lost a press conference. Left to right: Peter, moderator Bus Mosbacher, me and Eric Ridder.*

Constellation *is roaring for the line and* Sovereign *tacks ahead of her in hopes of blanketing or gaining a safe leeward.*

We on Constellation *are fearful of barging (the Committee boat is just out of the picture to the right) and hence bear off to pass to leeward.*

When Sovereign *also bears off there is room to pass to windward and, in a last second change of plan, I swing* Constellation *across her stern, clearing* Sovereign *by just a few feet.*

Constellation's *greater headway approaching the line allows us to gain this lovely position as the gun goes. Our bow is a half-length ahead, we have greater headway and are hard on the wind while* Sovereign *is forced to bear off to gain speed and keep her wind clear.*

The telephoto lens is deceiving. Constellation *is already two minutes ahead of* Sovereign *on the second leg of the first race in 1964.*

ingredients for a "yawner" they were here. But the strange part was that I could feel a growing excitement among our crew. The jib snapped home after every tack with the precision of a quarterback making a hand-off to his fullback. I was steering with as much intensity as if *Sovereign* were one length astern and gainng. We had decided long ago, as soon as we determined that *Constellation* was faster, that no matter how far ahead we

As Constellation *crosses the line in the last race of the 1964 match Rod and I instinctively give her a pat for a job well done.*

got we would never hold back in order to make the race look more respectable. We knew that if Peter Scott knew we were holding back he would not like it. Many times in the series we rooted for *Sovereign* to make it closer after we had a commanding lead. We agonized when we saw her make a desperation tack or jibe which we knew full well would put her even farther behind. But while we really wished she would do better we never had any part in making her look better, always trying to sail *Constellation* to her utmost. Still, some of the races, after the first mile or two, were pretty dull, not only for the spectator fleet but for us as well.

Why then the excitement we all felt on this last leg of what would surely be the last race in the nineteenth match for the America's Cup? Finally it dawned on me that we had all contracted "America's Cup fever." No other sailing event could engender such excitement when the out-

Only an America's Cup victory could engender such enthusiasm as we all felt on Constellation *after routing* Sovereign *by a huge margin in the final race of 1964.*

come was so obvious. But this was not just some other sailing event. This was the America's Cup, and we were about to win it and we suddenly wanted to win it in style.

Constellation foamed ahead, slicing through the seas left over from the previous day's fresh breeze. Many of us would never sail on her again or on any boat so deserving of being called a thoroughbred. We wanted to do her proud. And we did. We picked up more than three minutes on that last leg alone to win by fifteen minutes, thirty seconds.

And when we crossed the line, and heard the gun, both Rod and I instinctively and simultaneously patted *Constellation*'s topsides for a job well done, while the crew erupted with the enthusiasm one would expect from a come-from-behind victory of less than a length.

Sailing for the America's Cup can mean different things to different people. It can tear your heart out. It can bring strong men to the brink of a nervous breakdown and can leave scars which while diminishing through the years, will ever remain like a surgeon's most skilled incision. For persistent challengers like Sir Thomas Lipton and Baron Bich it can become an obsession, the more virulent the longer the quest goes unfulfilled. But for the fortunate few who have tasted victory, who have enjoyed the comradeship of a summer with an extraordinary group of teammates, and who have had the privilege of doing battle with other groups of extraordinary men, it becomes, for a while at least, the most important thing in life. Once it is all over, and you drift back into the mainstream of life, either licking your wounds or exulting for ever more in the greatest victory a sailor can have, you come to realize that America's Cup fever is nothing to laugh about. Once stricken, you won't ever get over it completely. But win or lose it is an unforgettable experience, and either way you might be the better for it.

AMERICA'S CUP COURSE

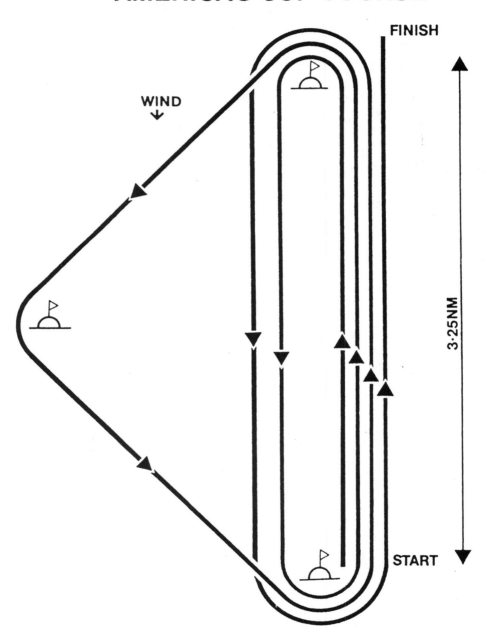

Chapter XV
1987 Forecast – A Battle Royal

In the 1981 edition of this book, in the chapter titled "When We Lose the Cup," I made a rash prediction that I am pleased to admit was at least half wrong. I forecast that when we did lose, interest in America to get the Cup back would exceed our zeal in defending it. In that respect I was dead right, except I didn't think it would reach such a feverish pitch. On the other hand, I forecast that interest from foreign nations would diminish. I knew that one thing that spurred them on was the desire to be the first to beat us. I forecast that "should we lose the Cup, competition will continue for a while as we design and build new boats to win it back. It is when we do win it back that I worry about the future. Will the challengers then be willing to spend the millions and exert the prodigious effort that is required to be the second nation to win the Cup from Americans? Maybe so, but maybe no. Most people know that Hilary and Tenzing were the first to scale Mt. Everest. But I have yet to find anyone who can name the second duo to do it . . . The great publicity the America's Cup enjoys is a big reason for competing for it. And publicity could wane after we have lost."

Picking a winner from this keen group of contenders is almost impossible. The closeness of this start and of the spinnaker reach several legs later at the 1986 World Championship shows how fierce the competition will be. Is it prophetic that Australia III is getting the start at the pin end and also is leading on the reach? Not necessarily so since many of the top contenders didn't compete.

It is now perfectly plain that interest everywhere is greater than ever before. It is now evident, based on the number of nations challenging in 1987, that whether or not America does regain the Cup, future competition will remain at fever pitch. True, the other nations would have loved to have been the first to knock us off and in that sense something will be lacking from all future challenges no matter who the defender is. But what has been gained is the realization that no nation is unbeatable and that it is possible to challenge for the America's Cup and to *win*. This increase in confidence has made it much more fun to challenge. That's why a prodigious effort has been launched by more nations than ever before. Even if the United States does regain the Cup there now seems to be no question but that competition will continue on a vast scale.

The title of this chapter indicates that perhaps I know who will win in 1987. Of course I don't, and neither does anyone else. There are simply too many top competitors. It is somewhat easier to pick what country might win, but even that is precarious. Still, it is interesting and perhaps illuminating to run down all the players and to assess their chances. But remember two things. First, the competition is between yacht clubs, not nations, and picking what club might win is near to impossible. Second, this forecast or assessment is being made in March 1986, after the '86 world championship but before a great many of the contending boats have ever been wet. Things could change pretty rapidly prior to the time the elimination races start in October 1986.

Originally, there were clubs from eight nations challenging the Australians—the United States, France, Canada, Great Britain, New Zealand, Italy, Germany, and Sweden. Germany and Sweden dropped out when they had difficulty raising the vast sums required to mount a meaningful challenge. The other six countries, however, are very much in it. They represent a total of fourteen yacht clubs and since many clubs are building more than one yacht, at least twenty-four boats are involved. Eventually each club must decide which one to enter the elimination races with, but with fourteen such entries the competition to gain the right to challenge the Aussies dwarfs any previous effort. And to meet this challenge the Australians have four defense syndicates with at least six new Twelves, making a minimum of thirty Twelve Meters vying for the Cup in 1987.

Picking a winner from this armada is virtually impossible, but for what it is worth here is the rundown of the various contenders and their chances as I see them.

Italy

The Italians have two clubs challenging:

YACHT CLUB COSTA SMERALDA *(Azzura)* Earlier, I considered this to be a strong contender, but am now less sanguine. I saw them racing *Victory 83* against a souped up *Magic* in Los Angeles in 1985 and was impressed by their sail handling and general savvy. In 1983, *Azzura* was fast and surprised everyone at Newport. Unfortunately the new boat looks slower. The skipper is Lorenzo Bortolotti and the helmsman is Stefano Roberti. Designer is Andrew Vallicelli. The fact that the Aga Kahn is head of their club and that a number of wealthy corporate sponsors have been lined up insures that they won't lack money. Two new Twelves that will bear the same name are on the way. Better late than never, but I fear this effort is too late.

YACHT CLUB ITALIANO *(Italia)* Aldo Migliaccio, skipper, Flavio Scala, helmsman. Like the other Italian entry this group is very well financed. At the moment that's all they seem to have going for them. Their Giorgetti e Magrini design appeared fast at the Twelve Meter Worlds but the crew work and general sailing was sloppy by America's Cup standards. They, too, are building a new boat, which might help their chances, but what they need most of all is to get their act together.

Canada

SECRET COVE YACHT CLUB *(Canada II)* The biggest thing lacking with this group is money. They are going with the same boat that couldn't quite cut it in 1983. But she's not really the same boat. Designer Bruce Kirby has made significant hull modifications and added a winged keel, and the result is nothing short of electrifying. Gary Jobson, who is impartial since he is tactician for Buddy Melges's *Heart of America,* says he has never seen a Twelve beat another one as much as the new *Canada II* beat *Clipper,* a very decent 1980 Dave Pedrick design. This comment gains added significance when one realizes Gary is well acquainted with *Mariner,* the real slow horse of 1974. Designer Kirby says he feels it better to optimize *Canada II* instead of building a new boat in the limited time available. In winds above fifteen knots she is already fast, below that perhaps suspect. Her skipper, Terry Neilson, has a tough job, but not a hopeless one. *Canada II* is a dark horse but she has already startled some keen observers.

ROYAL NOVA SCOTIA YACHT SQUADRON *(True North) True North* is a big Twelve. While she didn't shine at the 1986 Worlds she did show promise and designer Steve Killing has the luxury of sufficient funds to have a second boat built. Her biggest asset is having Hans Fogh as helmsman. Jeff Boyd, tactician of *Canada I* in 1983 has been named skipper. If he lets Fogh do his thing or if Fogh were to become top dog or if the new boat proves to be a big improvement this group could bear watching. Too many "ifs" there but then you never can be sure. Fogh is a winner, but probably not this time.

FLASH—A recent development after the above was written and just as this book goes to press is the joining of forces of the two Canadian groups. The two boats have raced against each other and *Canada II* was so vastly superior that only she will go to Australia. Paul Phelan has made a major financial contribution and hence for the very first time Kirby's design will have five sails and all the other goodies that make fast Twelves even faster.

Canada II was so much faster than *True North* and had already proved to be such a good boat that she must now be rated as a very strong contender, one that just could go all the way and become the challenger. I don't expect that to happen, but it just might.

France

SOCIÉTÉ NAVTIQUEDE MARSEILLE *(Challenge France)*   Little is known about this challenger except for the fact that skipper Yves Pajot is a world-class sailor and designer Daniel Andrieu has good credentials. Money is short, their Twelve has not (as of April 1, 1986) been launched. When launched, she will go directly to Freemantle and work up there. A definite long shot.

SOCIÉTÉ DES RÉGATES ROCHELAISES *(French Kiss)*   At the 1986 World Championship, *French Kiss* proved that the French were now far from pushovers in America's Cup competition. Skipper Marc Pajot is, like his brother Yves, a world-class sailor and he has a fine horse to work with. Designer Philippe Briand went for heavy air performance and in heavy air she is formidable. Whether *French Kiss* can do well enough to survive the elimination races, many of which will be in light air, is doubtful. If she is still alive in January, look out. The French can no longer be taken lightly.

Great Britain

ROYAL THAMES YACHT CLUB *(Crusader)*   The British have more than a stirring name. While funding is proving hard to come by and has delayed their program, they do have two new Twelves, one designed by Jonas Howlett who has good Twelve Meter credentials, the other a more experimental type by David Hollom. Skipper is Harry Cudmore, who proved his ability by winning the 1986 Congressional Cup. Look for *Crusader* to do well. She even has an outside chance of becoming the challenger.

New Zealand

ROYAL NEW ZEALAND YACHT SQUADRON *(New Zealand)*   If anyone told me a year ago that in the spring of 1986 I would be picking New

235

Winged keels are much in vogue. This is New Zealand *hauled out at the Worlds. Their lack of secrecy is refreshing.*

Zealand as a top contender to win the Cup I would have told him he was crazy. This country has a total population smaller than New York City. But it seems that almost all of them sail—not only sail but sail well. Moreover, they have top designers in Laurie Davidson, Bruce Farr, and Ron Holland. Their twenty-four-year-old skipper, Chris Dickson, fears no one. Funding is lavish, with seemingly all of New Zealand behind the effort, and their energy and dedication to the effort is extreme. In January 1986 John Bertrand told me to look out for this group. He proved to be spot on. They entered two new Fiberglass Twelves in the World Championship, less than two weeks after launching. They had never raced Twelves before, but they proceeded to finished second and seventh—a truly remarkable achievement. A third boat is now being built. Even if the third boat is no improvement, this is a group to fear. If the new boat is better than what they already have, the Kiwis could go all the way.

The United States

No less than six U.S. clubs are challenging. Originally there were several more, but when the realities of financing and logistics sunk in they fell by the wayside. The survivors are all sailed by superb helmsmen and crews. It is a far cry from the days when the New York Yacht Club was pitted against the world.

YALE CORINTHIAN YACHT CLUB *(Courageous)* It would be romantic to give this two-time defender a chance to regain the Cup. But it seems impossible. Her owner, Leonard Greene, has designed some new keel appendages, but they have only slowed her down. If money is forthcoming, a new boat may be forthcoming. Even if it is, I suspect it will be a case of too little and too late. Peter Isler, her skipper, is a fine sailor, but I look on this effort as a chance for him to gain Twelve Meter experience. He has since quit and joined the Stars and Stripes syndicate.

ST. FRANCIS YACHT CLUB *(U.S.A.)* Gary Mull is a fine designer with successful Six Meters to his credit and Tom Blackaller, her skipper, is a fearsome adversary. But the first *U.S.A.* seemed slow in early brushes against *Clipper* and *Canada I.* The group is at this writing building a more radical, or as they term it "revolutionary" Twelve. Revolutionary Twelves, with the notable exception of *Australia II,* seldom work. If theirs is not also an exception count this boat out.

CHICAGO YACHT CLUB *(Heart of America)* This challenge has two superlative things going for it—Buddy Melges and Gary Jobson. For many years I've considered Buddy America's number-one sailor, and Gary Jobson is demonstrably the best Twelve Meter tactician in the business. Their new boat, however (they have only one), won't be launched until June, and the designer Graham & Schlageter (with input from Jim Grutsky and C. Class catamaran star Duncan MacLane) lacks Twelve Meter experience. They might come up with a great design but to do so on a first effort would be remarkable. No one can get more out of a boat than Buddy, and he and Gary should team well. But I don't expect them to be able to pull it off. In match racing in particular you have to have a fast boat. If they happen to, this could be the boat to beat, but it's not a good bet.

A late development sure to hurt this challenge is the resignation of Gary Jobson, who bowed out for business reasons. Good as he is, Buddy needed Gary to become a top contender.

NEWPORT HARBOR YACHT CLUB *(Eagle)* Like *Heart of America, Eagle* will be the only boat for its syndicate. But there is a vast difference. *Eagle*'s designer is Johan Valentijn and there is no one with more recent experience and success with Twelves (barring Lexcen with *Australia II*) than Johan. Moreover, the fact that their new boat was only launched in April 1986 is no handicap because the skipper and crew have been sailing together on *Magic* for more than a year. Another plus is Gerry Driscoll, skipper of *Intrepid* in 1974, now their Director of Operations. And a final plus is that Rod Davis, multiple Congressional Cup winner, is her skipper. There is, in my mind, no finer skipper, including Melges, than Rod Davis. Perfecting one boat can work as well as building a number, and Valentijn should come up with a good one. *Eagle* should be *very* hard to beat.

SAN DIEGO YACHT CLUB *(Stars and Stripes)* Another hard one to beat will be *Stars and Stripes*. No one works harder than Dennis Conner, her skipper, and Dennis is determined to avenge his 1983 defeat. Funds are so expansive that five new boats have been built, all bearing the same name and all from a three-man team of distinguished naval architects—Britton Chance, David Pedrick, and Bruce Nelson. Their publicity releases indicate blazing speed for the four boats already launched, and this group has the added benefit of having *Liberty* as a trial horse so they know what they have. If the releases are not just a ploy to give Dennis a psychological lift the winner could come from this camp. Even if they are, don't count this group out. Robbie Haines, Soling class Olympic gold medalist, and Peter Isler have joined as alternate helmsmen.

NEW YORK YACHT CLUB *(America II)* This group was formed right after the Cup was lost and ever since 1984 has been training in Australia. Their first boat of three proved her speed by finishing third in the 1986 World Championship, despite costly breakdowns in two races when they were leading and despite losing a man overboard when a close sixth in another race. A third new Twelve, also from the board of Sparkman &

Stephens, was launched in May 1986. They are sure to benefit from all that sailing in Australia, a real edge over the other U.S. syndicates. John Kolius, their skipper, quit in the early fall of 1985 but has since rejoined, which is fortunate because he is about as good as they come. Look out for this one, which I rate as co-favorite with San Diego Yacht Club.

The Australia Defenders

ROYAL SOUTH AUSTRALIA YACHT SQUADRON *(South Australia)* This is a Ben Lexcen design based on *Australia II* and hence has to be a good boat. Fred Neill, her skipper, might be replaced by Phil Thompson. Sir James Hardy is giving them input. Thus far they haven't shown much. A long shot.

SYDNEY & QUEENSLAND YACHT CLUBS *(Eastern Australia)* This is a joint effort, but thus far not a promising one. Funding has been slow. Peter Cole is the designer of their sole boat due for launching in the spring of 1986. A well-known ocean racing yachtsman, Syd Fischer is syndicate head, but he is a genius if he can pull this off. Likely skipper is Larry Kleist.

ROYAL PERTH YACHT CLUB *(Kookaburra* and *Australia III)* The *Kookaburra* syndicate has already built two new boats and they are contemplating a third. Ian Murray is skipper and codesigner with John Swarbrick. They loom as the chief rival to Alan Bond's group to earn the defender's role. While they have a chance, the smart money is on Bond. *Kookaburra* brushed with *America II* in Australian waters and lost more than she won. Still this is a serious threat and could well defend.

Australia III is Alan Bond's charger, with which he hopes to defend the Cup. Based on *Australia III*'s victory in the 1986 Twelve Meter Worlds she is obviously a fine Twelve, but it must be remembered that not all of the varsity were there. In *Australia III* Ben Lexcen has designed a better all-around performer than *Australia II* (which, however, seems to retain an edge in light air). Colin Beashel is skipper and many other members of the 1983 crew are back, giving this group a real edge in experience.

239

Lexcen is at this writing doing further tank testing and if these tests reveal ways for improvement, a new boat will be built. Whether it be the present *Australia III* or a newer version, look for one or the other to be on the line when the match begins in 1987. FLASH—A new boat is building.

So there you have the lineup, as well as some indication of who might win. Let's stick our necks out and get a bit more specific.

From the defender's standpoint it looks to be *Australia III*. They have the talent, experience, backing, drive and general expertise to an extent no other Australian group comes close to having. And they have Ben Lexcen as designer—a tremendous plus.

Most Americans just assume that one of their boats will be the challenger. But never before has there been such a strong and concerted effort. With so many foreign boats yet to be tested in competition there is no sure way to be certain who might be most dangerous. One we now tend to overlook could come through on the wings of a new design and would beat all the American boats. With that caveat I would, at this writing, on one end dismiss the Italians and on the other most fear New Zealand.

It is not just national pride, however, that makes me pick a U.S. boat over those from all the challenging nations. We have a great group of skippers, the greatest ever assembled in America to go after the Cup. All our top designers are involved. We have enlisted the help of computer experts and aerospace technicians in design of some of our boats and their components. We are determined as never before to win and we have worked harder and longer to make winning possible. It seems unlikely that this major effort will fail and much more likely that an American boat will be the challenger.

But which American boat? With the exception of *Courageous*, I would say all of them have a chance. I put *America II, Stars and Stripes,* and *Eagle* at the top of the list. Beyond that it is simply too tough to call this far ahead, but my sentiments go with *America II*.

And then, when *Australia III* and an American boat do square off (assuming that will be the match-up), in that case, I'll pick the Americans to win. Going for Australia will be familiarity with the waters. Also going for them will be the fact that their boat will be selected and doesn't have to survive trials, which might be in light air as opposed to the heavier air expected in February.

But in my opinion, countering all that will be the fact that the challenger will have defeated the greatest array of Twelve Meters ever assembled. She will have raced over a period of more than three months and will be thoroughly battle-tested. She will be a great all-around boat—she simply has to be in order to survive the eliminations. An all-around boat could be the best bet after all, because the prevalent heavy airs of February are not always heavy at all.

But above all, if it is indeed an American defender, she will have desire on her side, desire to get the America's Cup back where we tend to feel it belongs.

Appendix

The Official Record of the America's Cup Races

1930-1983

The following details of all the matches from 1930 on are taken directly from the reports of the New York Yacht Club Race Committee. They tell more than just who won or lost each race. Since weather conditions are reported and since the time of each yacht is given at each mark one can ascertain the relative speed of both defender and challenger in different winds and on various points of sailing.

Note, for example, that *Sovereign* which was so badly trounced by *Constellation* in 1964 did gain a full minute on the next to last leg of the last race. She carried a different chute on that leg than in any previous race.

Note also that even that super J-boat *Ranger* lost ground to *Endeavour II* on at least one leg. *Ranger*'s greatest superiority was to windward.

The most interesting matches to compare times on are those we nearly lost—1934 and 1970 and to a lesser degree 1962 and 1980.

The Fourteenth Match 1930 *Shamrock V vs.* Enterprise

FIRST RACE—SEPTEMBER 13TH

Weather, cloudy; Tide, Ebb; Light Fog at start; Clearing before finish; Sea Smooth; Wind at start, N. × E., 9½ knots; Wind at finish, N.E., 8 knots; Course S. × W., 15 miles to leeward and return. Distance 30 miles.

	Start 12:55	
	Finish	Elapsed
Shamrock V	5.01.40	4.06.40
Enterprise	4.58.48	4.03.48
	Winner—*Enterprise*	

	Enterprise	*Shamrock V*
Times Rounding, Outer Mark	3.03.19	3.05.15
Elapsed Times, First Leg	2.08.19	2.10.15
Elapsed Times, Second Leg	1.55.29	1.56.25

The start of the race was postponed from 11.40 A.M. to 12.55 P.M. because of fog and lack of wind.

After finishing, each yacht signaled she would race the next weekday.

SECOND RACE—SEPTEMBER 15TH

Weather, clear; Tide, Flood; Light S.E. Ground Swell; Wind at start W.S.W., 7½ knots; Wind at finish, S.W. 10 knots; Course, Triangular, W.S.W.; S.E. × E.; N. ½ E. Distance 30 miles.

	Start 11:40	
	Finish	Elapsed
Shamrock V	3.50.18	4.10.18
Enterprise	3.40.44	4.00.44
	Winner—*Enterprise*	

	Enterprise	Shamrock V
Times Rounding, First Mark	1.20.18	1.26.16
Times Rounding, Second Mark	2.19.28	2.28.31
Elapsed Times, First Leg	1.40.18	1.46.16
Elapsed Times, Second Leg	59.10	1.02.15
Elapsed Times, Third Leg	1.21.16	1.21.47

After finishing, each yacht signaled she would race the next weekday.

About one ton of ballast was removed from *Shamrock V* after the first race. Professor Webb certified that this did not change her rating.

SEPTEMBER 16TH

The Race Committee made a trip outside of Newport Harbor at about 10:00 A.M. on the yacht *Javelin*. There was a thick fog and no wind. On returning to the harbor the Committee notified the yachts, *Enterprise* and *Shamrock V;* the larger yachts in the Fleet; the Coast Guard vessels and the sightseeing steamers that the race was called off for the day.

THIRD RACE—SEPTEMBER 17TH

Weather, clear; Tide, Flood; Sea, moderate S.W. Ground Swell; Wind at start, W.S.W., 12 knots; Wind at finish, S.W. 16 knots; Course, W.S.W., 15 miles to windward and return. Distance 30 miles.

	Start 11:40		
		Finish	Elapsed
Shamrock V		Disabled*	
Enterprise		3.34.16	3.54.16

Winner—*Enterprise*

	Enterprise	Shamrock V
Times Rounding, Outer Mark	1.53.33	*
Elapsed Times, First Leg	2.13.33	
Elapsed Times, Second Leg	1.40.43	

*At 12:24 P.M. *Shamrock V* parted main halyard at the masthead sheave. The Race Committee received a radiogram from yacht *Erin* reading:

"*Shamrock* Will Sail Tomorrow—Colonel Neill"

247

Enterprise signaled she would race the next weekday.

About one ton of ballast was replaced in *Shamrock V* after the second race. Professor Webb certified that this did not change her rating.

Fourth Race—September 18th

Weather, clear; Tide, Flood; Sea, light S.W. Ground Swell; Wind at start, W.N.W. 14 knots; at finish, W. 12 knots; Course, Triangular, W.N.W.; S. × E.; N.E. ½ E. Distance 30 miles.

Start 11:40

	Finish	Elapsed
Shamrock V	2.55.57	3.15.57
Enterprise	2.50.13	3.10.13

Winner—*Enterprise*

	Enterprise	Shamrock V
Times Rounding, First Mark	1.02.08	1.11.18
Times Rounding, Second Mark	1.54.00	2.01.47
Elapsed Times, First Leg	1.22.08	1.31.18
Elapsed Times, Second Leg	51.52	50.29
Elapsed Times, Third Leg	56.13	54.10

Newport, R. I., September 18, 1930.

George Cormack, Esq.,
 Secretary,
New York Yacht Club,
37 West 44th Street, New York.

Dear Sir:

We have to report that *Enterprise* won "the best four out of seven races" from *Shamrock V* and thereby the Match for the America's Cup.

Edmund Lang, *Chairman*
Colgate Hoyt, *Secretary*
Philip R. Mallory
Race Committee

The Fifteenth Match 1934 Endeavour vs. Rainbow

SEPTEMBER 15TH

Weather, Clear; Sea, Smooth; Tidal Current, turned S. × W. at the Lightship at 1:13 P.M. Wind, at start, S.E. × E., 6.8 miles per hour; at 5:10 P.M., S.E. × E., 7 miles per hour. Course, S.E., 15 miles to windward and return. Distance 30 miles.

Start—11:40

	Finish	Elapsed
Endeavour	D.N.F.	
Rainbow	D.N.F.	

	Endeavour	*Rainbow*
Times Rounding, Outer Mark	2.46.20	2.43.34
Elapsed Times, First Leg	3.06.20	3.03.34
Elapsed Times, Second Leg		

Each yacht signaled her consent to race the next weekday.

Neither yacht finished within the time limit of 5½ hours.

At the expiration of the time limit, *Rainbow* was about a quarter of a mile, and *Endeavour* was about one mile from the finish line.

FIRST RACE—SEPTEMBER 17TH

Weather, Cloudy; Sea, Choppy with moderate swell; Tidal Current, turned N. × E. at the Lightship at 9:22 A.M. Wind, at start, S.S.E., 16 miles per hour; at finish, S.S.E., 15 miles per hour. Course, S.S.E., 15 miles to windward and return. Distance 30 miles.

Start—11:55

	Finish	Elapsed
Endeavour	3.38.44	3.43.44
Rainbow	3.40.53	3.45.53
Winner—*Endeavour*		

	Endeavour	*Rainbow*
Times Rounding, Outer Mark	1.59.43	1.59.25
Elapsed Times, First Leg	2.04.43	2.04.25
Elapsed Times, Second Leg	1.39.01	1.41.28

249

After the course signals had been set the start of this race was postponed fifteen minutes because *Endeavour* was observed to be having difficulty in setting her mainsail, and it was apparent that if the start were not postponed it would result in *Rainbow* having had what would have amounted to a sail-over. In postponing this start the Race Committee was aware that under the agreed conditions of the match it had no power to do so and that such power could only be given it by the joint action of the representative of The Royal Yacht Squadron and The America's Cup Committee. As, however, immediate action by this Committee was imperative, if a sail-over for *Rainbow* was to be averted, this Committee acted as it did in the full confidence that its action would be approved by those having authority to authorize it.

After finishing each yacht signaled her consent to race the next day.

On September 16th *Endeavour* removed 1100 lbs. of ballast. Dr. Webb certified that this did not change her rating.

Second Race—September 18th

Weather, Cloudy; Sea, Moderate swell; Tidal Current, turned N. × E. at the Lightship at 10:32 A.M. Wind, at start, N.W., 14 miles per hour; at finish, N.W., 9.5 miles per hour. Course, Triangular, S. × W., N.W., E.N.E. ½ E. Distance 30 miles.

Start—11:40

	Finish	Elapsed
Endeavour	2.49.01	3.09.01
Rainbow	2.49.52	3.09.52

Winner—*Endeavour*

	Endeavour	*Rainbow*
Times Rounding, First Mark	12.36.37	12.36.53
Times Rounding, Second Mark	1.54.56	1.56.27
Elapsed Times, First Leg	0.56.37	0.56.53
Elapsed Times, Second Leg	1.18.19	1.19.34
Elapsed Times, Third Leg	0.54.05	0.53.25

After finishing each yacht signaled her consent to race the next day.

September 19th

Both yachts appeared at the starting line but on account of lack of wind, the Committee boat hoisted the signal "H" at 1:20 P.M. calling the race off for the day.

THIRD RACE—SEPTEMBER 20TH

Weather, Partly Cloudy; Sea, Smooth; Tidal Current, turned N. × E. at the Lightship at 12:37 P.M. Wind, at start, N.E. × E., 6.2 miles per hour; at finish, S.E. × S., 8.8 miles per hour. Course, S.W. × W., 15 miles to leeward and return. Distance 30 miles.

Start—11:40

	Finish	Elapsed
Rainbow	4.15.34	4.35.34
Endeavour	4.19.00	4.39.00

Winner—*Rainbow*

	Endeavour	*Rainbow*
Times Rounding, Outer Mark	2.00.38	2.07.17
Elapsed Times, First Leg	2.20.38	2.27.17
Elapsed Times, Second Leg	2.18.22	2.08.17

After finishing *Rainbow* signaled her consent to race the next day.

Endeavour signaled she would not race the next day.

On September 19th *Endeavour* removed 3360 lbs. of ballast. Dr. Webb certified that this did not change her rating.

FOURTH RACE—SEPTEMBER 22ND

Weather, Cloudy; Sea, Choppy with light swell; Tidal Current, turned N. × E. at the Lightship at 2:25 P.M. Wind, at start, E., 11.5 miles per hour; at finish, E. × S., 12.5 miles per hour. Course, Triangular, E., S.W. × S., N.N.W.½W. Distance 30 miles.

Start—11:40

	Finish	Elapsed
Rainbow	2.55.38	3.15.38
Endeavour	2.56.53	3.16.53

Winner—*Rainbow*

	Rainbow	*Endeavour*
Times Rounding, First Mark	1.05.48	1.05.25
Times Rounding, Second Mark	2.00.35	2.01.35
Elapsed Times, First Leg	1.25.48	1.25.25
Elapsed Times, Second Leg	0.54.47	0.56.10
Elapsed Times, Third Leg	0.55.03	0.55.18

251

After finishing each yacht signaled her consent to race the next weekday.

On September 21st *Rainbow* added 4000 lbs. of ballast. Dr. Webb certified that this did not change her rating.

Endeavour displayed Protest Flag.

Fifth Race—September 24th

Weather, Cloudy; Sea, Short chop; Tidal Current, turned N. × E. at the Lightship at 4:02 P.M. Wind, at start, N.E. × N., 14 miles per hour; at finish, N.E. × N., 18.5 miles per hour. Course, S.W. × S., 15 miles to leeward and return. Distance 30 miles.

Start—11:40

	Finish	Elapsed
Rainbow	3.34.05	3.54.05
Endeavour	3.38.06	3.58.06

Winner—*Rainbow*

	Rainbow	*Endeavour*
Times Rounding, First Mark	1.18.37	1.23.15
Elapsed Times, First Leg	1.38.37	1.43.15
Elapsed Times, Second Leg	2.15.28	2.14.51

After finishing each yacht signaled her consent to race the next weekday.

On September 23rd *Rainbow* added 1000 lbs. of ballast.

On September 23rd *Endeavour* added 3360 lbs. of ballast.

Dr. Webb certified that this additional ballast did not change the rating of either yacht.

Sixth Race—September 25th

Weather, Partly cloudy; Sea, Light swell; Tidal Current, turned N. × E. at the Lightship at 4:51 P.M. Wind, at start, N.E., 9.5 miles per hour; at finish, 12.5 miles per hour. Course, Triangular, S. × E., N.E., W.N.W.½W. Distance 30 miles.

Start—11:40

	Finish	Elapsed
Rainbow	3.20.05	3.40.05
Endeavour	3.21.00	3.41.00

Winner—*Rainbow*

	Rainbow	*Endeavour*
Times Rounding, First Mark	12.52.59	12.51.50
Times Rounding, Second Mark	2.12.28	2.15.12
Times Rounding, Third Mark	3.20.05	3.21.00
Elapsed Times, First Leg	1.12.59	1.11.50
Elapsed Times, Second Leg	1.19.29	1.23.22
Elapsed Times, Third Leg	1.07.37	1.05.48

Rainbow and *Endeavour* both displayed protest flags at the start. Both protests were withdrawn after the race.

Newport, R. I., September 25, 1934.

George A. Cormack, Esq.,
    Secretary,
New York Yacht Club,
37 West 44th Street, New York.

Dear Sir:

We have to report that *Rainbow* won "the best four out of seven races" from *Endeavour* and thereby the Match for the America's Cup.

Edmund Lang, *Chairman*
E. Vail Stebbins, *Secretary*
Clinton Mackenzie
Race Committee

The Sixteenth Match 1937 Endeavour II *vs.* Ranger

FIRST RACE—JULY 31ST

Weather, Cloudy, moderate fog at finish; Sea, Smooth; Tidal Current, turned north at Brenton Reef Lightship at 8:29 A.M. Wind at start, S. × E., 5 miles per hour; at 6:06 P.M. S.E. × S., 10.5 miles per hour. Course S. × E., 15 miles to windward and return. Distance 30 miles.

253

	Finish	Elapsed
Ranger	6.06.15	4.41.15
Endeavour II	6.23.20	4.58.20

Winner—*Ranger*

	Ranger	*Endeavour II*
Times Rounding, Outer Mark	4.14.49	4.21.03
Elapsed Times, First Leg	2.49.49	2.56.03
Elapsed Times, Second Leg	1.51.26	2.02.17

There were three 15 minute postponements because of lack of wind and to give the Coast Guard time to clear the starting line.

Each yacht signaled her consent to race the next weekday.

Second Race—August 2nd

Weather, Clear overhead, fog haze on surface; Sea, Smooth; Tidal Current, turned North at Brenton Reef Lightship at 10:49 A.M. Wind at start, S.W., 8.2 miles per hour; at 4:21 P.M. S.W., 11.5 miles per hour. Course triangular, S.W., E. × S., N. × W.½ W. Distance 30 miles.

Start—12:40

	Finish	Elapsed
Ranger	4.21.33	3.41.33
Endeavour II	4.40.05	4.00.05

Winner—*Ranger*

	Ranger	*Endeavour II*
Times Rounding, First Mark	2.26.57	2.37.25
Times Rounding, Second Mark	3.27.20	3.43.39
Elapsed Times, First Leg	1.46.57	1.57.25
Elapsed Times, Second Leg	1.00.23	1.06.14
Elapsed Times, Third Leg	0.54.13	0.56.26

After finishing *Endeavour II* requested one day postponement, which was immediately granted. *Ranger* signaled her consent to race the next weekday.

Third Race—August 4th

Weather, Clear overhead, fog haze on surface; Sea, Short chop; Tidal Current, turned North at Brenton Reef Lightship at 12:59 P.M. Wind at start, S.W., 11.5 miles per hour; at 4:34 P.M., S.W., 12.5 miles per hour. Course, S.W., 15 miles to windward and return. Distance 30 miles.

Start—12:40

	Finish	Elapsed
Ranger	4.34.30	3.54.30
Endeavour II	4.38.57	3.58.57

Winner—*Ranger*

	Ranger	*Endeavour II*
Times Rounding, Outer Mark	2.43.45	2.47.58
Elapsed Times, First Leg	2.03.45	2.07.58
Elapsed Times, Second Leg	1.50.45	1.50.59

After finishing each yacht signaled her consent to race the next weekday.

On August 3rd *Endeavour II* removed 5080 lbs. of ballast. Dr. Webb certified that this did not change her rating.

Fourth Race—August 5th

Weather, Clear; Sea, Smooth; Tidal Current, turned North at Brenton Reef Lightship at 2:58 P.M. Wind, at start, S.W., 12.5 miles per hour; at 3:47 P.M., S.W., 16 miles per hour. Course triangular, S.W., E. × S., N. × W. ½ W. Distance 30 miles.

Start—12:40

	Finish	Elapsed
Ranger	3.47.49	3.07.49
Endeavour II	3.51.26	3.11.26

Winner—*Ranger*

	Ranger	*Endeavour II*
Times Rounding, First Mark	1.57.45	2.01.50
Times Rounding, Second Mark	2.54.51	2.58.26
Elapsed Times, First Leg	1.17.45	1.21.50
Elapsed Times, Second Leg	0.57.06	0.56.36
Elapsed Times, Third Leg	0.52.58	0.53.00

At the start *Endeavour II* crossed the starting line nine seconds early and was recalled. She recrossed one minute and fifteen seconds after the starting signal.

Newport, R. I., August 5, 1937.

George A. Cormack, Esq.,
    Secretary,
New York Yacht Club,
37 West 44th Street, New York.

Dear Sir:
We have to report that *Ranger* won "the best four out of seven races" from *Endeavour II* and thereby the Match for the America's Cup.

Edmund Lang, *Chairman*
Walter L. Coursen, *Secretary*
George M. Pynchon
Race Committee

The Seventeenth Match 1958 Sceptre *vs.* Columbia

FIRST RACE—SEPTEMBER 20TH

Course: Windward-Leeward Twice Around
                Distance 24.0 miles
Wind: North ½ East 8 m.p.h.

Actual Time of Start	*Columbia*	12:30:10
Actual Time of Start	*Sceptre*	12:30:11
Time at First Mark	*Columbia*	13:54:41
Time at First Mark	*Sceptre*	14:02:17
Time at Second Mark	*Columbia*	15:47:16
Time at Second Mark	*Sceptre*	15:49:43
Time at Third Mark	*Columbia*	16:42:38
Time at Third Mark	*Sceptre*	16:50:10
Time at Finish	*Columbia*	17:43:56
Time at Finish	*Sceptre*	17:51:40

Winner—*Columbia*

Second Race—September 22nd

Course: Triangular
          Distance 24.0 miles
Wind: North ½ East 7 m.p.h.

Actual Time of Start	*Columbia*	12:21:32
Actual Time of Start	*Sceptre*	12:21:34
Time at First Mark	*Sceptre*	15:46:16
Time at First Mark	*Columbia*	15:48:01
Time at Second Mark	*Columbia*	16:52:04
Time at Second Mark	*Sceptre*	16:52:54

No race. Time limit expired at 17:50:00.
Sceptre signaled her unwillingness to start the next day.

Third Race—September 25th

Course: Windward-Leeward Twice Around
          Distance 24.0 miles
Wind: South West by West ¼ West 15 to 20 m.p.h.

Actual Time of Start	*Sceptre*	12:10:04
Actual Time of Start	*Columbia*	12:10:05
Time at First Mark	*Columbia*	13:09:28
Time at First Mark	*Sceptre*	13:11:51
Time at Second Mark	*Columbia*	13:45:27
Time at Second Mark	*Sceptre*	13:47:56
Time at Third Mark	*Columbia*	14:43:22
Time at Third Mark	*Sceptre*	14:51:07
Time at Finish	*Columbia*	15:19:07
Time at Finish	*Sceptre*	15:27:27

Winner—*Columbia*

Fourth Race—September 26th

Course: Triangular
          Distance 24.0 miles
Wind: South West by West 12 to 17 m.p.h.

Actual Time of Start	Columbia	12:10:10
Actual Time of Start	Sceptre	12:10:23
Time at First Mark	Columbia	13:28:44
Time at First Mark	Sceptre	13:34:14
Time at Second Mark	Columbia	14:20:31
Time at Second Mark	Sceptre	14:28:44
Time at Finish	Columbia	15:14:22
Time at Finish	Sceptre	15:21:27

Winner—*Columbia*

At the start *Sceptre* crossed the starting line two seconds early and was recalled. She recrossed twenty-three seconds after the starting signal.

Newport, R.I., September 26, 1958

W. Mahlon Dickerson, Esq.,
Secretary
New York Yacht Club,
37 West 44th Street, New York

Dear Sir:
The New York Yacht Club Race Committee reports that *Columbia* won "the best four out of seven races" from *Sceptre* and thereby the Match for the America's Cup.

John S. Dickerson, Jr., *Chairman*
Race Committee

The Eighteenth Match 1962 Gretel *vs.* Weatherly

First Race—September 15th

Course: Windward-Leeward Twice Around
       Distance 24.0 miles
Wind: 290 degrees—10 knots

Actual Time of Start	Weatherly	13:10:12
Actual Time of Start	Gretel	13:10:26
Time at First Mark	Weatherly	14:08:02

Time at First Mark	*Gretel*	14:09:37
Time at Second Mark	*Weatherly*	14:47:51
Time at Second Mark	*Gretel*	14:49:03
Time at Third Mark	*Weatherly*	15:42:58
Time at Third Mark	*Gretel*	15:46:16
Time at Finish	*Weatherly*	16:23:57
Time at Finish	*Gretel*	16:27:43

Winner—*Weatherly*

Gretel signaled her unwillingness to start the next day.

SECOND RACE—SEPTEMBER 18

Course: Triangular
 Distance 24.0 miles
Wind: 285 degrees—20–25 knots

Actual Time of Start	*Gretel*	12:20:11
Actual Time of Start	*Weatherly*	12:20:17
Time at First Mark	*Weatherly*	13:31:06
Time at First Mark	*Gretel*	13:31:18
Time at Second Mark	*Weatherly*	14:18:47
Time at Second Mark	*Gretel*	14:19:01
Time at Finish	*Gretel*	15:06:58
Time at Finish	*Weatherly*	15:07:45

Winner—*Gretel*

Gretel signaled her unwillingness to start the next day.

THIRD RACE—SEPTEMBER 20TH

Course: Windward-Leeward Twice Around
 Distance 24.0 miles
Wind: 010 degrees—9–12 knots

Actual Time of Start	*Gretel*	12:50:21
Actual Time of Start	*Weatherly*	12:50:24

259

Time at First Mark	*Weatherly*	14:00:04
Time at First Mark	*Gretel*	14:01:02
Time at Second Mark	*Weatherly*	15:10:28
Time at Second Mark	*Gretel*	15:33:45
Time at Third Mark	*Weatherly*	16:18:24
Time at Third Mark	*Gretel*	16:33:40
Time at Finish	*Weatherly*	17:11:16
Time at Finish	*Gretel*	17:19:56

Winner—*Weatherly*

Gretel signaled her unwillingness to start the next day.

Fourth Race—September 22nd

Course: Triangular
          Distance 24.0 miles
Wind: 175 degrees—8–10 knots

Actual Time of Start	*Weatherly*	13:05:19
Actual Time of Start	*Gretel*	13:05:23
Time at First Mark	*Weatherly*	14:34:55
Time at First Mark	*Gretel*	14:36:21
Time at Second Mark	*Weatherly*	15:31:25
Time at Second Mark	*Gretel*	15:32:13
Time at Finish	*Weatherly*	16:27:28
Time at Finish	*Gretel*	16:27:54

Winner—*Weatherly*

Gretel signaled her unwillingness to start the next day.

Fifth Race—September 25th

Course: Windward-Leeward Twice Around
          Distance 24.0 miles
Wind: 245 degrees—8–10 knots

| Actual Time of Start | *Gretel* | 13:10:09 |
| Actual Time of Start | *Weatherly* | 13:10:13 |

Time at First Mark	*Weatherly*	14:07:05
Time at First Mark	*Gretel*	14:09:09
Time at Second Mark	*Weatherly*	14:46:50
Time at Second Mark	*Gretel*	14:49:18
Time at Third Mark	*Weatherly*	15:46:01
Time at Third Mark	*Gretel*	15:49:40
Time at Finish	*Weatherly*	16:26:17
Time at Finish	*Gretel*	16:29:57

Winner—*Weatherly*

Newport, R.I., September 25, 1962

W. Mahlon Dickerson, Esq.,
   Secretary
New York Yacht Club,
37 West 44th Street, New York

Dear Sir:
   The New York Yacht Club Race Committee reports that *Weatherly* won "the best four out of seven races" from *Gretel* and thereby the Match for the America's Cup.

Julian K. Roosevelt, *Chairman*
Race Committee

The Nineteenth Match 1964 Sovereign *vs.* Constellation

First Race—September 15th

Course: America's Cup Course—24.3 Miles
Wind at Start: W × S—6–8 Knots

Times	*Sovereign*	*Constellation*
Start	12:35:00	12:35:00
1st Mark	13:19:20	13:17:31
2nd Mark	13:41:31	13:39:36
3rd Mark	14:05:03	14:03:13
4th Mark	14:49:11	14:46:11
5th Mark	15:27:47	15:22:56
Finish	16:11:15	16:05:41

Second Race—September 16th

Race postponed—due to insufficient and variable winds.

Second Race—September 17th

Course: America's Cup Course—24.3 Miles
Wind at Start: SSW—15–17 Knots

Times	Sovereign	Constellation
Start	12:10:00	12:10:00
1st Mark	13:02:05	12:58:22
2nd Mark	13:24:04	13:20:32
3rd Mark	13:45:00	13:41:38
4th Mark	14:36:16	14:30:55
5th Mark	15:18:41	15:06:13
Finish	16:17:12	15:56:48

Sovereign signaled her unwillingness to start the next day.

Third Race—September 19th

Course: America's Cup Course—24.3 Miles
Wind at Start: E ½ N—15–17 Knots

Times	Sovereign	Constellation
Start	12:10:00	12:10:00
1st Mark	13:03:10	12:59:03
2nd Mark	13:26:07	13:21:38
3rd Mark	13:45:56	13:41:23
4th Mark	14:34:39	14:29:07
5th Mark	15:04:36	14:58:47
Finish	15:54:40	15:48:07

Fourth Race—September 21st

Course: America's Cup Course—24.3 Miles
Wind at Start: E × N—8 Knots

Times	Sovereign	Constellation
Start	12:10:00	12:10:00
1st Mark	13:08:58	13:04:11
2nd Mark	13:37:43	13:32:22
3rd Mark	14:00:20	13:53:57
4th Mark	15:01:20	14:47:54
5th Mark	15:42:25	15:29:59
Finish	16:38:07	16:22:27

Newport, R. I., September 21, 1964

Arthur J. Santry, Jr., Esq.
New York Yacht Club,
37 West 44th Street, New York

Dear Sir:

The New York Yacht Club Race Committee reports that *Constellation* won "the best four out of seven races" from *Sovereign* and thereby the Match for the America's Cup.

F. Briggs Dalzell, *Chairman*
Race Committee

The Twentieth Match 1967 Dame Pattie *vs.* Intrepid

FIRST RACE—SEPTEMBER 12TH

Wind at Start—E × N¼N, 18 Knots . . . Wind at Finish—E × N¼N, 15 Knots

	Intrepid		Dame Pattie
Official Start		12:30:00	
Actual Start	12:30:16		12:30:06
1st Mark	13:15:45		13:17:35
2nd Mark	13:35:57		13:38:08
3rd Mark	13:52:40		13:55:30
4th Mark	14:39:07		14:43:33
5th Mark	15:08:56		15:14:02
Finish	15:55:03		16:01:01
Margin		00:05:58	

SECOND RACE—SEPTEMBER 13TH

Wind at Start—E × N¼N, 7 Knots . . . Wind at Finish—E × N¼N, 11–14 Knots

	Intrepid		*Dame Pattie*
Official Start		12:35:00	
Actual Start	12:35:15		12:35:14
1st Mark	13:22:09		13:23:02
2nd Mark	13:45:22		13:46:54
3rd Mark	14:03:24		14:05:27
4th Mark	14:48:23		14:50:19
5th Mark	15:20:49		15:24:12
Finish	16:04:21		16:07:57
Margin		00:03:36	

THIRD RACE—SEPTEMBER 14TH

Wind at Start—NE × E, 12 Knots . . . Wind at Finish—NE½E, 16 Knots

	Intrepid		*Dame Pattie*
Official Start		12:20:00	
Actual Start	12:20:07		12:20:06
1st Mark	13:04:29		13:05:50
2nd Mark	13:24:49		13:26:09
3rd Mark	13:44:15		13:45:59
4th Mark	14:28:10		14:31:30
5th Mark	14:58:11		15:01:46
Finish	15:40:14		15:44:55
Margin		00:03:41	

Dame Pattie signaled her unwillingness to start the next day.

SEPTEMBER 16TH

Race postponed due to hurricane Doria.

SEPTEMBER 17TH

Race postponed due to fog.

FOURTH RACE—SEPTEMBER 18TH

Wind at Start—SW, 12 Knots . . . Wind at Finish—SW × W, 8 Knots

	Intrepid		*Dame Pattie*
Official Start		14:00:00	
Actual Start	14:00:04		14:00:01
1st Mark	14:42:59		14:44:24
2nd Mark	15:03:07		15:04:59
3rd Mark	15:23:28		15:25:46
4th Mark	16:05:58		16:09:52
5th Mark	16:45:18		16:47:43
Finish	17:27:39		17:31:14
Margin		00:03:35	

Newport, R.I., September 18, 1967

Donald B. Kipp, Esq.
New York Yacht Club,
37 West 44th Street, New York

Dear Sir:

The New York Yacht Club Race Committee reports that *Intrepid* won "the best four of seven races" from *Dame Pattie* and thereby the Match for the America's Cup.

Henry H. Anderson, Jr., *Chairman*
Race Committee

The Twenty-First Match 1970 Gretel II *vs.* Intrepid

FIRST RACE—SEPTEMBER 15TH

Wind at Start—109°, 20 K . . . at Finish—110°, 12–15 K

	Intrepid	*Gretel II*	*Margins*	*Leader*
Actual Start	12:10:06	12:10:08	00:02	*Intrepid*
1st Mark	12:49:33	12:50:36	01:03	"
2nd Mark	13:11:17	13:12:25	01:08	"
3rd Mark	13:30:19	13:33:46	03:27	"
4th Mark	14:15:49	14:20:00	04:11	"
5th Mark	14:54:23	15:00:38	06:15	"
Finish	15:36:03	15:41:55	05:52	"

The weather mark was shifted 15° to starboard after the first leg.

Protests of both yachts before the start were disallowed.

Gretel II signaled her unwillingness to start the next day.

SEPTEMBER 17TH

Race postponed due to lack of wind.

SECOND RACE—SEPTEMBER 18TH

Wind at Start—201°, 9 K

	Gretel II	Intrepid	Margins	Leader
Actual Start	12:30:08	12:30:11	00:03	Gretel II
1st Mark	13:18:42	13:20:36	01:54	"
2nd Mark	13:47:13	13:47:33	00:20	"
3rd Mark	14:12:04	14:11:18	00:46	Intrepid

Race was abandoned after 3rd mark at 1452 hours due to thickening fog.

Gretel II signaled her unwillingness to start the next day.

SECOND RACE—SEPTEMBER 20TH

Wind at Start—238°, 6 K . . . at Finish—226°, 9 K

	Gretel II	Intrepid	Margins	Leader
Official Start	14:00:00			
Actual Start	Not Recorded			
1st Mark	15:08:33	15:07:51	00:42	Intrepid
2nd Mark	15:35:13	15:34:04	01:09	"
3rd Mark	15:58:32	15:56:50	01:42	"
4th Mark	16:54:28	16:53:16	01:12	"
5th Mark	17:44:29	17:45:19	00:50	Gretel II
Finish	18:37:03	18:38:10	01:07	"

Gretel II was disqualified for a foul after the starting signal and the race was awarded to *Intrepid*.

Both yachts signaled their unwillingness to start the next day.

Third Race—September 22nd

Wind at Start—236°, 10 K . . . at Finish—230°, 18 K

	Intrepid	Gretel II	Margins	Leader
Actual Start	12:10:09	12:10:14	00:05	Intrepid
1st Mark	12:53:42	12:54:28	00:46	"
2nd Mark	13:14:35	13:15:21	00:46	"
3rd Mark	13:36:47	13:37:43	00:56	"
4th Mark	14:20:27	14:21:20	00:53	"
5th Mark	14:53:56	14:55:12	01:16	"
Finish	15:34:43	15:36:01	01:18	"

Both yachts signaled their unwillingness to start the next day.

Fourth Race—September 24th

Wind at Start—076°, 10 K . . . at Finish—120°, 4–6 K

	Gretel II	Intrepid	Margins	Leader
Actual Start	12:10:21	12:10:13	00:08	Intrepid
1st Mark	12:54:56	12:54:27	00:29	"
2nd Mark	13:15:53	13:15:29	00:24	"
3rd Mark	13:36:52	13:36:12	00:40	"
4th Mark	14:19:52	14:18:56	00:56	"
5th Mark	14:52:25	14:51:23	01:02	"
Finish	15:33:59	15:35:01	01:02	Gretel II

Intrepid signaled her unwillingness to start the next day.

September 26th

Race postponed due to fog. Intrepid signaled her unwillingness to start the next day.

FIFTH RACE—SEPTEMBER 28TH

Wind at Start—360°, 9–10 K . . . at Finish—045°, 5 K

	Intrepid	*Gretel II*	*Margins*	*Leader*
Actual Start	12:10:11	12:10:10	00:01	*Gretel II*
1st Mark	12:56:47	12:57:31	00:44	*Intrepid*
2nd Mark	13:29:14	13:29:54	00:40	"
3rd Mark	13:58:39	13:59:18	00:39	"
4th Mark	14:55:25	14:56:16	00:51	"
5th Mark	15:55:22	15:55:42	00:20	"
Finish	16:39:03	16:40:47	01:44	"

The Twenty-Second Match 1974 Southern Cross vs. Courageous

FIRST RACE—SEPTEMBER 10TH

Course: America's Cup Course. Bearing to first mark 212°. Bearing to fourth and finish marks changed to 225°. Distance 24.3 miles.
Wind: At Start 212°, 11 knots. At Finish 222°, 7 knots.

	Courageous		*Southern Cross*	*Margins*
Official Start		14:10		
Actual Start	14:10:06		14:10:08	00:02
1st Mark	14:52:32		14:53:06	00:34
2nd Mark	15:18:15		15:19:37	01:22
3rd Mark	15:38:25		15:39:58	01:33
4th Mark	16:27:30		16:30:40	03:10
5th Mark	17:25:30		17:29:35	04:05
Finish	18:22:03		18:26:57	04:54
Elapsed Time	04:12:03		04:16:57	

Both yachts signaled their willingness to start the next day.

September 11th

The second race was postponed to a later date because of lack of wind.
Both yachts signaled their willingness to start the next day.

Second Race—September 12th

Course: America's Cup Course. Bearing to first mark 237°. Distance 24.3 miles.
Wind: At Start 237°, 11 knots. At Finish 236°, 16 knots.

	Courageous	Southern Cross	Margins
Official Start		12:10	
Actual Start	12:10:09	12:10:08	00:01
1st Mark	12:55:00	12:55:34	00:34
2nd Mark	13:17:54	13:18:22	00:28
3rd Mark	13:39:54	13:40:28	00:34
4th Mark	14:24:27	14:25:23	00:56
5th Mark	14:59:55	15:00:40	00:45
Finish	15:42:37	15:43:48	01:11
Elapsed Time	03:32:37	03:33:48	

Both yachts finished with protest flags displayed.
Both yachts signaled their willingness to start the next day.
September 13th—Course Signals for Race 3 were hoisted at 11:50, however, the race was postponed at 12:00 because of fog.
Both yachts signaled their willingness to start the next day.
September 14th—Race 3 was started but due to light wind neither yacht finished within the time limit which expired at 17:40.
Southern Cross requested a layover day the next day.

Third Race—September 16th

Course: America's Cup Course. Bearing to first mark 300°. Bearing to finish mark changed to 310°. Distance 24.3 miles.
Wind: At Start 305°, 12 knots. At Finish 308°, 11 knots.

	Courageous	Southern Cross	Margins
Official Start	12:10		
Actual Start	12:11:01	12:11:17	00:16
1st Mark	12:56:19	12:57:04	00:45
2nd Mark	13:18:49	13:20:14	01:25
3rd Mark	13:42:08	13:43:24	01:16
4th Mark	14:26:57	14:29:49	02:52
5th Mark	15:00:45	15:04:17	03:32
Finish	15:43:02	15:48:29	05:27
Elapsed Time	03:33:02	03:38:29	

Both yachts signaled their willingness to start the next day.

FOURTH RACE—SEPTEMBER 17TH

Course: America's Cup Course. Bearing to first mark 190°. Bearing to fourth mark changed to 215°. Distance 24.3 miles.
Wind: At Start 190°, 12 knots. At Finish 214°, 12 knots.

	Courageous	Southern Cross	Margins
Official Start	12:10		
Actual Start	12:10:07	12:10:27	00:20
1st Mark	12:51:51	12:53:10	01:19
2nd Mark	13:16:26	13:18:06	01:40
3rd Mark	13:38:20	13:40:09	01:49
4th Mark	14:22:20	14:26:22	04:02
5th Mark	14:59:23	15:03:53	04:30
Finish	15:42:25	15:49:44	07:19
Elapsed Time	03:32:25	03:39:44	

Courageous is the winner of the America's Cup.

The Twenty-Third Match 1977 Australia *vs.* Courageous

FIRST RACE—SEPTEMBER 13TH

America's Cup Course 24.3 miles. Weather leg 4.5 miles, 225 degrees.

Official Start 12:10:00

Yachts	Australia	Courageous	Deltas	Wind
Start	12:10:12	12:10:24	00:12 (A)	225, 12.5 k
1st Mark			01:08 (C)	
2nd Mark			01:16 (C)	
3rd Mark			01:23 (C)	
4th Mark			01:12 (C)	
5th Mark			01:18 (C)	
Finish			01:48 (C)	205, 17 k

The weather mark was moved for the 6th leg to 205 degrees.
Australia requested a lay day the next day.

SECOND RACE—SEPTEMBER 15TH

America's Cup Course 24.3 miles. Weather leg 4.5 miles, 050 degrees.

Official Start 12:10:00

Yachts	Australia	Courageous	Deltas	Wind
Start	12:10:06	12:10:07	00:01 (A)	050, 10 k
1st Mark	12:57:46	12:56:58	00:48 (C)	
2nd Mark	13:30:17	13:29:57	00:20 (C)	
3rd Mark	13:55:32	13:54:48	00:44 (C)	
4th Mark	15:13:51	15:03:06	10:45 (C)	
5th Mark	16:22:17	16:16:40	05:37 (C)	
Finish			At time limit.	125, 3 k

The weather mark was moved for the 4th leg to 110 degrees.
The time limit expired with *Courageous* approximately 570 yards and *Australia* approximately 2,280 yards from the finish.

SECOND RACE—SEPTEMBER 16TH

America's Cup Course 24.3 miles. Weather leg 4.5 miles, 190 degrees.

Yachts	Australia	Courageous	Deltas	Wind
Start	12:10:03	12:10:02	00:01 (C)	195, 11 k
1st Mark	13:00:06	12:58:06	02:00 (C)	
2nd Mark	13:21:57	13:19:57	02:00 (C)	
3rd Mark	13:50:33	13:47:55	02:38 (C)	
4th Mark	14:32:20	14:30:12	02:08 (C)	
5th Mark	15:11:46	15:10:40	01:06 (C)	
Finish	15:55:10	15:54:07	01:03 (C)	160, 15 k

The weather mark was moved for the 4th leg.

THIRD RACE—SEPTEMBER 17TH

America's Cup Course 24.3 miles. Weather leg 4.5 miles, 240 degrees.

Official Start 12:10:00

Yachts	Australia	Courageous	Deltas	Wind
Start	12:10:21	12:10:15	00:12 (C)	238, 8 k
1st Mark	13:02:44	13:00:54	01:50 (C)	
2nd Mark	13:42:33	13:40:02	02:31 (C)	
3rd Mark	14:08:41	14:05:37	03:04 (C)	275, 9–10 k
4th Mark	14:59:12	14:55:45	03:27 (C)	
5th Mark	15:42:33	15:40:36	01:57 (C)	
Finish	16:35:55	16:33:23	02:32 (C)	310, 8 k

The weather mark was moved for the 4th leg to 275 degrees.

FOURTH RACE—SEPTEMBER 18TH

America's Cup Course 24.3 miles. Weather leg 4.5 miles, 265 degrees.

Official Start 12:10:00

Yachts	Australia	Courageous	Deltas	Wind
Start	12:10:09	12:10:09	00:00	265, 14 k
1st Mark	12:54:16	12:53:32	00:44 (C)	
2nd Mark	13:14:34	13:13:46	00:48 (C)	
3rd Mark	13:34:54	13:33:58	00:56 (C)	
4th Mark	14:19:12	14:17:01	02:11 (C)	
5th Mark	15:01:17	14:58:42	02:35 (C)	
Finish	15:44:56	15:42:31	02:25 (C)	260, 9 k

Courageous successfully defended the Cup by winning four straight races. After the Race, in reply to the hoist CHARLIE-UNIFORM-EIGHT-ZERO, both yachts signaled "Affirmative."

The Twenty-Fourth Match 1980 Australia *vs.* Freedom

FIRST RACE—SEPTEMBER 16TH

Yacht assigned to Committee boat side of starting line: *Freedom*. Direction to 1st mark 090 degrees.

Official Start 12:10:00

Yachts	Freedom	Australia	Deltas
Start	12:10:29	12:10:24	00:05 (A)
1st Mark	13:06:22	13:07:14	00:52 (F)
2nd Mark	13:33:11	13:34:44	01:33 (F)
3rd Mark	13:53:30	13:55:26	01:48 (F)
4th Mark	14:38:53	14:41:07	02:14 (F)
5th Mark	15:12:44	15:15:01	02:17 (F)
Finish	15:58:32	16:00:24	01:52 (F)

Wind: At start 095 degrees, 10 knots. At finish 125 degrees, 12 knots.

The weather mark was moved and the course changed to 135 degrees for the 2nd weather leg.

Australia declined to race the next day.

SECOND RACE—SEPTEMBER 18TH

Yacht assigned to Committee boat side of starting line: *Australia*. Direction to 1st mark 345 degrees.

Official Start 12:25:00

Yachts	Freedom	Australia	Deltas
Start	12:25:06	12:25:16	00:10 (F)
1st Mark	13:16:07	13:16:49	00:42 (F)
2nd Mark	13:45:49	14:46:39	00:50 (F)
3rd Mark	14:10:18	14:11:27	01:09 (F)
4th Mark	15:05:32	15:07:14	01:42 (F)
5th Mark	—	17:37:49	—

273

Wind: At start 345 degrees, 6 knots. At time limit 240 degrees, 2 knots.

The weather mark was moved and the course changed to 355 degrees for the 2nd weather leg. The weather mark was moved and the course changed to 240 degrees for the 3rd weather leg. The time limit expired with *Australia* approximately 500 yards beyond the 5th mark and *Freedom* approximately 2,000 yards short of it.

Second Race—September 19th (Resailed)

Yacht assigned to Committee boat side of starting line: *Australia*. Direction to 1st mark 255 degrees.

Official Start 14:10:00

Yachts	Freedom	Australia	Deltas
Start	14:10:09	14:10:14	00:05 (F)
1st Mark	15:12:30	15:12:02	00:28 (A)
2nd Mark	15:43:45	15:43:30	00:15 (A)
3rd Mark	16:14:35	16:13:48	00:47 (A)
4th Mark	17:07:36	17:06:50	00:46 (A)
5th Mark	18:05:57	18:06:18	00:21 (F)
Finish	19:17:10	19:16:42	00:28 (A)

Wind: At start 250 degrees, 6 knots. At finish 245 degrees, 8 knots.

The weather mark was moved and the course changed to 235 degrees for the 2nd weather leg.

Freedom declined to race the next day.

Freedom protested *Australia* for improper running lights. The protest was rejected on a technicality when *Freedom* declined to offer evidence at the hearing.

Third Race—September 21st

Yacht assigned to Committee boat side of starting line: *Freedom*. Direction to 1st mark 250 degrees.

Official Start 12:10:00

Yachts	Freedom	Australia	Deltas
Start	12:10:02	12:10:05	00:03 (F)
1st Mark	12:58:57	12:59:42	00:45 (F)
2nd Mark	13:20:42	13:21:08	00:26 (F)
3rd Mark	13:44:58	13:45:18	00:20 (F)
4th Mark	14:30:03	14:30:54	00:51 (F)
5th Mark	15:02:04	15:02:12	00:08 (F)
Finish	15:45:07	15:46:00	00:53 (F)

Wind: At start 250 degrees, 12 knots. At finish 230 degrees, 16 knots.

The weather mark was moved and the course changed to 225 degrees for the 2nd weather leg.

Australia declined to race the next day. Protest flags were observed on both yachts approaching the 5th mark. Protests involving rule 54.3 were filed by both yachts. Both protests were disallowed.

FOURTH RACE—SEPTEMBER 23RD

Yacht assigned to Committee boat side of starting line: *Australia*. Direction to 1st mark 270 degrees.

Official Start 12:10:00

Yachts	Freedom	Australia	Deltas
Start	12:10:08	12:10:21	00:13 (F)
1st Mark	12:58:15	13:00:03	01:48 (F)
2nd Mark	13:22:55	13:25:46	02:51 (F)
3rd Mark	13:51:54	13:55:02	03:08 (F)
4th Mark	14:38:43	14:41:24	02:41 (F)
5th Mark	15:08:26	15:10:47	02:21 (F)
Finish	15:51:20	15:55:08	03:48 (F)

Wind: At start 270 degrees, 12 knots. At finish 320 degrees, 12 knots.

The weather mark was moved and the course changed for the 2nd and 3rd weather legs to 295 degrees and 325 degrees respectively.

Freedom declined to race the next day.

FIFTH RACE—SEPTEMBER 25TH

Yacht assigned to Committee boat side of starting line: *Freedom*. Direction to 1st mark 105 degrees.

Official Start 12:10:00

Yachts	Freedom	Australia	Deltas
Start	12:10:08	12:10:15	00:07 (F)
1st Mark	12:52:25	12:53:17	00:52 (F)
2nd Mark	13:14:24	13:15:28	01:04 (F)
3rd Mark	13:35:09	13:35:53	00:44 (F)
4th Mark	14:18:36	14:19:56	01:20 (F)
5th Mark	14:52:37	14:55:47	03:10 (F)
Finish	15:38:00	15:41:38	03:38 (F)

Wind: At start 115 degrees, 17 knots. At finish 110 degrees, 14 knots.

The weather mark was moved and the course changed to 115 degrees for the 2nd weather leg.

Freedom has successfully defended the America's Cup.

After the race the Committee boat hoisted the signals: "Well done *Enterprise/Freedom* Syndicate. See you in 1983."

The Twenty-Fifth Match 1983 Australia II *vs.* Liberty

FIRST RACE—SEPTEMBER 14, 1983

Bearings: 1st, 4th and 6th Legs 045°.
Wind: At start 045°, 18 knots. At finish 050°, 18 knots.

	Liberty	Australia II	Delta
Official Start: 12:10:00			
Actual Start	12:10:08	12:10:05	00:03 (A)
1st Mark	12:54:10	12:54:02	00:08 (A)
2nd Mark	13:14:24	13:14:14	00:10 (A)
3rd Mark	13:35:54	13:36:10	00:16 (L)
4th Mark	14:19:46	14:20:14	00:28 (L)
5th Mark	14:52:26	14:53:01	00:35 (L)
Finish	15:35:50	15:37:00	01:10 (L)

SECOND RACE—SEPTEMBER 15, 1983

Bearings: 1st and 4th Legs 030°, 6th Leg 050°
Wind: At start 030°, 17 knots. At finish 055°, 10–13 knots.

	Australia II	Liberty	Delta
Official Start: 12:10:00			
Actual Start	12:10:13	12:10:08	00:05 (L)
1st Mark	12:55:17	12:56:02	00:45 (A)
2nd Mark	13:16:50	13:17:21	00:31 (A)
3rd Mark	13:40:00	13:40:21	00:21 (A)
4th Mark	14:30:37	14:29:49	00:48 (L)
5th Mark	15:08:49	15:08:18	00:31 (L)
Finish	15:59:47	15:58:14	01:33 (L)

Protest flag observed on *Australia II* at finish. Protest disallowed. *Australia II* requested a lay day.

Third Race—September 17, 1983

Bearings: 1st Leg 155°, 4th and 6th Legs 215°.
Wind: At start 160°, 10 knots. At expiration of time limit 210°, 7 knots.

	Liberty	*Australia II*	*Delta*
Official Start: 12:10:00			
Actual Start	12:10:14	12:10:03	00:11 (A)
1st Mark	13:04:07	13:02:52	01:15 (A)
2nd Mark	13:34:47	13:32:47	02:00 (A)
3rd Mark	13:57:53	13:55:55	01:58 (A)
4th Mark	15:20:58	15:19:12	01:46 (A)
5th Mark	16:30:01	16:24:04	05:57 (A)

Time limit expired at 17:25:00 hrs.

Third Race—September 18, 1983

Bearings: 1st and 4th Legs 220°, 6th Leg 230°.
Wind: At start 225°, 7 knots. At finish 230°, 10 knots.

	Liberty	*Australia II*	*Delta*
Official Start: 14:00:00			
Actual Start	14:00:02	14:00:10	00:08 (L)
1st Mark	14:51:19	14:50:05	01:14 (A)
2nd Mark	15:14:50	15:13:58	00:52 (A)
3rd Mark	15:35:55	15:35:13	00:42 (A)
4th Mark	16:24:42	16:23:27	01:15 (A)
5th Mark	17:09:22	17:06:35	02:47 (A)
Finish	17:53:48	17:50:34	03:14 (A)

Liberty requested a lay day.

FOURTH RACE—SEPTEMBER 20, 1983

Bearings: 1st, 4th and 6th Legs 240°.
Wind: At start 235°, 10 knots. At finish 235°, 15 knots.

	Australia II	Liberty	Delta
Official Start: 12:10:00			
Actual Start	12:10:13	12:10:07	00:06 (L)
1st Mark	12:57:40	12:57:04	00:36 (L)
2nd Mark	13:18:20	13:17:32	00:48 (L)
3rd Mark	13:38:50	13:38:02	00:48 (L)
4th Mark	14:22:44	14:21:58	00:46 (L)
5th Mark	14:56:34	14:55:59	00:35 (L)
Finish	15:40:07	15:39:24	00:43 (L)

FIFTH RACE—SEPTEMBER 21, 1983

Bearings: 1st Leg 195°, 4th and 6th Legs 185°.
Wind: At start 190°, 18 knots. At finish 185°, 16 knots.

	Liberty	Australia II	Delta
Official Start: 12:10:00			
Actual Start	12:10:06	12:10:43	00:37 (L)
1st Mark	12:56:32	12:56:09	00:23 (A)
2nd Mark	13:15:28	13:15:05	00:23 (A)
3rd Mark	13:35:54	13:35:36	00:18 (A)
4th Mark	14:22:15	14:21:04	01:11 (A)
5th Mark	14:53:58	14:53:06	00:52 (A)
Finish	15:41:43	15:39:56	01:47 (A)

Australia II was recalled at the start.

SIXTH RACE—SEPTEMBER 22, 1983

Bearings: 1st Leg 335°, 4th Leg 295°, 6th Leg 265°.
Wind: At start 340°, 12 knots. At finish 260–290°, 16–19 knots.

	Liberty	*Australia II*	*Delta*
Official Start: 12:10:00			
Actual Start	12:10:14	12:10:21	00:07 (L)
1st Mark	13:00:18	12:57:49	02:29 (A)
2nd Mark	13:21:43	13:19:15	02:28 (A)
3rd Mark	13:55:38	13:51:52	03:46 (A)
4th Mark	14:35:30	14:32:08	03:22 (A)
5th Mark	15:06:49	15:02:41	04:08 (A)
Finish	15:45:01	15:41:36	03:25 (A)

Australia II requested a lay day.

Seventh Race—September 24, 1983

Postponed because of light winds.
Liberty requested a lay day.

Seventh Race—September 26, 1983

Bearings: 1st Leg 205°, 4th and 6th Legs 195°.
Winds: At start 205°, 8 knots. At finish 200°, 8 knots.

	Liberty	*Australia II*	*Delta*
Official Start: 13:05:00			
Actual Start	13:05:08	13:05:16	00:08 (L)
1st Mark	13:55:31	13:56:00	00:29 (L)
2nd Mark	14:18:53	14:19:38	00:45 (L)
3rd Mark	14:45:55	14:46:18	00:23 (L)
4th Mark	15:33:49	15:34:46	00:57 (L)
5th Mark	16:22:46	16:22:25	00:21 (A)
Finish	17:21:26	17:20:45	00:41 (A)

Australia II is the winner of America's Cup.